Dedication & Ackno

I dedicate this book to the God Almighty whom all praise is due.

I also acknowledge the love and the support from the many wonderful men and women who have served with me in preaching the gospel of Jesus Christ, especially those who proof read the manuscript of this book. Our labour in the Lord will not be in vain. We are going to heaven together, amen!

Building Your Life on the principles of God:

THE SOLID
FOUNDATION

Building Your Life on the principles of God:

THE SOLID FOUNDATION

Anthony Bright Atwam

authorHOUSE®

AuthorHouse™ UK
1663 Liberty Drive
Bloomington, IN 47403 USA
www.authorhouse.co.uk
Phone: 0800.197.4150

THE HOLY BIBLE, NEW INTERNATIONAL VERSION®, NIV® Copyright © 1973,
1978, 1984, 2011 by Biblica, Inc.® Used by permission. All rights reserved worldwide.

Published by AuthorHouse 12/16/2014

ISBN: 978-1-4969-9792-0 (sc)
ISBN: 978-1-4969-9791-3 (hc)
ISBN: 978-1-4969-9793-7 (e)

Contents

Chapter 1

Introduction

Sometimes life is a bit easier and beautiful if one knows what to do in any situation. The word of God provides such guidance or principles on all aspects of life, from family life, to career, from the salvation of the human soul to proper management of material resources; guidance for the young people and guidance for the older generation. What people should do in times of crisis and where to find answers to life's big questions such as, what is the meaning of life, what is my purpose in life, and how can one live a successful life.

Experts reveal the secret to happy and long life. Researchers believe they may have unlocked the secret to a longer life – a sense of meaning and purpose. They say that while keeping fit and eating well can help you live longer, having a purpose in life can be very important for long-term health. A new study by University College London, studied people with an average age of 65 and found that those who enjoyed "wellbeing" were likely to live longer. The study defined the key components of wellbeing as a sense of control, a feeling that what you are doing is worthwhile, and a sense of purpose in life. Many people are not happy in life because they are not sure whether what they are doing is worthwhile, but scripture can guide them into all these issues.

I am very pleased to have been able to write this book to encourage people to consider building their lives on God's principles: a solid foundation. It is my prayer that all those going through crisis will receive favour from God as they read this book. One of the things this generation lacks is spiritual faith to encourage and empower them to pursue life in godliness. I call such people '**The crying generation**'. These people desire good life, but they have no hope, or the courage to pursue their dreams. They lack courage mainly because of the mistakes of the previous generation who did not pass on any godly legacy to them. It is a fact of life that those who turn to God for help are blessed while those who abandon God, die tragically leaving no godly legacy behind. The crying generation has two options: either they become 'founding people', establishing godly families, a godly movement, a church, a business, or a godly nation in their generation with the help of God and passing on these godly legacy to their children or they continue to abandon God and pass on their misery, hopelessness, mistakes, and failures to their children.

Naturally, we don't look for best things in life (Romans 3:9-18). Best things in life are most of the time accidentally discovered. For example, Saul the first king of Israel was sent by his father to hunt for his lost donkeys. Days later, Saul came home as an anointed king of Israel (1 Samuel 9-11). In a similar incident, Paul was on his way to look out for the early Christians to persecute them, but had an encounter with Jesus Christ and became one of the best servants of God (Acts 9). God has a way of helping people to find some of the best things in life, and sometimes He uses His principles to guide people to discover what they are frantically searching for in life so that they will not continue to seek in a perpetual cycle. It is my prayer that, as you read this book you will discover good things in life, with the help of God. I have also discussed God's principles on how the younger generation can acquire wisdom to make good use of their resources, develop their character, and to receive blessings from the parents and older generations.

God's principles also provide guidance on proper attitude towards materialism. This book also discusses how the rich need God's guidance to help them manage their resources well, overcome greed, power thirst, and selfishness. The poor also need God to help them overcome their poverty and to have a decent living. I like how the word of God can help us to change to become better people in our conduct, in our thinking, grooming men and women to become suitable partners to each other in relationships and family life. God, through his word can change a person's social, economic, and spiritual life. These are all discussed in this book.

You see, when life is calm our foundations don't seem to matter. But when crisis come, our foundations are tested. Building your life is like building a house. If you build your life on good foundation it will be able to withstand the pressures of life. But if you build your life on a sandy foundation, you may lose everything in times of crisis. Many people are heading towards a life of failure, some out of stubbornness, some out of thoughtlessness and some out of ignorance. Through the sharing of the gospel, the Christian community should continue to help people to reflect on where their lives are heading towards, and also lead them to the true source of life- God and his principles. This book can be of such help.

In this book, one of my main arguments is that building one's life on God's principles is the best thing people should do. The reason is that God is the maker of heaven and earth, and as such he alone knows how best people should live their lives in order to live abundantly in this world. George Washington, the first American president (1732–1799) is quoted as saying, "It is impossible to rightly govern the world without God and the Bible". By implication, George Washington was saying that, we can undoubtedly govern any part of the world by ourselves, but to rightly govern, requires that we know God and His Word (the Bible). In the same way, you can build your life on any principle you like, but to have abundant life, you have to build your life on the principles of God. A fish taken out of its natural habitat, can survive, but only for a short time. In the same way, people who do not live under God's protection and influence can be described as a fish taken out of its natural habitat; they will survive but only for a short time. They may miss eternal life in heaven.

People who are privileged to have received proper guidance in life are able to do well in life both physically and spiritually. I once visited a couple who were going through marital crisis and I asked the woman how she wanted her man to treat her. Her answer was "I want my husband to respect me, not to be harsh on me". I then opened 1 Peter 3:7 which says "Husbands, in the same way be considerate as you live with your wives, and treat them with respect..." I turned and asked the man how he wanted his woman to treat him. His answer was "I want my wife to respect me and to take my opinions serious". Again, I opened 1 Peter 3:7 which says "Wives, in the same way be submissive to your husband's". God commands men not to be harsh on their wives, and women to be submissive. Much of the domestic abuse cases can be easily prevented if couples will build their relationships on the word of God. These couple I just talked about had been together for more than ten years but only got wedded after I gave them guidelines on relationships and marriage using scripture.

I believe many people wouldn't have gone through some problems in life if they were guided properly using the word of God. If you know what to do in order to go to heaven after death, you just go ahead and do it. If you know what to do to become successful in life, you just go ahead and do it. For lack of the right knowledge many people are suffering. In his book, *Knowing God*, J. I. Packer says "we become cruel to ourselves if we try to live in this world without knowing about the God whose world it is and who runs it". We as human beings, will benefit greatly if we will allow God to rule us, for God has a good plan for us because he knows what is best for us (Jeremiah 11:29).

People who do not know what to do in life especially in times of crisis suffer greatly. A CEO who was made redundant after twenty years of service lost his wife afterwards, his only dog was also killed in an accident. This man resorted to drinking till he died. How sad! It seems that this man did not build his life on good principles and so he could not bounce back when the tides of life were against him.

I believe it is a mistake for people to live their lives as if this world is an ideal perfect place where nothing tragic can happen. This world is not a perfect or a safe place and anything can happen unexpectedly.

Many people are surprised when something bad happens to them. It is a fact that your life will undergo crisis at some point. For example, many people's life shutters when they lose a loved one; sometimes they are not able to put the pieces together again. Unfortunately, many people are not able to cope in difficult times because their foundations are not strong enough. Some even commit suicide when they are going through life challenges. But there is hope for those who are willing to listen to God and to accept his offer of salvation through faith in His Son Jesus Christ.

The theme of this book is based on the words of Jesus Christ in the Holy Scriptures from Matthew 7:24-27. I have quoted this text as follows:

> Therefore everyone who hears these words of mine and puts them into practice is like a wise man who built his house on the rock. The rain came down, the streams rose, and the winds blew and beat against that house; yet it did not fall, because it had its foundation on the rock. But everyone who hears these words of mine and does not put them into practice is like a foolish man who built his house on sand. The rain came down, the streams rose, and the winds blew and beat against that house, and it fell with a great crash (Matthew 7:24-27).

The message in the book of Matthew chapters 5-7 is called the Sermon on the Mount because Jesus gave the sermon on a hill side near Capernaum in the present day Middle East. The surrounding scenery may have suggested the illustration in the text. As in all hilly countries, the streams of Galilee rush down the torrent-beds during the winter and early spring, sweeping all before them, overflowing their banks, and leaving beds of alluvial deposit on either side of the river. When summer comes their waters dry up, and what had seemed a river becomes a tract covered with debris of stones and sand.

It would be easier to build there instead of working upon the hard and rugged rock. So a stranger coming to build in the area might be attracted by the ready-prepared levelled surface of the sand. But the people of the land would know and mock the folly of such a builder, and he would pass into a by-word of reproach. On such a house, when the winter torrent comes again it will sweep it down in its fury.

In the same way, we are all strangers in this world. You were born into this world without knowing where you came from. You will die and be taken out of this world to an unknown destination, either heaven or hell. No one is a permanent resident of this word. We are all strangers. Therefore, we need someone who knows this world in and out to guide us through life. It can be tempting for us to build our houses (life) where the land seems already prepared and levelled instead of working on hard rugged rocky areas. God knows which principles; directions etc will be good for you to build your life on because he is the creator of the universe and He knows everything. Our duty is to listen to the advice God gives us, acknowledge Him in all our ways, else we may out of ignorance or disobedience end up building our lives on principles or lifestyles which have the potential to destroy us.

In civil engineering, a foundation is usually a stone or concrete structure that supports a building from underneath. In women's world, a foundation can be a woman's supporting garment or a cosmetic usually used as a base for makeup. In life or in philosophy a foundation is something such as an idea or a principle or a fact that provides support for life or something. There are many sources of principles of life; some are good others are not.

But why would people build their lives on principles or lifestyles which can destroy them? There are many reasons: perhaps to save time and to avoid the hard work of prayer, perseverance, patience, and commitment. Another reason could be that certain lifestyles seem attractive or certain lifestyles have higher status in the society than godly principles. Or maybe they haven't heard about the violent storms coming, or they have discounted the reports of impending disaster or may be because they think disaster can't happen to them. Whatever the reason is, those with no good foundation in life are short sighted, and they will be sorry one day if they don't reconsider how they have built their lives.

Sadly, through deception, discouragement, confusion, and ignorance Satan seems to be succeeding in turning many people's attention away from God and his word in these last days. 2 Corinthians 4:4 says 'The god of this age has blinded the minds of unbelievers, so that they cannot see the light of the gospel of the glory of Christ, who is the image of God'. The god of this age is Satan, and he is preventing many people from coming to God through faith in Jesus Christ. Please don't give the devil a chance to take you away from God.

The wind, the rain, the floods in the text represent collectively the presence of Satan, evil, troubles, suffering, persecution, and temptations of life. The wise people are those who built their house on the rock. In this context, the rock can be nothing else than the firm foundation of repentance and obedience to the word of God, which is Christ Jesus. I Corinthians 10:4 refer to Jesus Christ as the rock in scripture. Scripture refers to this rock which is Christ as 'the image of the invisible God, the firstborn over all creation. For by him all things were created: things in heaven and on earth, visible and invisible, whether thrones or powers or rulers or authorities; all things were created by him and for him' (Colossians 1:15–16). That is why Jesus could say in the parable that: 'Therefore everyone who hears these words of mine and puts them into practice is like a wise man who built his house on the rock'.

The two lives Jesus compares at the end of the Sermon on the Mount have several points in common: they both build, they both hear Jesus' teaching, and they both experience the same set of circumstances in life. The difference between them isn't caused by lack of information, but by one of them ignoring what Jesus said. Externally, their lives may look similar; but the lasting, structural differences will be revealed by the storms of life. The immediate differences in your life when following Jesus may not be obvious sometimes, but in times of crisis you will see how Jesus will come to your aid in a supernatural way.

Dear reader, please listen to Jesus' words on how to be saved, how to build a successful family life, and how to build your relationship with God. We must listen to Jesus' warning, because he knows the dangers in this world. These two sorts of hearers are represented as two builders. This parable teaches us to hear and do the sayings of the Lord Jesus Christ because He knows which part of the land is not suitable for building a house. In the midst of a devastating invasion only one thing will count: a living, confident relationship with God, the life giver. If you have such a relationship with him, then you can be assured that in times of crisis He will be there for you. Psalm 91:14–16 says 'Because he loves me, says the LORD, I will rescue him; I will protect him, for he acknowledges my name. He will call upon me, and I will answer him; I will be with him in trouble, I will deliver him and honor him. With long life will I satisfy him and show him my salvation.

We will look at what a principle is in a minute, but first let us look at what it means to build one's life on the principles of God. Practicing what is written in the Bible is what it means for someone to build their lives according to the principles of God. **Words Are Not Enough!** You can believe all the right things, yet still be dead wrong. James 1:22 says 'Do not merely listen to the word, and so deceive yourselves'. Jesus expressed the same notion in Matthew 7:21 saying 'Not everyone who says to me, 'Lord, Lord,' will enter the kingdom of heaven, but only he who does the will of my Father who is in heaven'. **Actions should follow Words.**

For example, if a man and a woman come together in sexual union, the result could be pregnancy if all conditions are met. And so, if a man and a woman want to have a child, all they need to do is to have sexual union[1] and to make sure the right conditions are in place. In the same way, it was God who instituted marriage, and knows what couples should do for the marriage to be successful. Our duty is to find out God's principles on every aspect of life and build our lives on them accordingly.

The first couple on earth were instructed by God to live a certain lifestyle: they were free to eat any fruit in the Garden of Eden where they were placed except the 'tree of the knowledge of good and evil' (Genesis 2-3). The first couple, made the wrong choice, the result was that sin entered the world. This sin has affected every aspect of this world. The first couple was warned of the dangers in the Garden of Eden, but they refused to obey. They were later thrown out of the Garden of Eden.

Similarly, God told Joshua to make sure he meditates on the word of God day and night so that he will be prosperous (Joshua 1:8-10). Joshua obeyed God and was prosperous throughout his lifetime.

Just before the Israelite entered the Promised Land, they were told how they should live their lives. They did not obey God's instructions and so they were scattered all over the world. The Bible prophesied the Jewish Diaspora because of disobedience (Deuteronomy 28-30). The Nation of Israel would dwell for many years outside of their country, the Promised Land. After this time had elapsed they would return to their ancient possession (Hosea 3:4-5). The predictions were exact and complete making the nation's return to their land a supernatural happening of our age. A modern miracle! They were dispersed for over 1,900 years. They are back there again today since 1967.

God told Saul the first king of Israel to carry out specific duties. Saul went and did the opposite. The result was that Saul was dethroned

---

[1] Although there are moral issues surrounding artificial Insemination, one can say that artificial insemination which is a deliberate introduction of sperm into a female's uterus or cervix for the purpose of achieving a pregnancy other than sexual intercourse is a knowledge derived or copied from what God has already established.

from his royal position and died in a battle (1 Samuel). The examples could go on and on and on. Life will definitely end well for you if you put into practice God's principles. God knows what will make your marriage succeed. God knows what is good for you and everyone in this world. God knows what will benefit a nation when they turn to him for help.'Now all has been heard; here is the conclusion of the matter: Fear God and keep his commandments, for this is the whole duty of mankind' (Ecclesiastes 12:13).

Does it mean that apart from scripture, people should not follow or practice any word of instructions from any discipline of life such as health, commence, culture, other religions or school of thought or history? The answer to this very question is that we live in a world where we are all influenced directly or indirectly by other things whether good or bad; other constitutions or philosophies. What is needed is guidance on what one has to allow to influence him or her. Some of this guidance will also be discussed later in this chapter.

We have just looked at what it means for one to build his or her life on the principles of God. Let us now look at what a principle is. A principle is a moral law or belief that helps you know what is right and wrong and that influences your actions. They are fundamental norms, rules, or values that represent what is desirable and positive for a person, group, organization, or community, and help it in determining the rightfulness or wrongfulness of its actions. They are fundamental truth or proposition that serves as the foundation for a system of belief or behaviour or for a chain of reasoning.

God's principles are timeless and work perfectly well in every generation, although each generation has its own unique challenges and things to contend for. All other principles in this world are derived from the main source; God. Some of the principles of God are: sowing and reaping, following what is clearly revealed, the abandonment of oneself to God, times and seasons, love for self, neighbour and God, the principle of small beginnings, faithfulness in someone's business, persevering in times of difficulty, labouring in

God's kingdom, the principle of asking, seeking, and knocking, the principles of God's promises, the principle of God's provision, the principle of God's promotion, the principle of praise, the principle of seedtime and harvest time, the principles of patience, just to name a few in this book. These principles have been applied and discussed in the various chapters in this book. Open mindedness and imaginative use of these principles in the Bible needs to be practised cautiously, seeking ways to listen, to learn and to discover God's will in any situation.

Although the principles of God are for the benefit of humanity, they also require certain things from us. It's very interesting to see people applying the principles of God in their lives without a relationship with God himself. The principles of God demands repentance, obedience and submission to the will of God in every situation, the worship of God and a day to day relationship with him till death. Scripture says, God's 'divine power has given us everything we need for life and godliness through our knowledge of him who called us by his own glory and goodness. Through these he has given us his very great and precious promises, so that through them we may participate in the divine nature and escape the corruption in the world caused by evil desires(2 Peter 1:3-4). Our duty is seek these provisions and make good use of them.

It is quite common to hear people dismiss an interpretation of the Bible by saying, 'that is your interpretation' or something like 'you are interpreting the Bible that way to make it fit your opinion'. It is true that Christians sometimes have different interpretations of the same biblical passage; it is also true that some interpretations are better than others. In chapter ten of this book, an attempt will be made to discuss how one can interpret and apply the word of God correctly. This is important because if you are going to build your life on what God has said, then it is important that you get the message right.

But where can people find some of these principles of God? What is the source(s) of these principles of God? These principles can be found in the Holy Bible, although some people argue that there are other principles of God which can be found outside the Bible. According to recent research, our society is experiencing more diversity in religion and ideologies due to globalisation and capitalism. Because of this, some argue that people can know the principles of God through reading the Bible and other religious writings. Others also argue that by studying nature they can have encounter with the God of the universe. Others believe that 'they are god' to themselves and therefore do not need any external authority to instruct them, although this notion can be very dangerous.

Some people look to nature to learn more about God's principles. For example, one can study the rising and the settling of the sun and base his or her daily activities on such phenomenon. Again this is not enough, nature does not provide all the information about God and how we are to live. We must also look elsewhere. In addition to all these sources, God has also spoken to humanity at different times and in various ways to different people in different generations. This spoken word of God is what Christians call 'the word of God', God's spoken word. This can be found in a book called the Bible. I know many people have questions about the Bible, and so I have endeavoured to answer some of these questions in the latter part of this chapter.

1.1 Setting the Scene

Gone were the days when our society was godly to the extent that people did not necessarily need to go to church to hear the word of God because the principles of God were taught, discussed, and practiced daily in people's lives. To some degree, men, women, and children in those days lived according to the word of God intentionally and unintentionally. The atmosphere was filled with the knowledge of God. People acknowledged God in their lives although many of them did not even read the Bible. Sometimes they just naturally do what the principles of God require. They show that what the principles of God require is written on their hearts. The way their minds judged them gave witness to that fact. Sometimes their thoughts found them guilty. At other times their thoughts found them not guilty.

But things have changed now. Our society is becoming anti-Godly and so principles such as love for neighbour and God, basic moral principles such as right and wrong which seemed to be common decades ago are now hidden if not completely vanished from our society. Even the little knowledge about God and morality, which God himself puts into our hearts as moral agents is either suppressed or obscured by the dark forces in the society.

It is interesting to note that, we spend much of our resources as a society to enact laws to criminalise certain behaviour than spending these resources to teach the right way people should live. Our educational system has little place for teachings on morals. Students are not taught what is right from wrong anymore. Bibles and prayers are not allowed in our schools anymore. Because of this and other reasons, many people in our day have not been exposed to the principles of God. There is less education or instructions on morality, these days. We spend more money and resources on the treatment and management of bad habits or behavioural problems which could otherwise be prevented by proper instructions.

For example, considerable amount of resources are spent on intervention policies and programmes, than on teachings on how people can live their lives responsibly and productively. We as society focus more on solving problems rather than on how to prevent problems arising. We wait till there is a problem, before we seek solutions. We wait till our young people become rebels, addicted to substance before we begin to manage them. It is not a surprise that our prisons are swelling daily with criminals. We wait till our relationships and marriages hit the rock before we begin to seek counselling.

There is famine in the land, famine of truth, famine of the word of God. There is darkness in our society. Darkness has to do with the inability to see good things in life or to understand what is going on in our world today. Darkness has to do with evil and uncertainty. The attempt by some groups of people in the society notably, the secularist and some humanist to suppress religion and the knowledge of God have not been very helpful in many ways, although they could not succeed to do so. These groups of people who tried to suppress the principles of God could not provide any alternative guidance for the people to build their lives on; they could not provide the society with any guiding principles on how people should live their lives. Because of this, many marriages and family lives have suffered simply because the people did not know how to manage their marriages. The young people have not had the opportunity to be brought up properly and this has resulted in an increase in teenage pregnancies, prostitution, crime and all kinds of anti-social behaviours.

If secularists and some humanists want the society to be void of Godly knowledge in public life, then they should have provided another way for people to live, but rather they left most of their followers in the dark; to live by the little knowledge of God they had received from the previous generations; depriving them from having access to the vast resources God has provided for humanity. It is however, comforting to hear that their propaganda to suppress the knowledge of God, faith, and religion in the society is proving futile. Truth is like the sun, you can shut it out for a time, but it won't go away.

Like most other sociologists of religion of his day, Peter Ludwig Berger (March 17, 1929) an Austrian-born American sociologist predicted in the 50's and 60's that the world would become secularized, due to capitalism and globalization. But as he went round the globe, he realized that religion was not going away. He realised that religion is on the increase instead. You see, God won't go away from the lives of the people, because He loves his creation. Harvey Cox, a retired

Professor of Divinity at Harvard, rightly makes a prophetic point in his book, *The Future of faith* as follows:

> The resurgence of religion was not foreseen. On the contrary, not many decades ago thoughtful writers were confidently predicting its imminent demise. Religion, we were assured, would certainly never again sway politics or shape culture. But the soothsayers were wrong. Instead of disappearing, religion – for good or ill- is now exhibiting new vitality all around the world and making its weight widely felt in the corridors of power.

An artist will not abandon his own work. In the same way God won't abandon His creation. God created the world to be part of his creation. No human agenda can suppress the knowledge of God. Prophetically Habakkuk 2:13-14 says, 'Has not the LORD Almighty determined that the people's labor is only fuel for the fire, that the nations exhaust themselves for nothing? For the earth will be filled with the knowledge of the glory of the LORD, as the waters cover the sea'. Jesus said,'

And this gospel of the kingdom will be preached in the whole world as a testimony to all nations, and then the end will come(Matthew 24:14). Colossians 1:6 says' All over the world this gospel is bearing fruit and growing, just as it has been doing among you since the day you heard it and understood God's grace in all its truth'.

In Greek mythology, it is believed that the gods need the people to survive. Without the people worshipping and sacrificing to these smaller, man-made gods, these gods won't survive. And so, if one wants to do away with these gods, all they have to do is to discourage people from worshipping them, the result will be that these gods will cease to exist. But the God who created the heavens and the earth is the Great God. God does not need our worship or acknowledgment to exist. He is of himself. He is eternal. His very existence does not depend on us acknowledging or worshipping him. He is not made by human hands because he himself gives all mankind life and breath and everything else. For in him we live and move and have our being. Since we are God's offspring, is it a mistake for people to think that the divine being is like gold or silver or stone—an image made by man's design and skill.

It should rather be seen as a privilege for mankind to participate and have fellowship with God because He can even cause stones to worship him if mankind refuse Him worship (read Matthew 3:9 and Luke 19:40). **Don't let the stones Worship God in your place.** Scripture says 'Worship the LORD your God and his blessings will be on your food and water. I will take away sickness from among you, and none will miscarry or be barren in your land. I will give you a full life span… I will make all your enemies turn their backs and run' (Exodus 23:25-27). Why don't you make the worship of God a priority today? Start attending church service, and ask the pastor for further guidance on how to worship God in spirit and in truth (John 4:23-24).

Some people even think that God does not exist because they cannot see him. There are many reasons to believe that God exist. I will discuss some of these reasons in the following paragraphs. The fact that one cannot see something does not mean that, that thing does not exist. It is important for the reader to bear in mind that, it is not everything in this world that can be seen or even tasted. You cannot see 'your thought' with your eye but it is there. We can smell the presence of some things; others can be touched, while others can only be heard. For example the note C on the piano, can be heard but can't be smelled. We can hear music, but cannot smell music. We can taste food, smell food, see food, but cannot hear or listen to food. The fact that we cannot listen to food does not mean food does not exist, all it means is that we can know or proof the existence of a particular food by tasting, smelling, seeing or touching.

The nature of an object determines the mode of perception. For example, it is not right to conclude that colours do not exist because you cannot smell colours, or taste colours. In the same way it is wrong to conclude that you cannot believe in God because you cannot see God. ***God, is by definition an infinite spirit*** (John 4:23-24). It is not part of the nature of a spirit to be visible as a material object would be. Commenting on the nature of God as an infinite spirit, J.P Moreland in his book *Scaling the Secular City*, says that 'it is a category fallacy to ascribe sensory qualities to God or fault him for not being a visible object. This is faulting God (an invisible spirit) for not being a visible object'. And so those who say they cannot believe in God because they cannot see God, do not really understand the world they live in.

God expresses his attributes in many different ways to help people to know and to understand him. You can know God by hearing- his word; you can know God by sight- through his Son Jesus Christ; you can know God by touch- through what he has created; you can know God by feeling- through his church. You can look at nature, the way the universe is ordered is even a testimony to the notion that some intelligent designer is behind it sustenance. Design demands a Designer, Intelligence demands an Intelligent Creator, life Demands a Life giver, matter demands a Maker, the Bible's Supernatural attributes Demand a Supernatural Author, the Historical, Miracle-Working, Resurrected Jesus demands a Supernatural explanation, Morality Demands a Moral Law Giver.

There are certain things that can't exist unless something else exists along with them. Commands for example are like that; commands can't exist without something else existing that commanded them. In our society, we have laws and commands because some people made them. The laws at your work place do not exist on their own. In the same way, it is God who commanded us to love one another, not to steal, not to murder, not to lie, to forgive people when they sin against us, to help others etc. The source of all these commands is God. This is what some theologians called 'The Moral Argument'. The moral argument appeals to the existence of moral laws as evidence of God's existence. According to this argument, there couldn't be such a thing as morality without God. If there is no God, then everything is permissible. But since there are moral laws, then not everything is permissible. This proves that God exist, He has no beginning or end. He is immortal.

Building your life on the word of God is a choice. In life, you become what you decide to become, although you may face some challenges before you see your dreams come true. Some people decide to become teachers and so end up becoming teachers. Some also decide to become farmers; they end up becoming farmers. Life is full of choices. Some people make heaven a goal in life, so end up in heaven after death. The 17th-century mathematician and philosopher Blaise Pascal, once told his friends, "If I believe in God and life after death and you do not, and if there is no God, we both lose when we die. However, if there is a God, you still lose and I gain everything." I think this is a good advice to those who deny the existence of God either by confession or by their lifestyle. They should be encouraged to believe in God, so that in case there is God, they will not be condemned on the judgment day. But if they continue to live in unbelief and later find out after they are dead that there is God, they will be in serious trouble. Scripture wisely warns mankind this:

> For we must all appear before the judgment seat of Christ, that each one may receive what is due him for the things done while in the body, whether good or bad (2 Corinthians 5:10).

> Be happy, young man, while you are young, and let your heart give you joy in the days of your youth. Follow the ways of your heart and whatever your eyes see, but know that for all these things God will bring you to judgment (Ecclesiastes 11:9).

The subject of judgment after death where every person will meet God to give an account of things done in this world is something I think everyone should seriously think about. God is making sure everyone in this world hears about this message and his offer of salvation through faith in Jesus Christ where men and women receive forgiveness of sins and eternal life.

Peter Ludwig Berger who predicted that our society would become secularized later admitted humorously on a number of occasions, concluding that the evidence from his collected data as he toured part of the world in fact proved otherwise, that religion is not going away. By the late 1980s, Berger publicly recognized that religion (both old and new) was not only still prevalent, but in many cases was more vibrantly practiced than periods in the past. While recognizing that religion is still a powerful social force, he points to the fact that pluralism and the globalized world fundamentally have changed how the individual experiences faith. Formal religion is being replaced by an individual's search for a personal religious preference, according to his research. This trend is what Mr Harvey Cox; calls 'the Age of Spirituality'.

Many people are seeking God and spiritual things themselves, than through the established religions. A casual survey of any general bookstore- includes at least one prominent section devoted to spirituality: "Devotional Literature" "Metaphysics" "New Age" "Self-Help" etc. Most of the volumes found on popular bookstores are practical in nature; some loosely related to religious traditions and focused on experience of one sort or another. There is a hunger for God and spiritual things these days.

Undoubtedly, there has been an increase in people's interest in spirituality in the 21st century. From the 1960s, a significant portion of the population particularly those in the West began to experiment with new forms of consciousness and communication that took the inner life seriously. Thomas G. Plante's article on *Integrating Spirituality and Psychotherapy: Ethical Issues and Principles to Consider,* reports that professional and scientific psychology appears to have rediscovered spirituality and religion during recent years, with a large number of conferences, seminars, workshops, books, and special issues in major professional journals on spirituality and psychology integration. Journals such as The *American Psychologist, Annals of Behavioural Medicine,* and *Journal of Health Psychology,* among others, have recently dedicated special issues to this important topic.

With the world in such disarray, humanity spontaneously looks for answers in unexpected places or neglected places, one of which involves reconnection with our spiritual traditions. Many people have turned to sources unfamiliar in the West. Some looked to the East, experimenting with transcendental meditation, yoga, and apprenticeship with gurus. The subject of spirituality is thoroughly discussed in chapter three of this book.

The reason why many people are turning to the practice of spiritually can be a subject for future research. But what can be said here is that, the suppression and ridiculing of faith and the knowledge of God by some groups of people seems to have forced many people to seek God not in public spaces, but privately. Many people feel 'ashamed' to declare their faith in the public, particularly those in the West. A survey among leaders who are Christians revealed some disturbing trend. Only about half of the nations' leaders who are Christian share their faith with others according to a research. The chief reason is the fear of rejection or being labelled a religious zealot.

According to *The Telegraph*[2] newspaper, the former attorney general Dominic Grieve had this to say on the suppression of the Christian faith:

> He fears that aggressive secularism is pushing the Christian faith out of the public space. Britain is at risk of being sanitised of faith because an "aggressive form of secularism" in workplaces and public bodies is forcing Christians to hide their beliefs, the former attorney general has warned. Dominic Grieve said he found it quite extraordinary that people were being sacked or disciplined for expressing their beliefs at the work place. He described Christianity as a powerful force for good" in modern Britain and warned that Christians should not be intimidated and excluded for their beliefs. He said that politicians and public figures should not be afraid of "doing God" and

---

[2]   23 August, 2014 edition

that they have a duty to explain how their beliefs inform
their decisions.

Mr Grieve, a practising Anglican, said that Britain is "underpinned" by Christian ethics and principles. He criticised the Tony Blair era when Alastair Campbell, the then communications director in Downing Street, famously said "we don't do God" amid concerns that religion would put off voters. David Cameron once described his own faith as being like "Magic FM in the Chilterns", meaning his faith can come and go. However, earlier this year (2014) the Prime Minister said he has found greater strength in religion and suggested that Britain should be unashamedly "evangelical" about its Christian faith.

Formal religion is being replaced by an individual's search for a personal religious preference. As I said earlier, one of the main reasons is the attempt by some group of people to push faith out of the public space, although there could be other reasons like the effect of globalisation.

Modern spirituality is centered on the "deepest values and meanings by which people live." It embraces the idea of an ultimate or an alleged immaterial reality, or 'a higher being'. It envisions an inner path enabling a person to discover the essence of his/her being. Spirituality is the search for what cannot be seen. This search for the unknown can be both rewarding and at the same time perilous especially if not guided properly. Since the practice of spirituality may involve an interaction between one's spirit and some divine spirit, one of my main concerns has been the type of spirit people expose themselves to.

There are good spirits, and there are also bad spirits. Which spirit have you exposed yourself to? Bad spirits ultimately bring misfortunes into the lives of those who consult them or operate with them. God's Spirit ultimately brings blessings to those who are led by Him, here and the life after. Unfortunately, many spiritual seekers are not guided properly in their practice of spirituality. This can have serious consequences. The word of God can provide the best guidance and answers to what spiritual searchers seek. 1 John 4:1 says 'friends do not believe every spirit, but test the spirits to see whether they are from God'. Dear reader, please make sure you expose yourself to good spirit. God's Spirit is the good Spirit and will bring many blessings to you. Some of the blessings of God's Spirit include: love, joy, peace, patience, kindness, goodness, faithfulness, gentleness and self-control.

We should begin to ask ourselves the question, how we can live our lives in a way that minimises creating more problems for ourselves? We should probably agree with the Psalmist's rhetoric question in Psalm 119:9: 'How can a young man keep his way pure? And he answers thus 'By living according to your word'. The psalmist continues by saying that 'The unfolding of your words gives light; it gives understanding to the simple. I open my mouth and pant, longing for your commands. Turn to me and have mercy on me, as you always do to those who love your name. Direct my footsteps according to your word; let no sin rule over me' (Psalm 119:130-133).

People often wonder if following God's law will restrict them, but experience shows that God's law liberates us—by freeing us from the destructive impact of sinful behavior, and by introducing us to the mind-expanding realm of God's wisdom, so that we will not walk in darkness or do things that will harm us. Like the author of Ecclesiastes, the psalmist had looked around and seen limits to everything in this world. Only in following God's commands, he says, can a person escape the frustrating sense of despair or running into trouble.

It is true that some messages in the Bible can be harsh or hostile, but you see, unless you tell a patient their sickness they may not be willing to accept medication. So it is with the Bible, it tells us who we truly are and then offers us a cure. If a doctor suddenly appears on a television news program announcing in an excited voice, 'a cure for the Paraguayan flu', who would notice? For his discovery to impress us so deeply that we would seek the vaccination, he would first need to prove the terrible danger of the unknown virus. The word of God does the same. It reveals our weaknesses and sin and it also offers a cure. So, please don't be offended when the preacher man or the Bible tells you that you are a sinner. Preachers of God's word have many roles. They can serve as a watchmen warning the people of their sins:

> Son of man, I have made you a watchman for the house of Israel; so hear the word I speak and give them warning from me. When I say to the wicked, 'O wicked man, you will surely die,' and you do not speak out to dissuade him from his ways, that wicked man will die for his sin, and I will hold you accountable for his blood. But if you do warn the wicked man to turn from his ways and he does not do so, he will die for his sin, but you will have saved yourself (Ezekiel 33:7-9).

You don't hire a watchman to fight off robbers single-handed; he is responsible for sounding the alarm. In this text, God assigned the prophet Ezekiel the watchman's role. It's tragic when someone dies for his or her sins, but when he or she dies without being warned, that is inexcusable—for the watchman was assigned to warn the person to repent. Preachers have the duty to encourage, inspire, and at the same time warn the people if they are going astray. Scripture says that, later, Jesus found the disabled man who was healed at the temple and said to him, "See, you are well again. Stop sinning or something worse may happen to you" (John 5:14). The word 'repentance' means to change for the better. This man had to stop sinning or something worse may happen to him.

Paul's message in the book of Romans is the great news about God's amazing grace: a complete cure is available to all. As I said earlier on, people won't seek a cure until they know they are ill. Thus, the book of Romans begins with one of the darkest descriptions in the Bible. The writer concludes, "There is no one righteous, not even one." The entire world is doomed to spiritual death unless a cure can be found. This cure is available to all who will believe the gospel of Jesus Christ.

The closest some people have come to benefiting from God's principles is to live under the shadows of their parents and the previous generations who built their lives on the principles of God. Some people are alive today or are doing well in life today because of how godly their parents were. These people are benefiting from their parent's and the previous generation's loyalty to God. These people are benefiting from the spiritual investments of the previous generations. This is one of the reasons why someone can argue that one does not need to build their lives on the word of God in order to become successful in life. This principle is made clear in the Decalogue as follows:

> I the LORD your God, am a jealous God, punishing the children for the sin of the fathers to the third and fourth generation of those who hate me, but showing love to a thousand generations of those who love me and keep my commandments (Exodus 20:5-6).

The Decalogue or the Ten commandments is a basic set of rules carrying binding authority. They also reveal to some extent the nature of God is to humanity. When God is pleased with one person, He blesses the children and the grand children of that person to many generations. This explains why some people seem to be doing well in life although they don't go to church or acknowledge God in their lives. However, this privilege is short lived. There will come a time when those who benefit from the spiritual investments of their parents have to fend for themselves.

On the other hand, if God is not pleased with one person, such hatred can be passed on to that person's children and the future generations of that person, unless the children or the future generations of that person turn to God and worship him. This is one of the many reasons why each and everyone should seek God for themselves. You may not know how your fore parents lived. Whether they lived to please God or whether they made themselves enemies of God. You have a personal duty to seek the blessings of God for yourself, and for your children's children (Proverbs 13:22).

The second reason why someone can argue that one does not need to build their lives on the word of God in order to become successful in life is because of what I call 'God's common Grace or Kindness'. Sometimes, many people who seemed blessed in this world may think that their own hard work is what have earned them what they have and where they are today. This is God's kindness towards them. It is the character of God to send rain upon the wicked and also send rain upon the righteous (Matthew 5:45). The motive for such acts of kindness is to encourage people to turn to him, the Father of the universe. The book of Romans 2:4 says 'or do you show contempt for the riches of his kindness, tolerance and patience, not realizing that God's kindness leads you toward repentance'.

Sometimes, secular agencies and even the government are very happy to accept the physical contributions from churches such as food banks, shelter for the homeless, youth mentoring programmes etc but are unwilling to engage with or accept the reasons why these material contributions were being offered to the society by the church. When this happen, it is like asking someone who is entering your house to leave something essential about himself or herself outside the door of your house. For example, our love for Jesus Christ as our saviour is the reason why we Christians do good deeds to our fellow human beings, because Christ's love for us compels us to do so. The society is happy to accept the physical contributions made by churches, but are not willing to accept Jesus Christ as Lord and saviour. This is what I call 'the acceptance of religious capital and the rejection of spiritual capital'[3].

---

[3] Religious capital and spiritual capital are terms used by Dr Chris Baker in his paper *The post secular public square, spiritual and progressive politics of hope, 6th June 2013*

Religious capital is the practical contribution to individual, local and national life by churches and other faith groups. Spiritual capital is the motivating basis of faith, belief, and values that shapes the actions of churches. Spiritual capital energises religious capital by providing a theological identity, worshipping tradition, and also a value system, moral vision, and a basis of faith. For people to get the best value from scripture, faith in God, and the church, my suggestion in this book is that, people should accept both the religious capital and spiritual capital aspects of the church. This will encourage churches to do more for the society.

Often times, the church becomes the final institutions left in areas of deprivation in the society. The church serves the homeless, drug addicts, prostitutes, people with mental problems, people suffering from abuse etc. We can see this in Jesus' manifesto and ministry in Luke 4: 18-19 and John 6. "The Spirit of the Lord is on me, because he has anointed me to preach good news to the poor. He has sent me to proclaim freedom for the prisoners and recovery of sight for the blind, to release the oppressed, to proclaim the year of the Lord's favor.

John chapter 6 shows the full cycle of people's response to Jesus. At first, excited by his miracle of feeding the 5000, folks tried to make him king. But Jesus escaped. The next day He rebuked them for having an interest only in physical concerns, not in spiritual truth (John 6:26-29). He used the miracle of the feeding to give an important lesson on the bread of life, using words that were later applied to the Lord's Supper, or the Eucharist. These words, however, disappointed the sensation-seeking crowd that many turned away from him. As the bread of life (John 6:35), Jesus would nourish his people far better than any miraculous meal. Sadly many people have interest only in physical concerns, not in spiritual truth.

1.2 Scripture and its usefulness

Let us now define what Scripture is. Scripture is the sacred writings of Christianity contained in the Holy Bible. In worship services, public and private readings, Christians often turn to Scripture for guidance: to the stories of Abraham, Moses, to the Psalms, to the prophecies, to the life of Jesus, to the letters of Paul, and to the vision of John etc.

So how did we get the Bible? The first hand-written English language Bible manuscripts were produced in the 1380's AD by John Wycliffe, an Oxford professor, scholar, and theologian. The question most people ask is, how did the people of old live according to God's standard since they did not have the Bible in their day? Before the Bible was written, God used to speak to individuals, groups of people, and nations in various ways, either through dreams, or by an angel or by a human messenger, usually through the prophets. For example, the city of Nineveh did not have the Bible, so when God wanted them to repent, he sent Jonah there to proclaim his message to them. The people obeyed the message, and built their lives based on what Jonah told them. God has many ways to reach people who do not have the Bible with His principles, even in our day. God could have also put his principles in the heart of people (Romans 2:14-15). These people knew the word of God intuitively because God has put his word in them. These people have the desire to obey God's word because it was in them.

During the first twenty-five hundred years of human history, there was no written revelation. Those who had been taught about the principles of God, communicated their knowledge to others orally, father to son through successive generations. The preparation of the written word began in the time of Moses. Inspired revelations were then embodied in an inspired book. This work continued during the long period of sixteen hundred years, from Moses the historian of creation and the law, to John the recorder of the most sublime truth of the Gospel.

We should therefore see the Bible as a collection of the word of God spoken to different people at different times written over a period of about 1500 years. Believers in the twenty first century are privileged to have copies of this book. Believers in the earlier days did not have all the books we have in the Bible today, they only had portions of what we have today, but what they had was enough to give them the light of salvation they needed in their day.

Can scripture or the Bible be trusted? Many people are of the opinion that the Bible was written and translated by human beings so it cannot be trusted. There are others who are also of the opinion that the Bible is contradictory or is not error free. Some people also have questions with the translation of the Bible into various languages and versions. Due to space constraint, I have briefly discussed few of these questions here. We have people who are experts in interpreting the constitution of a particular country. In the same way the church of God has people who have been trained in matters regarding the interpretation of scripture and to answer any questions concerning the Bible. It is suggested that those who have questions about the Bible can also attend Sunday school in a local church to find answers to their questions.

It is true that the Bible was written in human language by human beings. You see, after creation, God has been using human beings as instruments or vessels to communicate his truth to us, although there are instances whereby God used angels to communicate to humanity. Everything we see around us in this world is done by a human being because God has given us the abilities to do them. Deuteronomy 8: 18 say 'it is he [God] who gives you the ability to produce wealth, and so confirms his covenant, which he swore to your forefathers'. In the same way, God gave certain men and woman the abilities (the grace) to write and translate the Bible into different languages and versions. 2 Peter 1:20-21 summaries this notion as follows:

> Above all, you must understand that no prophecy of Scripture came about by the prophet's own interpretation. For prophecy never had its origin in the will of man, but

men spoke from God as they were carried along by the
Holy Spirit.

God inspired the writers of the books in the Bible so we can say
that their message is authentic and reliable. God used the talents,
education, experience, cultural background and His Holy Spirit in
guiding each writer's mind in such a way to ensure that their message
is authentic and reliable. I think the problem has to do with the
interpretation, understanding, and application of the Bible. Different
people have different interpretations of the Bible. But these issues
have been discussed in chapter ten in this book.

Some reasons people should build their lives on scripture:
Scripture is very useful as guidance, correcting, and training in all
righteousness. Scripture tells us how to be kind to our fellow human
beings, how to pray effectively, how to escape temptation and trials.
At the same time it tells us how to seek and worship God for more
of his blessings and so on. In this section we will look at more of
the reasons why people should build their lives according to the
principles of God.

Firstly, every system of belief or practice in this world is derived
or borrowed from what the Christian tradition calls scripture. In
other words, every system of belief comes from scripture either
partially, wholly, or in adulterated form. For example, in the field
of medicine, technology or any of the innovative disciplines of life,
scripture reminds us the source of human abilities to make all the
inventions we see around us (read Genesis 1:27-30; Deuteronomy
8:17-18). Our Justice or legal system which is aimed at upholding
fairness in society both in business and for individuals derived its
origin and inspiration from scripture (read Exodus 23:1-9), although
many legal systems are silent on their original source of inspiration.
Gerald R. Thompson in his book, *Legal Foundations: The Framework
of Law*, has this to say on how Biblical principles of law and the Bible
itself were used and acknowledged in the documentary history of
England and America:

> The use of the Bible in Anglo-American jurisprudence should not be underestimated. In structuring a society to secure the greatest liberty and promote the greatest happiness, the Bible was viewed not only as relevant, but also as authoritative guidance for the task.

The three sets of such documents which were inspired by biblical principles are: (1) organic English documents; (2) American colonial documents; and (3) early state constitutions. The reader can find out more about these documents which helped shaped and secured the British and the American societies.

The notion of caring for and about others is a common thread running through many of the world's established religions and communities. And this notion of love for fellow human beings is a commandment from God found in the Holy Scriptures which has been passed on down the generations. Someone who identified herself as a Buddhist said 'one of the central teachings of Buddhism is compassion'. 'Love thy neighbour as thyself and love for God is a central principle in the Christian faith tradition too. And seek to be in harmony with all your neighbours; live in amity with your brethren is a tenet of Confucianism- a system of philosophical and ethical teachings founded by Confucius, a Chinese philosopher. To 'love' is a commandment from God who expects his creation to love one another and himself. 'To love one another' is not the only guidance from God to us. There are many more principles of God which we need to find out for our benefit. This is the second of the many reasons people need to turn to God and to build their lives according to his word.

The third reason is that, scripture is comprehensive and dynamic. Comprehensive because in scripture, God has given humanity all that we need for life and godliness in every generation (1 Peter 1:3-4). For example Daniel who served as a prophet to the exiles from 605-535BC and also as an administrator in past empires during the reigns of Nebuchadnezzar, Belshazzar, Darious, and Cyrus was told by the Lord that he had given him enough vision and message for his time, he did not need to understand every vision he has seen, some were for the future generations (Daniel 12:8-9). Every generation has enough truth to build their lives on.

Scripture is also dynamic in the sense that there are certain important issues in life which the written word seems silent on. Sometimes true understanding and application of scripture in a particular situation can be difficult for people. This is where the dynamic nature of Scripture plays a vital role. God's Spirit helps spiritual seekers to discover more about scripture itself, more about themselves, more about this world, and more about God. Jesus says in John 16:12-13:

> I have much more to say to you, more than you can now bear. But when he, the Spirit of truth, comes, he will guide you into all truth. He will not speak on his own; he will speak only what he hears, and he will tell you what is yet to come.

The Spirit of God will lead and help people to understand more about the word of God concerning any problem they will have.

Should people build their lives on scripture alone? As I said earlier on in this chapter, we don't live in a completely godly world; hence it is practically impossible for one to be guided in life by scripture alone. Because of this, there are many things, belief systems, and ideologies which influence our lives at the work place, in colleges and in universities, and even our social and spiritual lives. What is needed, are guidelines to help people decide what they can allow to influence the way they live. The next section discusses some of these guidelines. Scripture provides guidelines on which ideas, beliefs, or lifestyles we should allow to influence our lives.

1.3 Guidelines on what you should allow to influence your life

There are many sources of teachings, ideas, and lifestyles which influence many people's lives and which are not bad *per se*. However, some of these belief systems which people allow themselves to be influenced by are very dangerous. The following guidelines can help people to accept or reject any source of information, belief system, idea, teachings or life style which might be dangerous to their very existence.

First, any book or any source of a particular belief system, idea, philosophy, lidestyle or religion which challenges the Golden Rule and the Ten Commandments can be very dangerous for humanity. Such ideology should not be embraced. The **Golden Rule** or **ethic of reciprocity** is an ethical code or a morality code which essentially states that 'one should treat others as one would like others to treat oneself'. This concept can be explained from the perspective of psychology, philosophy, sociology and religion. Psychologically, it involves a person empathizing with others. Philosophically, it involves a person perceiving their neighbour as also "an I" or "self." Sociologically, this principle is applicable between individuals, between groups, and also between individuals and groups. For example, a person living by this rule treats all people with consideration, not just members of his or her group. Any religion, school of thought or life style which does not promote this rule should be seen as dangerous.

The **Ten Commandments**, also known as the **Decalogue**, are a set of biblical principles relating to ethics and worship of the almighty God, which play a fundamental role in Judaism and Christianity. They include instructions to worship the only true God and to keep a rest day or the Sabbath;[4] as well as prohibitions against idolatry, blasphemy, murder, theft, dishonesty, and adultery. The Ten Commandments is a very good 'principle' to follow because it will ultimately lead you to Christ Jesus for the salvation of your soul.

The second guidelines on what you should allow to influence your life in addition to scripture is that, any book or any source of

---

[4]   The New Testament treats the Sabbath day in a significantly different way than the Old Testament does and it is not required for Christians today. Christians who choose to keep the seventh-day Sabbath, and Christians who do not choose to do so, should be tolerant of each other's convictions.

a particular belief system, philosophy or religion which promotes hedonism, can be very dangerous for humanity unless well balanced. Such ideology should not be embraced. **Hedonism** is a school of thought that argues that pleasure is the only intrinsic good. This is the idea that all people have the right to do everything in their power to achieve the greatest amount of pleasure. A lifestyle which only aims at achieving pleasure can be dangerous in so many ways. It can compel a person to become covetous, selfish, restless, greedy, foolish, and sometimes a murderer. People who hold the view that pleasure should be the highest good in life can do anything foolish or dangerous to achieve pleasure. Proverbs 21:17 says 'He *who loves pleasure will become poor; whoever loves wine and oil will never be rich'*. Ethical hedonism is said to have been started by Aristippus of Cyrene, a student of Socrates. He held the idea that pleasure is the highest good. People who live for pleasure normally die a foolish death (read Luke 12:13-21). Does it mean that people should not experience pleasure? Pleasure can be good if it is well balanced with good behaviour and other vital issues of life such as godliness, self-control, purity, kindness, decency, obedience to God etc.

Thirdly, any book or a source of a particular belief, or lifestyle which provides instructions or rituals for magic acts, 'abnormal sex', witchcraft, destruction, and rebelliousness is very dangerous and can destroy people's life easily. These practices are invocations for Satan. Scriptures warns in 1 Timothy 4:1-2: 'that in later times some will abandon the faith and follow deceiving spirits and things taught by demons'. The practice of magic art, witchcraft, rebelliousness, and immoral sexual lifestyle are dangerous. Some people indulge in these practices out of ignorance; they don't know that such practices are detestable to God. God is not happy with people who do these things. Those who indulge in them will miss heaven unless they repent. Rebelliousness, magic arts, witchcraft, unhealthy sexual lifestyles are all not good because they are some of the character traits of Satan.

God wants mankind to live a life of purity, love, peace, gentleness, respect, self discipline, and joy. Healthy sexual life is recommended by the Lord, where every man is to have a wife and vice versa. Single people are encouraged to seek a partner leading to marriage. It is better for single people to marry than to burn with passion.

Fourthly, any book or any source of a particular belief system, idea, philosophy or religion which teaches that God is not an external entity who deserves to be worshipped, but teaches that 'god' is something that each person creates as a projection of his or her own personality is very dangerous for people to build their lives on. Such belief system teaches people that they are 'god' themselves, there is no God anywhere! Such teachings should be looked at with suspicion. Scripture says 'In the beginning God created the heavens and the earth' (Genesis 1:1). There is only one true God. No human being should assume the place of God either in their own lives or in the society. God is great; we are his creation, his offspring by nature and his adopted sons and daughters through faith in Jesus Christ (Ephesians 1:4-6).

Fifthly, any book or a source of a particular belief should be seen as incomplete if it does not lead people to Jesus Christ as the Son of God who died, rose again for the sins of the world. If you follow any tradition or belief and that tradition or belief does not lead you to Jesus Christ as your saviour, the advice is that you must on your own, seek Christ for the salvation of your soul. Jesus Christ is the fulfilment of all promises from God. 2 Corinthians 1:20 says 'For all of God's promises have been fulfilled in Christ with a resounding "Yes!" And through Christ, our Amen (which means "Yes") ascends to God for his glory.

The book of John 6:45 says 'it is written in the Prophets: *'They will all be taught by God.' Everyone who listens to the Father and learns from him comes to me* [Jesus]. Hebrews 1:1-12 says 'In the past God spoke to our forefathers through the prophets at many times and in various ways, but in these last days he has spoken to us by his Son, whom he appointed heir of all things, and through whom he made the universe. God is speaking to the world through his Son Jesus

Christ. Any source of belief, tradition or philosophy which does not lead people to Christ should be seen as incomplete. 2 John 1:9 says 'Anyone who runs ahead and does not continue in the teaching of Christ does not have God; whoever continues in the teaching has both the Father and the Son'.

This chapter is an introduction of this book, *Building your life on the principles of God, the solid foundation*. Let us look at how scripture can guide people to receive help in times of personal crisis in the next chapter.

Chapter 2

Guidance on receiving help in times of Personal crisis

The God who created the world knows that humanity needs help. That is why He sent his only begotten Son to die for the sins of the world. He sent his Holy Spirit upon those who will believe in Him to strengthen them, to comfort them, to counsel them, to teach them and to lead them into all truth. Some people need encouragement to continue the good works they are doing, others need prayers for healing and deliverance, and others need wisdom to lead and to live wisely whereas some people need strength to overcome their weakness and depression, for example. There are some who may need protection from Satan and evil people and others have a need to find a marriage partner to overcome their loneliness, while some need to be snatched from hell fire. Generally, everyone receives help one way or another from God whether knowingly or unknowingly. But those who have decided to hope and trust in God in covenantal terms receive *extra* help from Him in times of crisis.

> Do you not know? Have you not heard? The LORD is the everlasting God, the Creator of the ends of the earth. He will not grow tired or weary, and His understanding no one can fathom. He gives strength to the weary and increases the power of the weak. Even youths grow tired and weary, and young men stumble and fall; but those who hope in the Lord will renew their strength. They

will soar on wings like eagles; they will run and not grow
weary, they will walk and not be faint (Isaiah 40:28-31).

It is a fact of life that we can all grow tired and weary. But those
who have hope in the God who created the heavens and the earth
will receive extra strength from Him in such times. What God has
in mind is that he will continue to supply us with more resources
as we depend on Him. This is one of the many reasons why people
have to build their lives on God's principles. God's principles work
all the time. Help is available. The problem is that many people
have turned their back on God and are consequently going through
unnecessary suffering.

We are not living in a trouble free world. Good people suffer. Bad
people suffer. Some of these problems come to us by our own choices.
We can also suffer from tragedies and harms as innocent victims.
Sometimes, ignorance which is defined as a lack of education or
awareness can makes us commit mistakes that harm our relationships,
marriages, careers and much more. Many people do not know what
to do when they are in crisis. Some even end up committing suicide
because they think their world has come to an end when they have
exhausted all means and are unable to do anything else to help
themselves. Some also resort to drugs and rough living because they
have no hope anywhere. But the good news is that there is always
help available to us! Especially for those who believe in God!

People who commit suicide do so because they have no hope
when they fail in some aspect of life. A friend of mine whose brother
committed suicide said he thinks his brother did so because the
brother thought he had failed in life. He had no hope in anything
else, how sad! I strongly believe he would be alive today if he had
been putting his faith in God. God knows the condition of our world
and how people are suffering. But He has got a solution to all these
problems. Our duty is to find out God's plans for this dying world,
and what we have to do in order to cope with the challenges we
face in life.

In this chapter we will discuss some of God's principles that can help us in times of crisis. We will also look at three main reasons why people should not give up in life. God has many ways to help people in crisis. I will only discuss some of these sources of help from God here, namely the Angelic help, the promised Son, the promised Holy Spirit etc. We will also discuss how people can practically receive help from God in times of crisis. It appears some people who believe in God do not receive help from him in times of crisis. Probably you may have known a believer who went through a serious crisis yet it appeared the person did not receive help from God. I have few lessons to discuss with such people in this chapter. God has been helping many people in times of crisis to overcome whatever challenges they have encountered. It is my prayer that as you read this book God will help you to overcome any crisis or challenges you face.

2.1 How people can receive help from God in times of crisis

Those who need help from God should call upon Him in prayer in times of personal crisis, for whoever *shall call upon the name of the Lord shall be saved.* They must believe when they ask God for help. There may be times when you have to tell your church to help you in prayers.

Some people want to believe in God if they can see evidence like the doubting Thomas, who would only believe in the resurrection of Jesus Christ if he saw the nail marks in Jesus' hands and put his finger where the nails were, and put his hand into Jesus' side. (John 20:24-29). Others too are able to believe or have faith when they hear the message about what God can do for them, for '*faith comes to people from hearing the message about God, and the message is heard through the word of Christ*' (Romans 10:17).

One of the keys to supernatural experiences in the lives of people who received help from God, is their belief in God, and this is one of my aims for writing this book; that men and women will have faith in the true God who created the heavens and the earth, and build their lives on His word. I heard a testimony of a Pastor in the US who was diagnosed of cancer. Do you know what this Pastor did? He selectively read all the scriptures in the Bible which talk about the healing power of God and how God miraculously healed people who were sick. A couple of weeks later, he revisited the hospital and was told that the cancer has disappeared. Reading the scriptures regularly can help you develop faith for supernatural miracles.

As you read this book I pray that you will hear the voice of God speaking to you right now so that you will have faith to receive an answer or solution to any problem you have, in Jesus name. For Jesus *says: You may ask me for anything in my name and I will do it* (John 14:13-14). You can pause for a moment, and pray to God to have mercy on you, and to help you in any difficult situation you find yourself in, believe that God will answer you as you pray.

> Do not be anxious about anything, but in everything, by prayer and petition, with thanksgiving, present your requests to God. And the peace of God, which transcends all understanding, will guard your hearts and your minds in Christ Jesus.

Prayer to God can be said by both believers and unbelievers. Many people and nations have found peace in times of crisis by praying to God and asking for help.

Obviously not all prayers are answered, and so how can we pray for answered prayers? Hebrews 5:7 says 'During the days of Jesus' life on earth, he offered up prayers and petitions with loud cries and tears to the one who could save him from death, and he was heard because of his reverent submission'. Jesus prayed with tears to God, and because of his submission to the Father, his prayers were answered. Many people want God to answer them when they are in trouble, but they are not willing to submit their lives to Him. Sometimes to receive help from God, you have to submit your life to him and pray passionately, sometimes with tears.

2 Chronicles 7:13-14 says, "When I [the Lord] shut up the heavens so that there is no rain, or command locusts to devour the land or send a plague among my people, if my people, who are called by my name, will humble themselves and pray and seek my face and turn from their wicked ways, then will I hear from heaven and will forgive their sin and will heal their land'. In this text the subject of humility in prayer is emphasized. Scripture also tells us to turn from our wicked ways if we want God to hear us from heaven.

Let us now discuss some of the reasons why people should not give up on life no matter what they go through in the next paragraphs.

2.2 Three reasons why people should not give up

The first reason why people should not give up in life is the fact that things or situations change. The second reason is that there are good people in this world who are ready to help you. The third reason is that there is hope, for those who believe in God.

Things change; this is a good reason why people should keep on going no matter their problem or level of suffering. As hard as it may be to believe, a distressing circumstance – even one that seems beyond your control- may be temporary. In fact, your situation can change for the better unexpectedly. Consider these three faithful people mentioned in the Bible who suffered despair to the point of not wanting to go on. But because of their faith in God they survived and finished well in life.

Moses said:

> If this is how you are going to treat me, put me to death right now—if I have found favor in your eyes, and do not let me face my own ruin' (Number 11:15).

Elijah's season of despair:

> Elijah was afraid and ran for his life. When he came to Beersheba in Judah, he left his servant there, while he

himself went a day's journey into the desert. He came to a broom tree, sat down under it and prayed that he might die. I have had enough, LORD, he said. Take my life; I am no better than my ancestors' (1 Kings 19:3-4).

Job's profound expressions of pain and despair:

Why did I not perish at birth, and die as I came from the womb? (Job 3:11). Oh, that I might have my request, that God would grant what I hope for, that God would be willing to crush me, to let loose his hand and cut me off (Job 6:8-9).

If you read the Biblical accounts about these people, you will find out that their circumstances changed for the better- and in ways that they could not have foreseen. This is one of the many reasons why people should not give up, no matter what they go through. God will come to their help. The Bible says this concerning Job:

The LORD blessed the latter part of Job's life more than the first. He had fourteen thousand sheep, six thousand camels, a thousand yoke of oxen and a thousand donkeys. And he also had seven sons and three daughters. The first daughter he named Jemimah, the second Keziah and the third Keren-Happuch. Nowhere in all the land were there found women as beautiful as Job's daughters, and their father granted them an inheritance along with their brothers. After this, Job lived a hundred and forty years; he saw his children and their children to the fourth generation. And so he died, old and full of years (Job 42:12-17).

Someone may ask, 'but what if my circumstances cannot change?' For example, suppose you have a chronic illness. Or what if your case is an irreversible situation, such as the breaking up of marriage or relationship or the death of a loved one? Dear reader, even in such cases, there is something you can do to move on in life positively: one way is that, in learning to accept what you cannot change, you become more likely to view things from a more positive standpoint.

Such impossible situations could open a new chapter in your life. A song writer once said 'God makes rivers in the desert'.

The second reason why people should not give up in life is because there is help available. The bible says' *'Cast all your anxiety on him because he cares for you'* (1 Peter 5:7). Paul tells the Philippian church *'not to be anxious about anything, but in everything, by prayer and petition, with thanksgiving, present your requests to God. And the peace of God, which transcends all understanding, will guard your hearts and your minds in Christ Jesus'* (Philippians 4:6-7). Prayer is **one** of the means by which you can receive help from God. There are good people both in the church and outside the church who are willing to help you, so don't give up! Look for truly godly people and let them help you. All you have to do is to tell them in confidence your problem and learn to receive help from them.

Church fellowship can provide such godly group of people to turn to in times of need. Brown *et al.*, in their research into depression in women in the Hebrides Islands of Scotland, discovered that religious communities could be protective for women against depression. They offered support, friendship and a place where problems and concerns could be aired and worked through. However, culturally, men did not express themselves in this way and tended not to be involved in religious communities. Instead they drank excessively and became involved in acts of violence, according to the same research. The word of God encourages people to belong to the church fellowship so that they can call on the leaders for help in times of crisis:

> 'Is any one of you sick? He should call the elders of the church to pray over him and anoint him with oil in the name of the Lord. And the prayer offered in faith will make the sick person well; the Lord will raise him up. If he has sinned, he will be forgiven. Therefore confess your sins to each other and pray for each other so that you may be healed. The prayer of a righteous man is powerful and effective' (James 5:14-16).

The third reason why people should not give up in life no matter what they go through is because there is hope, especially for those who believe in God.

What is hope? Hope is defined as a *desire with expectation of obtainment or a desire for something to happen.* Hope encourages us in times of despair & difficulty. People can have hope or become hopeful in this world by knowing the good things in store for them in the future. If you know that there is something good for you tomorrow, you will not complain too much if you are going through some personal crisis today. Knowledge about God is powerful. People should seek to know some of the good things in our world so that they can be hopeful, especially about their future. The Bible promises a lot of such hopes. This hope is not just a collection of mere wishful sayings. God fully purposes to bring to fruition any promise He has made.

> 'As the rain and the snow come down from heaven, and do not return to it without watering the earth and making it bud and flourish, so that it yields seed for the sower and bread for the eater, so is my word that goes out from my mouth: It will not return to me empty, but will accomplish what I desire and achieve the purpose for which I sent it'(Isaiah 55:10–11).

God is committed to seeing that what he says comes to pass. *'The LORD said to me, "You have seen correctly, for I am watching to see that my word is fulfilled'* (Jeremiah 1:12). You may also be familiar with this message sent to the exiled Israelites' who were discouraged:

> 'For I know the plans I have for you, declares the LORD, "plans to prosper you and not to harm you, plans to give you hope and a future'(Jeremiah 29:11).

No matter how bad your situation is, there is hope for you. Your duty is to seek this hope in the Lord. For example, on a personal level, Jesus has promised to save, provide, protect and be with all those who will believe in Him (John 6:37–40; Matthew 11:28–30). On the cosmic level, this world will become a better place one day. People should not live in fear that this world is coming to an end. God says He is preparing a New heaven and a New earth for the human race (Revelation 21:1-5). So there is hope for our world. This promise should encourage people to live a fulfilling and positive life in this world. You cannot enjoy life or achieve anything substantial if you have no hope. Hopeless people live reckless lives because they think there is nothing good in store for them. They usually say, *"Let us eat and drink, for tomorrow we die"* (1 Corinthians 15:33). True hope encourages people to live a careful and godly lifestyle. This is one of the reasons you have to build your life on God's word, His principles.

> 'Dear friends, now we are children of God, and what we will be has not yet been made known. But we know that when he appears, we shall be like him, for we shall see him as he is. Everyone who has this hope in him purifies himself, just as he is pure' (1 John 3:2-3).

Those who have hope live a decent life because they know something good is in store for them in the future. Our leaders should point out these things to the people so that they can have hope. The youth of today live anyhow because they have no hope in the future.

The world has been designed by its creator in such a way that in any time of crisis or trouble there is always help or a solution at hand, no matter the problem. Some of these kinds of help can come to us through people; some too can come from God himself. Experience and research have confirmed that the kind of help we receive from our leaders or other people sometimes do not really address our problems. There are many reasons why this is so. Evidently, the main reason given by most people is that human beings are mortal and limited in power and abilities. I love how Mr. Rowan Williams, the former Archbishop of Canterbury describes the human limitations and dependency:

> The sense that human beings are limited and dependent is not, for religious believers, something humiliating or disempowering; it is simply an acknowledgment of the

way things are which, like any apprehension of the truth,
is liberating because it delivers us from aspiring to mythic
goals of absolute human control over human destiny.

God bless your soul Mr Williams for these revelations! There are many dimensions of life where you don't have absolute control. Nobody has absolute control over spiritual things except the almighty God. For example, one of the reasons why treatment of depression can be difficult is because of the spiritual dimensions aspect of this illness. Even an initial and intuitive reflection on depression reveals it to be an inherently spiritual condition. Depression main symptoms of profound hopelessness, loss of meaning in life, often perceived loss of relationship with God or a higher power, low self-esteem, the search for meaning, and the general sense of purposelessness, all indicate a level of distress which clearly has spiritual connotations. As John Swinton and Harriet Mowat make the case in their book, *Practical Theology and qualitative research*, "There is therefore a sense of spiritual crisis inherent within depression that will not necessary be alleviated by psychotherapy or pharmacology, particularly if the true nature of the crisis go unnoticed". The main point I am making here is that, human beings are limited in many ways, hence the need to seek God for help especially in areas where we have no absolute control.

Before I continue to the next section, let me state these five facts about life to guide our thoughts:

1. Everyone has weaknesses and limitations. So don't use your weaknesses or limitations as an excuse. Seek help.

2. There is no ideal environment to pursue your dreams; you have to create one for yourself.

3. Every problem you will encounter in this world has a solution.

4. Your duty is to find out how to get things done in life instead of complaining or being idle or giving up.

5. You have a personal responsibility towards the welfare of your social, economic and Spiritual needs.

Read these positive attitudes from these two men:

> As Jesus approached Jericho, a blind man was sitting by the roadside begging. When he heard the crowd going by, he asked what was happening. They told him, "Jesus of Nazareth is passing by." He called out, "Jesus, Son of David, have mercy on me!" Those who led the way rebuked him and told him to be quiet, but he shouted all the more, "Son of David, have mercy on me!" Jesus stopped and ordered the man to be brought to him. When he came near, Jesus asked him, "What do you want me to do for you?" "Lord, I want to see," he replied. Jesus said to him, "Receive your sight; your faith has healed you." Immediately he received his sight and followed Jesus, praising God. When all the people saw it, they also praised God (Luke 18:35-43).

> 'In a similar situation, a man called Zacchaeus wanted to see who Jesus was, but being a short man he could not because of the crowd. So he ran ahead and climbed a sycamore-fig tree to see him, since Jesus was coming that way. When Jesus reached the spot, he looked up and said to him, "Zacchaeus, come down immediately, I must stay at your house today"'.(Luke 19:1-10).

The lesson here is that these two men, all had weaknesses and limitations, but that did not stop them from achieving what they wanted. In the same way, you must not allow your weakness, environment or limitations to prevent you from achieving your dreams. Have a positive mindset, make use of any opportunity that comes your way, seek godly solution and take the appropriate steps to solve any problem you have with the help of God.

As Mr Williams said, we should not feel ashamed of our failures due to our weakness and limitation but rather it is important that we look elsewhere for help, we should look up to something greater than ourselves, to the all powerful God- **'the God who created the universe and his Son Jesus Christ'**. But is God really powerful and all able as people claim? The answer is emphatically YES. You can know someone through his name, through what he has done for other people, and through what he himself says about himself. Join me through the following, as I discuss what God can do in your life and also in the lives of all those who will call upon his name.

God can heal you of any sickness. God can restore peace and unity in your family and relationships. If you are jobless, know that God can help you get a job so that you can live a responsible life. If you have lost hope in everything, know that God has good news for the hopeless. If you are loaded with sin and guilt, you don't need to remain in this situation. Because while you were still a sinner Christ Jesus died for your sins, God made Jesus Christ, who did not sin, to become a sin offering for **you** so that you might become the righteousness of God (Romans 5:6-9; 2 Corinthians 5:21). There are many benefits you will receive in times of difficulty if you build your life on the principles of God- that is, putting God's words into practice.

2.3 Sources of Help from God in times of crisis

The writer of the book of Hebrews assures those who built their lives on the word of God that: *'you have come to Mount Zion, to the heavenly Jerusalem, the city of the living God. You have come to thousands upon thousands of angels in joyful assembly, to the church of the firstborn, whose names are written in heaven. You have come to God, the judge of all men, to the spirits of righteous men made perfect'* (Hebrews 12:22-23). You are surrounded by a host of heavenly support; to help you in times of need. There are many means God can use to help you in times of crisis. I will only discuss four of these assistances from God here, namely the promised Son, the angelic help, the promised Holy Spirit, fellow believers, and even help from nature.

1. The Promised Son, Jesus Christ the saviour of the world

God really loves the world, and so at the right time he sent his only Son to come and help the human race.

> For God so loved the world that he gave his one and only
> Son, that whoever believes in him shall not perish but
> have eternal life (John 3:16).

Unless a person communicates to you, in speech or gestures or even facial expressions, you can't get to know him or her. What goes on behind the mask of skin will always remain a mystery. God, too, was a mystery until he broke His silence. He spoke once, and all creation sprang to life—quasars, oceans, whales, giraffes, orchids, and beetles. He spoke again, says John, and this time the Word took the form of a man, Jesus Christ. John's book tells the story of that Word who became flesh. In the words of John, the reason Jesus became man was to help the human race deal with their plight caused by Satan, sin, oppressions, sickness, fear, hopelessness:

> He who does what is sinful is of the devil, because the
> devil has been sinning from the beginning. The reason
> the Son of God appeared was to destroy the devil's work
> (1 John 3:8).

The book of Hebrews goes further than any other New Testament book in explaining Jesus' human nature. Why was it so important that Jesus shared our humanity? The answer is that because Jesus came to help humanity in need! The book of Hebrews stresses three more reasons: (1) so that, in dying, he could free us from the power of death (Hebrews 2:14-15); (2) so that, by becoming the final sacrifice for sin, he could reconcile us to God (Hebrews 5:8-9); and (3) so that, in experiencing temptation, he can better help us with our own temptations (Hebrews 2:18).

Jesus Christ is a gift from God to humanity. Jesus came the first time in human form to teach humanity many things about God and to live an exemplary life. He was crucified so that his blood could forgive the sins of the world especially those who will believe in Him. In death, he went to the spirits of those who are dead long ago and rose from the dead on the third day so that He can be the Lord of both the dead and the living (Romans 14:9; 1 Peter 3:18-20). He ascended to heaven after forty days (Acts 1:9-11). He will come back the second time to take believers with Him to paradise! (John 14:1-3).

Before we discuss how to receive help from Jesus, let us look at one another way to receive help from God.

2. The Promised Holy Spirit

God has promised to bless all people with his Spirit in the last days. The Holy Spirit empowers us, gives us wisdom and leads us to the truth. Let us read this text together:

> No, this is what was spoken by the prophet Joel. In the last days, God says, I will pour out my Spirit on all people. Your sons and daughters will prophesy, your young men will see visions, your old men will dream dreams. Even on my servants, both men and women, I will pour out my Spirit in those days, and they will prophesy. (Acts 2:16-18).

Before Jesus' ascension to heaven, He promised to ask the father to send the Holy Spirit to his people:

> 'If you love me, you will obey what I command. And I will ask the Father, and he will give you another Counselor to be with you forever— the Spirit of truth...'(John 14:15-17).

It is true that God has promised humanity the Holy Spirit, but the question I want to ask is do humanity really need the Holy Spirit? To answer this question, I think it will be helpful for us to look at the three main functions of the Holy Spirit. We will first look at the role of the Holy Spirit in the world; second, the role of the Holy Spirit in the life of people who have received God's Spirit; and thirdly the rediscovery of spirituality by scholars, politicians and unbelievers in the 21st century.

A. The role the Holy Spirit plays in the world

In the beginning God created the heavens and the earth. According to the creation account, *'the earth was formless and empty, darkness was over the surface of the deep, and the Spirit of God was hovering over the waters'* (Genesis 1:1-2). Usually, darkness and the sea or the waters has to do with evil. And so if the Spirit of God was hovering over the water, then it may suggest that, the Spirit of God was policing the world at that time. Jesus says *"When he comes, he will convict the world of guilt in regard to sin and righteousness and judgment"* (John 16:8). When you look at the three global role of the Holy Spirit, no one will tell you that humanity needs the Holy Spirit. The three global task of the Holy Spirit are: (1) convicting the world of its sin and calling it to repentance, (2) revealing the standard of God's righteousness to anyone who believes, because Christ would no longer be physically present on earth, and (3) demonstrating Christ judgment over Satan.

There are many reasons why people and nations need to be righteous. Proverbs 11:4 says *'wealth is worthless in the day of wrath, but righteousness delivers from death'*. Proverbs 11:8 says' *'the wicked man earns deceptive wages, but he who sows righteousness reaps a sure reward'*. Proverbs 14:34 says' *'Righteousness exalts a nation, but sin is a disgrace to any people'*. Build your life on the righteousness of God by putting His word into practice. So far we have looked at the global task of the Holy Spirit. Let us now look at the role of the Holy Spirit in individual's life. We need the Holy Spirit! A song writer wrote this song about the Holy Spirit:

> Come, Holy Spirit, I need you
> Come, sweet Spirit, I pray
> Come in your strength and your power
> Come in your own special way

B. The role of the Holy Spirit in individual's life

The Holy Spirit who is the same as the Spirit of God or the Spirit of Christ is involved in our salvation from beginning to the end. According to John 3:5-6, we are 'born again' by the Holy Spirit and water. Romans 8:9 say *'if anyone does not have the Spirit of Christ, he does not belong to Christ'*. Acts 1:8 Jesus says *'and you will receive* power when the Holy Spirit comes on you; and you will be my witnesses in Jerusalem, and in all Judea and Samaria, and to the ends of the earth'*. In John 14:15-17, Jesus says *"If you love me, you will obey what I command. And I will ask the Father, and he will give you another Counselor to be with you forever— the Spirit of truth. The world cannot accept him, because it neither sees him nor knows him. But you know him, for he lives with you and will be in you"*. In 2 Timothy 1:7 Paul reminded Timothy that 'God did not give us a spirit of timidity, but a spirit of power, of love and of self-discipline'.

Someone may ask, 'how can one receive the Holy Spirit?' The answer is, when you give your life to the Lord and accept Jesus as your Lord and saviour, God's Spirit comes and dwells in you. Acts 2:38 says *'repent and be baptized, every one of you, in the name of Jesus Christ for the forgiveness of your sins. And you will receive the gift of the Holy Spirit'*. Ephesians 1:13 says *'and you also were included in Christ when you heard the word of truth, the gospel of your salvation, having believed, you were marked in him with a seal, the promised Holy Spirit'*. The Bible always encourages us to be continuously filled with the Holy Spirit, and this can be done through prayer. We human; we leak, so there is a need to ask the father in prayer to fill us with more of His Spirit, especially in those times when you feel weak or discouraged. Acts 4:31 says' *'after they prayed, the place where they were meeting was shaken. And they were all filled with the Holy Spirit and spoke the word of God boldly'*. Another reason why humanity needs the Holy Spirit is the subject matter in the next section.

C. Rediscovery of Spirituality by ordinary people, scholars & politicians

The rediscovery of spirituality by ordinary people, scholars & politicians in the twenty first century is an indication of humanity's need of the spirit of God, although many people are seeking spiritual things from wrong and dangerous sources. Many people are now turning to spiritual things. As Thomas G. Plante rightly makes the point: *'Professional and scientific psychology appears to have rediscovered spirituality and religion during recent years, with a large number of conferences, seminars, workshops, books, and special issues in major professional journals on spirituality and psychology integration'.*

The study and practice of spirituality is gaining such great momentum. It is fast becoming a household word not only in Churches, but in mosques, synagogues and other religious communities. It does not stop there, it is swiftly spreading in corporate America, in medicine, in the academy, and in the global marketplace of ideas and practices. For example, spirituality has been linked to high levels of effort, performance, ethics and job satisfaction in business organizations so much so, that, more recently spirituality is seen as an important foundation for effective business. For social workers, spirituality is an important motivator for entering the profession and a source of support for caregivers. In education, Astin *et al.* findings indicate that ' students performance in academic and intellectual realm is enhanced if their faculty employ student centred pedagogical practices and put a priority on student's personal and spiritual development'. In the field of heath care, Spirituality is commonly recognized as an important component of effective care, especially in the care of the terminally ill and the elderly.

The growing interest in spirituality by ordinary people, scholars and politicians in the twenty first century is an indication of humanity's need of the Spirit of God to provide us with the answers we seek. But we thank God that he has made his Spirit available to all who will seek him. Let us look at another way God can help those who call upon Him times of crisis.

3. The Angelic help:

An angel (from the Greek word – *ángelos*) is a supernatural being or spirit, often depicted in humanoid form with feathered wings on their backs and halos around their heads, found in various religions and mythologies. The theological study of angels is known as "angelology". The term "angel" has also been expanded to various notions of spirits found in many other religious traditions.

Other roles of angels include protecting and guiding human beings, and carrying out God's tasks. In Zoroastrianism and Abrahamic religions they are often depicted as benevolent celestial beings who act as intermediaries between Heaven and Earth, or as guardian spirits or a guiding influence. Hebrews 1:14 says *'Are not all angels ministering spirits sent to serve those who will inherit salvation?'* There have been many instances where God sent angels to help human beings. Let us look at some of the roles of angels in the next paragraphs.

Israel needed guidance: here God commanded an angel to lead the Israelites:

> 'See, I am sending an angel ahead of you to guard you along the way and to bring you to the place I have prepared. Pay attention to him and listen to what he says. Do not rebel against him; he will not forgive your rebellion, since my Name is in him. If you listen carefully to what he says and do all that I say, I will be an enemy to your enemies and will oppose those who oppose you'.
> (Exodus 23:20-22).

Mary & Joseph: God sent an angel to announce the birth of baby Jesus to the father Joseph and the mother Mary (Matthew 1:18-21).

Jesus before the crucifixion: God sent angels to strengthen Jesus before his crucifixion:

> 'He [Jesus] withdrew about a stone's throw beyond them, knelt down and prayed, Father, if you are willing, take this cup from me; yet not my will, but yours be done. An angel from heaven appeared to him and strengthened him'. (Luke 22:41-43).

Warning about angels: angels are **not** to be worshipped or contacted, prayed to, or called upon in any way. **God alone** should be worshipped and prayed to through Jesus Christ (Colossians 2:18; Revelation 22:8-9). Angels are God's servants usually sent by God alone to serve those who will receive salvation (Hebrews 1:14).

In earlier times, people freely accepted the existence of angels and accorded them honor and respect. Jewish people retold stories of how angels had assisted Abraham, Moses, Elijah, Balaam, and Daniel. In fact, several New Testament letters warn Jewish Christians against the common practice of worshiping angels. To prove its argument about Christ being superior, the book of Hebrews shows that angels served God's purposes, and that they are not to be worshipped.

Someone may ask, if angels are not to be contacted by any human being why is the author of this book discussing angels in this section? The first reason for discussing the subject of angels in this section is to let you know how God loves the human race to the extent that He can sometimes use angels to serve humanity, especially those who will call upon him (Hebrews 1:14). Angels can deliver your blessings, sometimes faster than human being. Please take note; there are times when God will send angels to help you. The second reason for discussing the subject of angels in this book is that Scripture enjoins us not to forget to entertain strangers, for by doing so some people have received blessings from God, blessings brought to these people by angels (Hebrews 13:2). The lesson here is that you have to be a nice person so that you won't miss a blessing, in case God sends an angel to deliver a blessing to you.

Let me briefly touch on the subject of demons before we move to our next section. Demons are fallen angels who work with Satan to do evil (Revelation 12: 7-12). Any angel who does not serve Christ and his kingdom is a demon! Demons are evil spirits who torment people on earth. A prayer of command in the name of Jesus Christ can drive a demon away from someone. Let us look at how this prayer of command can be done:

> *'Once when we were going to the place of prayer, we were met by a slave girl who had a spirit by which she predicted the future. She earned a great deal of money for her owners by fortune-telling. This girl followed Paul and the rest of us, shouting, "These men are servants of the Most High God, who are telling you the way to be saved". She kept this up for many days. Finally Paul became so troubled that he turned around and said to the spirit, "In the name of Jesus Christ I command you to come out of her!" At that moment the spirit left her'. (Acts 16:16-18).*

In the book of Acts chapters 16, 21, and 28, Dr Luke, the author, uses "we" in writing, for he accompanied the apostle Paul on some of his missionary trips. His close association with Paul meant he had immediate access to many of the miracles done by Paul and here, Luke tells us how Paul drove out an evil spirit from a slave girl by a prayer of command: *'In the name of Jesus Christ I command you to come out of her! At that moment the spirit left her'*. This *'prayer of command'* to cast out an evil spirit from people should only be exercised by born again strong matured believers who are filled with the Spirit of God. It can be fatal for people who are not born again or matured to engage in prayer of command to drive out evil spirits. Let us read this account:

> *'Some Jews who went around driving out evil spirits tried to invoke the name of the Lord Jesus over those who were demon-possessed. They would say, "In the name of Jesus, whom Paul preaches, I command you to come out. Seven sons of Sceva, a Jewish chief priest, were doing this. One daythe evil spirit answered them, "Jesus I know, and I know about Paul, but who are you? Then the man who had the evil spirit jumped on them and overpowered them all. He gave them such a beating that they ran out of the house naked and bleeding. When this became known to the Jews and Greeks living in Ephesus, they were all seized with fear, and the name of the Lord Jesus was held in high honor'* (Acts 19:13-17).

The sons of Sceva were impressed by Paul's work, whose power to drive out demons came from the God's Holy Spirit, not from witchcraft, and was obviously more powerful than theirs. They discovered, however, that no one can control or duplicate God's power. These men were calling on the name of Jesus without knowing the person. The power to change lives comes from Christ. It cannot be tapped by reciting his name like a magic charm. God works his power only through those **He** chooses.

So far, we have looked at how God can use angels to help us in times of need. Let us look at another help God has made available to the human race in times of crisis.

4. Support from the Environment in times of need

Those who believe in God can receive help and support from the environment in times of difficulty. Someone may ask, how? The world is designed by the creator in such a way that nature can react positively or negatively according to the deeds of the people. God can use nature to protect His people or work in favour of His people. Do you know what happened to the world at the time when Jesus Christ was falsely accused and was crucified by evil people about 2000 years ago? The Bible says *'there was a great earthquake, the sun stopped shinning and darkness came over the whole land for three hours'* (read Matthew 27:50-54; Luke 23:44-49). All these phenomena were the responses of the earth and the sun to the wickedness of those who killed the saviour of the world. Nature will plead the case of those who have built their lives on the principles of God.

Can we then conclude that all the earthquakes and other environmental disasters are the result of people's wickedness? The answer is YES and NO. There are other reasons. The lesson here is that, if you believe in God, God can cause nature to come your aid in times of difficulty. Those who killed Jesus did not know that by crucifying Him, they were fulfilling a prophecy. According to God's plan for the world, *"This is what is written: The Christ will suffer and rise from the dead on the third day, and repentance and forgiveness of sins will be preached in his name to all nations, beginning at Jerusalem"* (Luke 24:44-47).

Let us look at another example in the Bible where nature helped Jesus:

> *'The dragon stood in front of the woman who was about to give birth, so that he might devour her child the moment it was born. Rev. 12:4 ...Then from his mouth the serpent spewed water like a river, to overtake the woman and sweep her away with the*

torrent. **But the earth helped the woman** *by opening its mouth and swallowing the river that the dragon had spewed out of his mouth'* (Revelation 12:4; 15-16).

In the text just read, we see the earth opened its mouth and swallowing the river to prevent the woman and the child Jesus from drowning. The view of Christ's birth in Revelation 12 gives a glimpse into the pattern of the entire book of Revelation. John, the writer is fusing things seen with things not normally seen. In daily life, two parallel histories occur simultaneously: one on earth and one in heaven. Every inch of this planet is claimed by God and counterclaimed by Satan. Sometimes the "war in heaven" can break out into actual violence on earth, as it did when Jesus came. We normally experience only the visible, everyday effects of this struggle.

But, as we are living out our lives on earth, the supernatural universe is simultaneously at war. The book of Revelation draws the contrasts sharply: good versus evil, the Lamb versus the dragon, Jerusalem versus Babylon, the bride versus the prostitute. Those who belong to Christ have gone into battle on God's side; and He has guaranteed them victory. God will not lose the war, but we must make certain not to lose the battle for our own souls. Please don't waver in your commitment to Christ. A great spiritual battle is being fought and there is no time for indecision. But those who hope in the Lord will be victorious and receive eternal life.

Let us look at another example where God used nature to give victory to someone- Joshua. The sun stopped in the middle of the sky and delayed going down about a full day:

'On that day the LORD gave the Amorites over to Israel, Joshua said to the LORD in the presence of Israel: "O sun, stand still over Gibeon, O moon, over the Valley of Aijalon. So the sun stood still, and the moon stopped, till the nation avenged itself on its enemies, as it is written in the Book of Jashar. The sun stopped in the middle of the sky and delayed going down about a full day' (Joshua 10:12-13).

How did the sun stand still? Of course in relation to the earth, the sun always stand still- it is the earth that travels around the sun. But the terminology used in the book of Joshua should not cause us to doubt the miracle. After all, we are not confused when someone tells us that the sun rises or sets. The point is that the day was prolonged, to give Joshua and his fighting men enough sunlight to totally defeat their enemies.

In this section we have looked at a few examples where God caused nature to support people who have faith in Him. We have also discussed how the earth opened its mouth and swallowed the river that Satan had spewed out of his mouth to overtake the little child Jesus and his mother with the torrent (Revelations 12:13-17). The earth helped the woman to escape the harm Satan wanted to inflict on her. In a time of famine, God caused a bird to send food to the prophet Elijah (1 Kings 17:1-6). There are many things in nature God can use to help people who love Him, who have faith in Him, and who worship Him. It is my prayer that you put your hope in God, and start building your life on the principles of God if you are not already doing so.

5. Help from fellow believers in times of need

But what happens when a person going through difficult times does not have enough faith to pray alone to God for help? Even when a medical doctor falls sick, he will need his fellow doctor(s) and other health professionals to treat him or her. In the same way, God has made provisions for those who cannot pray to Him alone in times of difficulties. In times of trouble, those who are enduring a time of difficulty are to inform the leaders of the church so that they can pray and anoint that person with oil, and the prayer offered in faith will heal that person (James 5:13-16). This however, means that faith in God must not be a private affair alone, but that collective faith of other believers is necessary for anyone who needs help from God in times of crisis. This is what I call 'Group faith'. This is one of the many reasons you should join a local church.

What is group faith? This is the situation where a group of people's faith can help you in times of difficulty, usually when you are unable to help yourself. There are many examples in scriptures and real life situations where people in crisis benefited from this 'group faith'. For example, a paralytic received healing because of his friend's faith (Mark 2:1-5). Dorcas was raised from the dead because the church pleaded with Peter to pray for her resurrection (Acts 9:32-43). When Peter was put in jail for preaching the gospel, it was the church members who prayed for Peter's release from Prison (Acts 12: 1-17). In this particular incident, although Peter was able to pray for someone to come back to life, when he was in trouble his very own prayer was not enough to get him out of the difficulty he was in. As you can see, you can receive a lot of help from your fellow believers.

This is one of the main reasons why scripture enjoins believers to meet together regularly (Hebrews 10:24-25). Believers who do not make attending church services regularly are depriving themselves of many blessings. For example, when believers meet together in prayers or worship, God comes in the power of the Holy Spirit, and once God's Spirit is present, healing, deliverance, and other supernatural miracles can take place (Luke 5:17-28). I will encourage you to find a good church and start attending service regularly, especially in these difficult and hard times. Move with people who are productive, who will help you know God; people who are purpose driven; people who are willing to change for the better.

The church is such an important place to benefit from this kind of group faith (Hebrews 12:22). You must be committed to the church so that the church will be willing to seek God's favour on your behalf in times of crisis. Don't wait till you find yourself in difficult situations before you join a local church or fellowship. As you build your life on God's principles, you will find yourself among other people who have also made the same commitment to God. These people or believers can be a great source of help to you especially in times of need.

2.4 Lessons for people who have not receive their desired help from God although they claim to believe in God.

In times of crisis there is more help readily available from God to His children. Unfortunately, during these times of crisis many people tend to focus on the wrong issues. They demand answers as to why they are suffering instead of focusing on the help available to them during their time of difficulty. In the next four paragraphs, I will be explaining why it appears some people who believe in God do not receive the type of help they expect from God in times of crisis. Probably you may have seen a believer who went through a serious crisis yet it appeared the person did not receive the needed help from God. The truth is that, some of these people received help from God in times of crisis, but probably not the type of help they asked from the Lord. God in His own wisdom gives what He thinks is best, and what God gives us is far better than what we wish for ourselves. But this only becomes clearer to us after the crisis is over. The explanations in the following paragraphs will be of great help to many people going through challenging times.

Isaiah 57:1 says' *'the righteous perish, and no one ponders it in his heart; devout men are taken away, and no one understands that the righteous are taken away to be spared from evil'.* This is the first reason why some believers do not receive healing from God or die in an accident. Sometimes, God wants to save these people from evil, and so He allows them to die, in order for them to enter paradise. Have you lost a loved one through accident or sickness whom you think deserved to have been rescued by God? Take heart! God knows best! By now they are in a safer place with God resting their souls provided they accepted the Lord into their lives. Heaven is a better place than this earth. Therefore, make it your ambition to be there. Let us look at the second reason why some believers do not receive help from God in times of crisis. The Bible uses the word discipline to describe another reason why believers seem to go through times of crisis.

The second reason why some believers appear not to receive the type of help they need from God in times of crisis is that God may be using their situation to instill discipline in them. Hebrews 12:5-13 say:

> And you have forgotten that word of encouragement that addresses you as sons: "My son, do not make light of the Lord's discipline, and do not lose heart when he rebukes you, because the Lord disciplines those he loves, and he punishes everyone he accepts as a son. Endure hardship as discipline; God is treating you as sons. For what son is not disciplined by his father? If you are not disciplined (and everyone undergoes discipline), then you are illegitimate children and not true sons. Moreover, we have all had human fathers who disciplined us and we respected them for it. How much more should we submit to the Father of our spirits and live! Our fathers disciplined us for a little while as they thought best; but God disciplines us for our good, that we may share in his holiness. No discipline seems pleasant at the time, but painful. Later on, however, it produces a harvest of righteousness and peace for those who have been trained by it. Therefore, strengthen your feeble arms and weak knees. Make level paths for your feet, so that the lame may not be disabled, but rather healed.

Some believers go through crisis because God is disciplining them. This usually happens when they commit a serious sin against God or someone. King David experienced this kind of discipline when he took someone's wife and killed the man (2 Samuel chapters 11 -12). Let us look at the third reason.

God has a way of humbling His children, so that they will not be proud or consider themselves better than other fellow human beings. Sometimes God does this by intentionally allowing the believer to go through a time of which is not the result of any personal sin. The crisis cannot separate the believer from the love of God because God's grace will be sufficient for the person. The apostle Paul experienced this kind of crisis in his life (2 Corinthians 1:10). He had thorns in his flesh, the result of what he calls the messenger of Satan sent to torment him because he 'was caught up to paradise. He heard inexpressible things in heaven, things man is not permitted to tell'. So in order to keep him from becoming conceited because of these surpassingly great revelations, God allowed a thorn to be in his flesh. Paul said, 'three times I pleaded with the Lord to take it away from me but he said to me, "My grace is sufficient for you, for my power is made perfect in weaknesses'. Therefore, Paul says 'I will boast all the more gladly about my weaknesses, so that Christ's power may rest on me'.

Bible scholars don't agree on the precise nature of Paul's "thorn in the flesh." Some suggest a physical ailment, such as an eye disease, malaria, or epilepsy. Others interpret it as a spiritual temptation, or a sequence of failures in his ministry. The Bible gives no clear evidence on the precise nature of this affliction. Regardless, Paul stresses that God permitted the thorn to continue, despite his prayers for relief, to teach him an important lesson about grace, humility, and dependence.

The fourth reason why sometimes believers seem not to receive the type of help they need from God in times of crisis is the fact that, crisis, suffering, trials, and temptation can sometimes help believers to become mature if handled properly. James 1:2-5 says' *consider it pure joy, my brothers, whenever you face trials of many kinds, because you know that the testing of your faith develops perseverance. Perseverance must finish its work so that you may be mature and complete, not lacking anything'.* Trials, suffering, and problems can produce maturity in us. People who have put their faith in God, yet experiences trials and suffering should not be discouraged because the end result is always good. What should people do in such situations? James continues to say that '*if any of you lacks wisdom, he should ask God, who gives generously to all without finding fault, and it will be given to him'.* We need wisdom in times of trials and suffering to make wise decisions.

So far we have looked at four reasons why it appears some people who have put their faith in God do not receive help in times of crisis. The conclusion is that, these people receive help from God in times of crisis, but not the type of help they asked from the Lord. Those who have put their faith in God should not be worried if their problems persist, but they should continue to trust God, because God has good reasons for allowing them to experience what they are going through.

2.5 Some people do not receive help from God at all, why?

Let us now look at some of the reasons why some people do not receive help at all from God. Faith in God is a necessary requirement to receive help from Him in times of crisis. Jesus confirmed the importance and necessity of faith when he said: *'if you have faith as small as the tiniest seed' (mustard seed for example), nothing will be impossible for you'* (Matthew 17:20). I believe it is important for me to clearly state here that not everyone who claim to believe or have faith in God receive help from Him. There are many reasons why this is so.

To help you follow what I am about to discuss, please keep in mind that the way God works is different from the way human beings do things: *'For my thoughts are not your thoughts, neither are your ways my ways, declares the LORD. As the heavens are higher than the earth, so are my ways higher than your ways and my thoughts than your thoughts'* (Isaiah 55:8-9).

God works in His own time, seasons and according to His own principles. Someone who is in crisis may call on God for help; the person may receive help instantly or sometimes later, or sometimes no help at all. This is because certain conditions must be met before God can grant the needed help. If you go to your bank for a loan or for any credit facility, the bank will make sure you first satisfy certain conditions before they grant you your request. God works with higher principles than even your bank, and so it is important that people take their time to know God at a relationship level and to understand how He works. This is not what we see these days, the most common practices among those who claim to know God, is what I call the *'magic formula'*. This is the practice whereby believers keep God far away from their lives and only cry out to him for help when they are in crisis. This is not a good practice. God desires to have a spirit to spirit loving relationship with his people.

The second reason why people who claim to believe in God don't receive help in times of crisis, is that they do not ask God for help when they are in crisis (James 4:2), they think God should automatically grants them their desires without even asking, this is not how God works. What many people do not know is that there are certain things in this world that can be received from God only when we ask. Many professing believers are ignorant of this. Jesus, during one of his teachings on prayer taught the disciples to ask God to give them their daily bread, and to lead them not into temptation… (Matthew 6:11-13). *'Ask and it will be given to you; seek and you will find; knock and the door will be opened to you. For everyone who asks receives; he who seeks finds; and to him who knocks, the door will be opened'* (Matthew 7:7-8).

The third and the most subtly reason why people do not receive help from God in times of crisis is because of wrong motives: The Bible says *'When they ask, they do not receive, because they ask with wrong motives, that they may spend what they get on their pleasures'* (James 4:3). What many people forget is that God is a just God who does not support or endorse bad agenda. If your motive for asking is not right God will not grant what you ask, although you may be in a time of crisis, and so, the advice is that you must *always* ask God what is right, avoid selfishness; avoid asking something that will hurt your neighbor.

There fourth and most obvious reason why people do not receive help from God is lack of faith in what God can do for them. Although some people claim to believe in God, they have doubts as to whether God will do it for them what they are asking (James 1:5-8). Sometimes, this happens when there is a feeling of guilt or unworthiness on the part of the believer before God. Some people think that because of their sins or something bad they have done, God will not answer their prayers, and so although they may pray alright, they do not have confidence or trust in God. And without faith, it is impossible to please God (Hebrews 11:6). Believe that anything you ask from God will be done according to His will, do not doubt, have faith in God. There are many ways people can increase their faith in God.

2.6 How people can increase their faith in God

There are different levels of faith. Some people seem to have greater faith than others. *'The apostles said to the Lord, "Increase our faith"'* (Luke 17:5). Let us look at some of the means to develop a greater faith in God.

1. The Ministry of Jesus

If people's lack of faith in God is due to their sins, then how can they overcome this? Two suggestions will be offered in this section. The book of Hebrews 4:15-16 offers the first suggestion:

> For we do not have a high priest who is unable to sympathize with our weaknesses, but we have one who has been tempted in every way, just as we are—yet was without sin. Let us then approach the throne of grace with confidence, so that we may receive mercy and find grace to help us in our time of need.

In this text, the writer points his readers to Jesus' ministry as the means by which the people could approach God with confidence so that they may receive mercy and find grace in times of their need.

Those who have received Jesus Christ into their lives as their Lord and personal savior, repented of their sins, and who have done their baptism can approach God for help with full assurance that their sins are forgiven. Every known sin must be confessed to God in prayers. This will clear your mind of guilt feelings: *'if we claim to be without sin, we deceive ourselves and the truth is not in us. If we confess our sins, he is faithful and just and will forgive us our sins and purify us from all unrighteousness'* (1 John 1:8-9). Confess your sins to God in prayers, He will forgive, and grants you your request.

Think of this: a young man fell into sin and contracted a horrible disease and was afraid to tell anyone. The only thing ahead of him was death. He met a minister of God who offered to pray for him. The Minister quoted this scripture: *'Fools, because of their transgression and iniquities were afflicted. Their soul abhorred all manner of food and they draw near to the gates of death' (Ps 107:17)*. The young man cried out, 'I am that fool'. He broke down and confessed his sins. The moment he repented a great abscess burst, God sent power into his life and delivered him. Oh! If people will repent and turn to God, God will stretch out His hand to bless and save them!

2. Knowing What God can do

Secondly, knowing what God do in your life can increase your faith in Him. You can know what God can do by looking at some of the attributes of God, how God works, and how God has blessed some people. We will first look at the power of God.

The power of God: You can know more about God's power for example by studying the book of Genesis which has record accounts of the creation events, how the world including human beings were created. You see, if you know the power of God, it will be easier for you to believe in God, so that you can receive help from Him, *'for all things are possible for those who believe'*(Mark 9:23). So please take your time to read and reflect on the handiwork of God in the following sections.

How God made the first person can teach us a lot:

> Then the Lord God formed man from the dust of the ground and breathed into his nostrils the breath or spirit of life, and man became a living being (Genesis 2:7).

This is how the first person in the world was created. Does it surprise you? Begin to think of God as someone who is supreme, He is all powerful, all knowing, his ways are beyond understanding, God is not like us, He is of different essence (Isaiah 55: 8-9). If God could make a human being from the dust and breathe his Spirit into him so that what was made out of dust could live, what else can't He do? Of course you may ask, if God is all that powerful, why do people have problems or why doesn't He help people? These are all valid questions; and there are answers to such questions. To help you find answers to some of these questions, I recommend a book by R.C. Sproul to you. The title is *Surprised by Suffering: The role of Pain and Death in the Christian Life*. Let us look at how God made the second person on earth- the woman, in the next section.

How God made the second human being on earth:

> The LORD God said, "It is not good for the man to be alone. I will make a helper suitable for him...So the LORD God caused the [first] man to fall into a deep sleep; and while he was sleeping, he took one of the man's ribs and closed up the place with flesh. Then the LORD God made a woman from the rib he had taken out of the man, and he brought her to the man (Genesis 2:18-22).

God performed a simple divine anesthetic on the first man created in order to get a sample of him to form the woman. The lesson here is that, if God could make a woman from the rib of the first man then know that God can replace any part of your body that is not working properly. Healing and restoration is possible for those who will believe in the power of God.

We are still looking at how knowing God's creative work can increase your faith in Him because faith in God is such a necessary requirement to receive help from Him. The Bible says '*...and without faith it is impossible to please God, because anyone who comes to him must believe that he exists and that he rewards those who earnestly seek him*' (Hebrews 11:6).

God gave the first man and the woman the ability to reproduce and to make wealth

> God blessed them [Adam and Eve]. He said to them, "Have children and increase your numbers. Fill the earth and bring it under your control...Adam made love to his wife Eve. She became pregnant and gave birth to Cain. She said, "With the LORD's help I have had a baby boy." Later she gave birth to his brother Abel (Genesis 1:28; 4:1-2).

From this time on, the human race has been populating through the union of a man and a woman. One of the unchanging attributes about human beings is that by default, God has put certain abilities, limited though, into us to reproduce, to be creative and innovative with or without His help (Deuteronomy 8:18).

When God created man, He empowered him, although He did not give mankind everything; this is one of the reasons why human beings are not able to do everything. But God made provision for people who will need His help to come to him for more abilities. Jesus emphasized this truth when He taught us how to pray effectively to the Father; 'give us this day our daily bread' (Matthew 6:11-13). The lesson here is that if you lack daily necessities, any ability, talent or skills to solve a problem, you can go to God in prayers and ask Him. For example, Jesus told his disciples to go to Jerusalem to wait to be filled with power coming from the Spirit of God so that they could preach the gospel effectively.

Read what God told the prophet Jeremiah:

> Call to me [God] and I will answer you and tell you great and unsearchable things you do not know (Jeremiah 33:3).

Those who believe in God should not suffer in silence but should call on God for help. Even as we seek God's help in everything, I would like to bring to your attention that it is not everything we will receive in our lifetime or dispensation (Daniel 12:8-9). Moses said *'secret things belong to the LORD our God, but the things revealed belong to us and to our children forever, that we may follow all the words of this law'*(Deuteronomy 29:29). There are certain knowledge, ideas, information, or revelations which were not available to people in past generations, but which are available to us today (1 Peter 1:1-12). In the same way, we may not know or have all the answers to the problems facing us as individuals, as families or even as a nation, but future generations may have solutions to them. This is one of the ways God works. God grants grace in His own time. But we can be sure that what He will give us, will be sufficient if we continue to trust Him.

God just spoke and things came in to being, May God speak into your life today!

In Genesis chapters 1 and 2, you can see God's creative power at work. How God spoke and things came into being. For example:

And God said, "Let there be light," and there was light. God saw that the light was good and he separated the light from the darkness (Gen 1:3-4).

If God could just speak and light came into being, what else can't He do? Similarly in Exodus 14, we saw how through God's power, the red sea parted for the Israelite to pass through. Testimonies like this should encourage you to put your trust in God. The apostle Paul told the Roman church, in the book of Romans 15:4:

'For, everything that was written in the past was written to teach us, so that through endurance and the encouragement of the Scriptures we might have hope'.

I will conclude this section by drawing your mind once again to what God can do for you personally in times of crisis. In Genesis

1-2, we are told that it is God who created the heavens and the earth including everything we see around us today. This should encourage you to believe in God, to give you a new and fresh beginning in your life if that is what you need. May be you have had a very bad past life, don't stay in that situation and continue in misery; come to God today for help!

3. Faith comes by hearing the word of God

Someone may ask, what is faith? Faith is a trust in God, which allows God to act on your behalf. Paul says Romans 10:17 that, *'consequently, faith comes from hearing the message, and the message is heard through the word of Christ'*. John says *'Jesus did many other miraculous signs in the presence of his disciples, which are not recorded in this book. But these are written that you may believe that Jesus is the Christ, the Son of God, and that by believing you may have life in his name'* (John 20:30–31).

The more you hear about God's word the more your faith in God grows. The word of God tells us many things about God. It tells us what He did in the past, what He is doing now, and what He will do in future. We have a lot of testimonies of how God helped people in the past in times of crisis. Reading about all these testimonies can increase your faith in God. This is also one of the reasons why you must attend church service regularly to hear sermons and to participate in Sunday school lessons. Your faith increases the more you hear God's word.

The danger in trusting people for help

I will conclude this section by briefly discussing some of the dangers involved in trusting people. We are commanded by God to love people and God himself (Matthew 22:37). But we are to trust in God alone because He never fails (Proverbs 3:5). There are many people who put their trust in people, especially in times of difficulty only to be disappointed. If someone has failed to help you in the past, please don't be disappointed because the person you trusted in is only a human being. To be human means, he or she is a fallen creature, limited in whatever he or she can do. Read God's word on this:

> This is what the LORD says: "Cursed is the one who trusts in man, who depends on flesh for his strength and whose heart turns away from the LORD. He will be like a bush in the wastelands; he will not see prosperity when it comes. He will dwell in the parched places of the desert, in a salt land where no one lives. "But blessed is the man who trusts in the LORD, whose confidence is in him. He will be like a tree planted by the water that sends out its roots by the stream. It does not fear when heat comes; its leaves are always green. It has no worries in a year of drought and never fails to bear fruit" (Jeremiah 17:5-8).

A curse is an offensive word that people say when they are angry. You see, buy two identical plants in a nursery, plant one in a desert, and one by a river. For a few days they'll look alike, but what happens after a few weeks? That's the image the prophet Jeremiah uses. The person who trusts in human beings will end up like a shriveled bush (Jeremiah 17:6), while the person who trusts in God will be like a tree that has its roots sunk deep beside a stream (Jeremiah 17:8).

Someone may argue that he or she has received help from people without necessarily believing in God. Good! It is your attitude towards the person or the object you received the help from that matters. If you put your trust in the object or the person who helped you, then God says this is dangerous. You should see the person or the object that helped you in that time of crisis as a means or a vessel God used to help you. There are many ways God can help those who trust in Him. God can intentionally empower someone to assist you in times of need. God can send his angels to be with you in times of need. But you are not encouraged to put your faith (trust) in the vessel God used to bless you. Rather we are to show appreciation to the people who God uses to bless us. We are to thank them for availing themselves to be used by God.

The truth is that people who do not put their trust in God may be disappointed by the people they trust. Those who trust in human beings more than God will be impoverished and spiritually weakened with time, because they will have no strength to draw on. But those who trust in the Lord will have abundant strength, not only for their own needs, but even for the needs of others. God has already given humanity His Son, Jesus as a sin offering. And God has promised His Holy Spirit to His children in these end times to empower us to build His kingdom, to give us self-control to manage our unhealthy emotions, and to lead us, His children into all truth. Worship Him, pray to Him, study His scriptures, and do good deeds to others. God should be your utmost priority in life.

What is priority? The word priority means being regarded or treated as more important than others. For example "the safety of the country takes priority over any other matter." God, money and family life are all important in life but they are not equal in value and significance. In order of priority which one comes first in your life? To some people, God takes priority over money and family life. To others, money takes priority over God and family life:

> No one can serve two masters. Either he will hate the one and love the other, or he will be devoted to the one and despise the other. You cannot serve both God and Money (Matthew 6:24).

Jesus says we can serve only one master. We live in a materialistic society where many people serve money. They spend all their lives collecting and storing it, only to die and leave it behind. Their desire for money and what it can buy, far outweighs their commitment to God and spiritual matters. Whatever you store up, you will spend much of your time and energy thinking about. Don't fall into the materialistic trap, because 'the love of money is the root of all kinds of evil' (1 Timothy 6:10).

The litmus test: can you honestly say that God and not money or any other thing is your master? One test is to ask which one occupies more of your thoughts, time and effort. Your priority is determined by how you live your life. Many religious people profess

God as the utmost priority in their lives but the way they live betrays them.

I will give two main reasons why you must put God first in everything. First, it is a principle of life that the enemy, if he wants to attack you, harm you or destroy you, will attack your most valuable asset, what you really love or treasure. The enemy is not interested in what you don't like or treasure. He is interested in where your heart is, what is dearest to your heart. For example if money is what you treasure most in life, the enemy will attack your finances. If you consistently have financial problems, it could be that you love money more than God that is why you seem to be having financial problems. If your spouse or your child is the most valuable thing in your life, I want you to know that they will be the target of the enemy. So put God first, after all the enemy cannot defeat God in your life.

The story of Job in the Bible is both a moral and a spiritual lesson to us all. Unknown to him, Job a man God Himself considered pure and righteous was involved in a cosmic test, a contest proposed in heaven but staged on earth. In this extreme test of faith, the best man on earth suffered the worst calamities. Satan had claimed that people like Job love God only because of the good things God provides them. 'Remove those good things', Satan challenged God, and Job's faith would melt away along with his riches and health. But Job proved to Satan that he loved God more than the material riches. Job was able to stand through all these horrendous trials because He treasured God in his heart.

If your relationship with God is the most treasured thing, the enemy will try to attack you from that angle, but he cannot succeed, because nothing will be able to fight against God (Psalm 2:1-5). That is why it is advisable to put your trust and hope first in God. Jesus said 'for where your treasure is, there your heart will be also' (Luke 12:34).

So far in this section we have looked at the fact that people who build their lives on the principles of God can receive help in times of crisis from God. We have also discussed four reasons why some believers appear not to receive help from God in times of crisis and many more issues. Let us discuss the subject of spirituality in the next chapter.

Chapter 3

Spirituality:
Scripture as a guide

Spirituality is a word that has come into vogue this century. The good news is that, the practice of spirituality or developing one's spiritual life offers many benefits if guided properly. Statistics reveal that substantial numbers of UK population are hungry for meaning to life. In 1999, the Henley Centre published, *The Paradox Prosperity,* a detail research project sponsored by the Salvation Army, which gives an overview of the current scene. The research concluded that:

> There is a growing demand for some sort of **alternative approach to life,** for new answers to old questions. This has led to the emergence of a renewed emphasis on spirituality. There is a recognition that true 'wealth' comes from spiritual as well as material resources, and people are drawing up alternative scale of 'value' that will restore meaning to their lives. 27% of people claim to have successfully changed their spiritual life and a further 20% would like to do so.

Please beware of the difference between spirituality and spiritualism. **Spiritualism** is a belief that spirits of the dead residing in the spirit world have both the ability and the inclination to communicate with the living. In this book, our interest is in the subject of spirituality not spiritualism. In this chapter in particular, we will be discussing how scripture provides answers to everything spiritual searchers seek.

We will also look at some of the dangers involved in the practice of spirituality and how people can overcome them.

Modern **spirituality** is centered on the "deepest values and meanings by which people live." It embraces the idea of an ultimate being or an alleged immaterial reality. It envisions an inner path enabling a person to discover the essence of his/her being. Life's 'big questions' that preoccupy many people such as "Who am I? What are my most deeply felt values? Do I have a mission or purpose in my life? Why am I in this world? What kind of person do I want to become? What sort of world do I want to help create?" are essentially spiritual questions. In this book, when I speak of people's spiritual quest, I am essentially speaking of people's efforts to seek answers to these questions.

One of my main points in this chapter on spirituality is that, what people are seeking for in their practice of spirituality has been provided for in the Holy Scripture. Scripture says God's 'divine power has given us everything we need for life and godliness through our knowledge of him who called us by his own glory and goodness. Through these he has given us his very great and precious promises, so that through them you may participate in the divine nature and escape the corruption in the world caused by evil desires' (2 Peter 1:3-4). All that seekers need to do is to turn to the word of God for answers. Scripture provides the best guidance for all spiritual seekers.

On the other hand spiritualism which is the act of consulting the dead is condemned by God in scripture. Leviticus 19:31 says:

> Do not turn to mediums or seek out spiritists, for you will be defiled by them. I am the LORD your God'. Many people do not know that consulting the dead or spirits or engaging in witchcraft or magic acts is something God hates; this is because it is harmful to those who indulge in them. Deuteronomy 18:10-11 says 'Let no one be found among you who sacrifices his son or daughter in the fire, who practices divination or sorcery, interprets omens, engages in witchcraft, or casts spells, or who is a medium

or spiritist or who consults the dead. Anyone who does
these things is detestable to the LORD'.

God says this in Micah 5:12: '1 will destroy your witchcraft and you
will no longer cast spells'. But why do people consult the dead on
behalf of the living when they can directly go to God in prayers?
The answer is that some people do so without knowing that such
practices are detestable to God. Others too were born with it while
others follow such practices as a tradition.

You see, the attempt by secularists to do away with the knowledge
of God in public life or to suppress the truth in our society has also
compelled some people to begin to seek spiritual things in different
ways, sometimes from wrong and dangerous sources. There are some
people too who are ignorant of the knowledge of the true God that is
why they seek help from sources outside the kingdom of God. There
is the great God in heaven, who created the heavens and the earth.
He alone is to be worshipped and sought after by the means He has
prescribed. You can know more about this God by reading the Bible,
by going to church, by learning more about Jesus Christ, His Only
begotten Son who died for the sins of the world.

Many people confuse the voice of God and other voices from the
dark world. Strange and audible voices have led many people to harm
themselves. So what should people do when they hear dead people
speaking to them in their dreams? What should people do when they
hear strange voices? My suggestion in this book is that such people
should find a Bible believing church and seek help from the church
pastor or the church leaders.

My primary reason for writing this chapter is that spirituality is
fundamental to people's day to day lives. Another reason for writing
this chapter is the recent interest in spirituality by many people
and the many benefits the practice of spirituality offers if guided
properly. From the 1960s a significant portion of the population
particularly those in the West, began to experiment with new forms
of consciousness and communication that took the inner life seriously.

Thomas G. Plante's article on *Integrating Spirituality and psychotherapy: Ethical Issues and Principles to Consider,* reports that Professional and scientific psychology appears to have rediscovered spirituality and religion during recent years, with a large number of conferences, seminars, workshops, books, and special issues in major professional journals on spirituality and psychology integration. Journals such as *The American Psychologist, Annals of Behavioural Medicine,* and *Journal of Health Psychology,* among others, have recently dedicated special issues to this important topic.

This is not a surprise to some of us at all. There are many reasons why people are turning to the practice of spirituality in this twenty-first century, a trend which will continue way beyond this century. According to research, the practice of spirituality is a recent moving away from dogmatic[5] religion.

Harvey Cox, a retired Professor of Divinity at Harvard, says this recent move away from dogmatic religion is best explained against the backdrop of three distinct periods of church history. First, we had the Age of Faith followed by the Age of Belief, and then the Age of the Spirit, what some people call spirituality in our day. The first three centuries of Christianity when the early church was more concerned with following Jesus' teachings than enforcing what to believe about Jesus is referred to as the *age of faith.* The age of belief marked a significant shift between the fourth and the twentieth century when the church focused on orthodoxy and correct doctrine. The age of the spirit is a trend that began about fifty years ago and is increasingly directing the church of tomorrow where Christians are ignoring dogma and breaking down barriers between different religions. Spirituality seems to be replacing formal religion. People are seeking what they refer to as 'a higher being' whom Christians call God, and ethical guidance through the practice of spirituality.

---

[5] **Dogma** is a principle or set of principles laid down by an authority as incontrovertibly true

Before we look at what spirituality is and the different types of spirituality, let us first look at some of the benefits of the practice of spirituality in the next section.

3.1 Some benefits of the practice of spirituality

As some of you will recall, Karl Marx, a hugely influential revolutionary thinker and philosopher viewed religion as an "opiate [drug]" that took the edge off the pain of life; Sigmund Freud who became known as the founding father of psychoanalysis thought 'religion was a fantasy-escape mechanism employed by weak people in search of security'. Emile Durkheim, a founding figure in the field of sociology believed that religious rituals, especially for "primitive" people, were a way of maintaining collective order. All these views are rooted in deprivation theories[6] of one sort or another but I see these theories as indicators, telling us why we all need God in our daily lives.

There are many benefits individuals, families, and the nation will enjoy if God's principles are what influence their actions. I believe this is one of the main reasons why many people are turning to the practice of spirituality in this century. David J. Houston and Katherine E. Cartwright's article on *Spirituality and Public Service* reports that, 'spirituality has been linked to high levels of effort, performance, ethics and job satisfaction in business organisations'. The report also says spirituality is also seen as an important foundation for effective business leadership. For social workers, spirituality is an important motivator for entering the profession and a source of support for caregivers.

In healthcare, spirituality is commonly recognised as an important component of effective care, especially care of the terminally ill and the elderly. A statement by the World Health Organisation

---

[6]   **Deprivation** is the lack of resources to sustain the diet, lifestyle, activities and amenities that an individual or group are accustomed to or that are widely encouraged or approved in the society to which they belong.

encouraging health professionals to incorporate spirituality into their practice goes like this:

> 'Health professions have largely followed a medical model which seeks to treat patients by focusing on medicines and surgery and gives less importance to beliefs and to faith. This reductionist or mechanistic view of patients as being only a material body is no longer satisfactory. Patients and physicians have begun to realize the value of elements such as faith, hope and compassion in the healing process. The value of such 'spiritual elements in health and quality of life has led to research in this field in an attempt to move towards a more holistic view of health that includes a non–material dimension, emphasizing the seamless connections between mind and body'. (WHO, Consultation on Spirituality, Religion and Personal Beliefs, 1998)

In education, Astin *et al.* research indicates that student's performance in the academic and intellectual realm is enhanced if their faculty employ student centred pedagogical[7] practices and put a priority on student's personal and spiritual development. Students are therefore encouraged to take their spiritual life seriously. The same research project suggests the apparent need for spiritual development in colleges and universities. Two thirds of the students who participated in the research expressed a strong interest in spiritual matters. Well over half reported that their professors never encouraged discussions on religious or spiritual matters, and about the same proportion reported that professors never provided opportunities to discuss the purpose and meaning of life. I hope this book will help raise the awareness of the vital role that spirituality can play in student's learning and development.

Research has also shown that people who have a strong spiritual life are able to cope with life's problems more easily than people with

---

[7] Pedagogy is the method and practice of teaching, especially as an academic subject or theoretical concept.

weak or no spirituality. For example, Walter Hollenweger, who is described by some Pentecostals as the founding father of academic research into Pentecostalism makes this point about William Seymour: 'it was his spirituality which enabled him to prevent his heart from becoming bitter in spite of constant humiliation, both from Christians and non Christians and later from white fellow-Pentecostals.

These benefits of the practice of spirituality are a tip of the iceberg. Spirituality is also now associated with mental health, managing substance abuse, marital functioning, parenting, and coping. The practice of spirituality can lead both spiritual searchers to receive many benefits from God if they are guided properly. Throughout this book, I have identified strategies which you might find helpful in seeking answers to life's big questions from the word of God.

We have been using the term 'spirituality so far in this chapter without defining what spirituality is. Let us look at what spirituality is in the next section.

3.2 What is spirituality?

The term spirituality has no direct equivalent in Scripture and did not emerge historically as a well-defined branch of theology until the 18th century when Giovanni Scaramelli (1687-1752) of the Society of Jesus established ascetical and mystical theology as a science of Spiritual life.

The term spirituality is used in various senses by different scholars and Christian traditions, partly because the spiritual life itself is very complex. Kees Waaijman points out that "spirituality" is only one term of a range of words which denote the praxis of spirituality. Some other terms are "Hasidism, contemplation, asceticism, mysticism, perfection, devotion and piety".

There is no single, widely-agreed definition on spirituality. Social scientists have defined spirituality as the search for "the sacred", for that which is set apart from the ordinary and worthy of veneration, "a transcendent dimension within human experience...discovered in moments in which the individual questions the meaning of personal existence and attempts to place the self within a broader ontological context.

In this section, I will attempt to provide a variety of definitions of what spirituality is, used in academic research. These are illustrated by the following sample definitions cited from an article by Houston and Cartwright[8]. My main interest in all these definitions is to bring to the fore the truth that what people seek in the practice of spirituality is in fact what God has promised to offer humanity although many people are rejecting these blessings from God.

> Benner sees spirituality as the human response to God's gracious call to a relationship with himself.

For Canda and Furman:

> Spirituality relates to a universal and fundamental aspect of what it is to be human- to search for a sense of meaning, purpose, and moral frameworks for relating with self, others, and the ultimate reality [God].

For Hill and Pargament:

> Spirituality can be understood as a search for the sacred, a process through which people seek to discover, hold on to, and, when necessary, transform whatever they hold sacred in their lives.

Astin et al. define Spirituality this way[9]:

> Spirituality, as we have defined it, is a multifaceted quality. It involves an active quest for life's big questions; a global worldview that transcends ethnocentrism and egocentrism;

---

[8] Cited in Houston, D. J., & K. E. Cartwright, (2007) 'Spirituality and Public Service', *Public Administration Review*, 67 (1), pp. 88-102

[9] In 2003, Alexander Astin, Helen Astin, and Jennifer Lindholm embarked on a seven-year journey to examine how student's spiritual qualities change during their undergraduate studies and what role the college experience plays in facilitating their spiritual development. Their major findings are reported in the book, *Cultivating the spirit: How College Can Enhance Students' Inner lives.*

a sense of caring and compassion for others coupled with a lifestyle that includes service to others; and a capacity to maintain one's sense of calm and centeredness, especially in times of stress.

Houston and Cartwright say:

Among the many definitions of Spirituality that appear in the literature, four components are common. The first is a belief in transcendence, something greater than oneself; the second is interconnectedness or the relational dimension of spirituality. The third common component is a feeling of love and compassion for others and their life circumstances and fourthly, a sense of purpose and meaning in the earthly world.

I have heard some people say 'I am spiritual but not religious'. Let us now look at the differences between spirituality and religion in the next section.

Spirituality and Religion

What do people mean when they say 'I am spiritual but not religious'? What some of these people mean when they say I am spiritual but not religious is that they don't belong to any religion; nevertheless they worship God or seek a higher being in their own way.

There are many reasons why people do not want to associate themselves with any particular religion these days. **Religion seems to have caused more trouble than good, some people say.** There is a class of people who are of the opinion that religion has done more harm than good to the human race and so they will not attend to religion nor believe in God. Before I discuss this subject further, it is important for us to distinguish between what people do in the name of God, and what God expects people to do in His name. I will elaborate on the former first.

There are many people who do things in the name of God or in the name of their religion. Some of these people have good intentions, although they can sometimes make mistakes. There are others who use the name of God to advance their own personal selfish agenda. These are the people who use religion or the name of God to cause a lot of trouble, because of their own selfish ambitions.

Let us continue our discussion on the difference between religion and spirituality. Despite the impressive volume of research that has been amassed to distinguish spirituality from religion in today's era, there remains little definitional congruence among authors. The terms spirituality and religion can sometimes be used interchangeably, or treated as mutually exclusive, or viewed as distinct yet interdependent constructs.

Some people define spirituality as the narrow band of searching for meaning prior to latching on to any particular beliefs, practices, or structures. But religion or philosophy is invoked after specific values, beliefs, practices, and institutions come into play. For the same reason that religion has been characterized as being dead when devoid of a spiritual core, spirituality is a quest or a search until it finds embodiment in beliefs, values, and/or practices. Sometimes once spirituality finds substance, it becomes religion or philosophy. Once spiritual seekers find what they are looking for, they somehow stop the search and start practicing or believing what they have found routinely. This is one of the main reasons we have different sects, and even sects within different religions.

I think every religion should encourage it adherents to seek God for themselves because there are still a lot of mysteries God wants to reveal to humanity. Religion without spirituality can deny the search for the divine.

Some spiritual seekers may be religious in one sense. Many of these religious spiritual seekers may embark on their individual spiritual journey as a result of some kind of dissatisfaction in what their church or denomination believes or does. When people become dissatisfied with their church, sect, or religion, this can make them seek the truth outside their church or religion for themselves. In Christianity for example, we have different movements, denominations, and churches as a result of people seeking for the truth in their generation. This is another reason why the subject of spirituality is in vogue in the 21st century.

3.3 The Quest: What spiritual searchers seek

When one considers the reasons why people practice spirituality, it is easy to conclude that what God promises humanity in scripture is exactly what people are seeking for. So what are some of the things people are searching for in their practice of spirituality? In this section, we will look at how scripture can provide such guidance.

The first is a belief in transcendence; something greater than oneself. The second aspect of spirituality is the 'interconnectedness or the relational dimension of life'. The third component of spirituality is a feeling of love and compassion for others and their life circumstances. The fourth is finding peace or calmness in times of hardship. The fifth component of spirituality is a sense of purpose and meaning in the earthly world. Let us discuss the first thing spiritual searchers seek in their practice of spirituality in the next section.

1. The belief in a higher being

The first thing spiritual searchers seek in their spirituality is a belief in transcendence; something greater than oneself. Some people who practice spirituality say they are seeking something cosmically greater than themselves. Here, the seeker does not know exactly what he or she is seeking. Usually they refer to this unknown as a 'higher being'.

One website reported, 'we're out to find an authentic experience or tradition, a way to live more passionately, profoundly, and truthfully. Our wandering and reading and adventures express our desire to connect to something bigger than ourselves'. So my question is what is it that which is bigger than ourselves which people are seeking? **My answer is God**! The same website reports that 'today, people equate spirituality with growth, discernment, experience, and authenticity," says Jerome P. Baggett, associate professor of religion and society at the Jesuit School of Theology at Berkeley. "They're saying, 'Yes, I want to have a connection to the sacred, but I want to do it on my own terms—terms that honour who I am as a discerning, thoughtful agent and that affirm my day-to-day life'.

What is it that which is greater than oneself or sacred? Many people refer to a 'higher being' as the one they seek or worship or relate to. As I said earlier on, my personal belief is that this is God. The dictionary defines the 'sacred' as something worthy of religious worship, very holy'. God is the one who is Holy and worthy of our worship. These people refer to God as a higher being because they do not know him yet. To such people the word of God says in Isaiah 55:6-7, 'seek the LORD while he may be found; call on him while he is near. Let the wicked forsake his way and the evil man his thoughts. Let him turn to the LORD, and he will have mercy on him, and to our God, for he will freely pardon. People who are seeking a higher being should turn to the God of the Bible, they do not need to seek further, He is right before their eyes, and He will be found by them.

Some people may also think that there is a divine being greater than the God who created the universe, hence their quest to seek this higher being. The God who created the universe is greater than any spirit or human being or god. He is greater than any god or idol or any supernatural being. This is what God says about himself: 'For the LORD your God is God of gods and Lord of lords, the great God, mighty and awesome' (Deuteronomy 10:17).

Many people worship what they do not even know, they want to have a connection to the divine or someone greater than themselves but unless they receive direction they may end up worshipping the wrong object. John, who wrote the book of Revelation in the Bible, says that he nearly worshipped an angel instead of the true God: 'I, John, am the one who heard and saw these things. And when I had heard and seen them, I fell down to worship at the feet of the angel who had been showing them to me. But the angel said to me, "Do not do it! I am a fellow servant with you and with your brothers, the prophets and all who keep the words of this book, Worship God' (Revelation 22:8-9). Unless people are directed to the true God, many people out of ignorance will end up worshipping angels or something else. This is the reason why sometimes people may need a spiritual guide or a shepherd to help them find their way out around spiritual things. If not, it is possible that many people will miss the way.

As part of his missionary journey in Europe, the apostle Paul gave a remarkable speech to a gathering of philosophers in the sophisticated university city of Athens in the first century. But as he walked around and looked carefully at their objects of worship, he even found an altar with this inscription: TO AN UNKNOWN GOD. And so he told them 'now what you worship something as 'unknown' I am going to proclaim to you' (Acts 17:23). Many people have altars, gods, higher beings or worship things they do not know. God has revealed himself to humanity. People should seek this God. His name is Jehovah. He has revealed himself to many godly men and women in the past and in the present time. These people have documented their experience with this God in the Bible. For example, when Gideon had an encounter with this God centuries ago, the writer of the book of Judges tells us this:

> When Gideon realized that it was the angel of the LORD, he exclaimed, Ah, Sovereign LORD? I have seen the angel of the LORD face to face! But the LORD said to him, Peace! Do not be afraid. You are not going to die. So Gideon built an altar to the LORD there and called it **The LORD is Peace**. To this day it stands in Ophrah of the Abiezrites (Judges 6:22-23).

From this account, we now know that God is peace because someone has experienced peace with this God.

The various concepts of God that make him greater than anything else in all creation may include the following: God's attributes of omniscience, describes his infinite knowledge:

> For my thoughts are not your thoughts, neither are your ways my ways declares the LORD. As the heavens are higher than the earth, so are my ways higher than your ways and my thoughts than your thoughts (Isaiah 55:8-9).

The omnipotence of God describes his unlimited power:

> Jeremiah 32:27: Behold, I am the LORD, the God of all flesh: is there anything too hard for me?

> Psalms 33:8-9: Let all the earth fear the LORD: let all the inhabitants of the world stand in awe of him. For he spoke and it was done; he commanded, and it stood fast.

The omnipresence of God describes his ability to be everywhere:

> For where two or three come together in my name, there am I with them." (Matthew 18:20).

The omnibenevolence of God describes his perfect goodness:

> A certain ruler asked him, "Good teacher, what must I do to inherit eternal life? Why do you call me good?" Jesus answered. "No one is good—except God alone (Luke 18:18-19).

The divinity of God describes the fact that he is a spirit being, and therefore must be regarded as sacred and holy:

> John says God is spirit, and his worshipers must worship in spirit and in truth (John 4:24).

> Paul say therefore since we are God's offspring, we should not think that the divine being is like gold or silver or stone—an image made by man's design and skill. In the past God overlooked such ignorance, but now he commands all people everywhere to repent (Acts 17: 29-3).

All these attributes suggest that the 'higher being' people seek in their practice of spirituality is God. The good news is that God has seen people's desires, their longings to be connected to him. That is why God is already inviting people who are seeking the sacred to worship him in spirit and in truth as John writes: 'Yet a time is coming and has now come when the true worshipers will worship the Father in spirit and truth, for they are the kind of worshipers the Father seeks. God is spirit, and His worshipers must worship Him in spirit and in truth' (John 4:23-24). God, through the prophet Isaiah, issues an open invitation to "all...who are thirsty." Anyone can eat and drink this meal, free of charge. The only requirement is that they come. In Isaiah 55:6 Isaiah urges everyone to take this opportunity of forgiveness while it is so freely available.

2. Finding calmness or peace in times of hardship

Many people practice spirituality in order to find calmness or peace in times of hardship or when they are under duress. When God designed the human personality, he put different desires in us. He put the desire to be at peace in us and this search for peace is becoming a global phenomenon. If life has meaning, how can one find peace in this troubling world where everything seems uncertain? Scripture offers many ways to find peace depending on the situation you find yourself.

In times of duress, problems, sickness, or uncertainty, God has told us what to do to find peace and calmness and this is the focus of this section. Philippians 4:6-7 says:

Do not be anxious about anything, but in everything, by prayer and petition, with thanksgiving, present your requests to God. And the peace of God, which transcends all understanding, will guard your hearts and your minds in Christ Jesus.

The peace of God— (like the righteousness of God) is the peace which God gives to every soul who rests on Him in prayer. This peace includes peace with God, peace with men, and peace with self.

Those who want peace must make sure they have peace with God, with everyone, and with themselves. This peace is "through Christ Jesus," for "He is our peace (Ephesians 2:14), as "making all one," and reconciling everyone to God. The comprehensiveness and beauty of the passage has naturally made it the closing blessing of our most solemn church service of "Holy Communion" with God and man.

Many people do not have peace because they are not at peace with God. If you want peace with God, go to Him in prayers and ask for forgiveness, through Jesus Christ. Some people too, are not at peace with themselves; because sometimes these people are loaded with quilt. Please learn to forgive yourself, by praying to God and encouraging yourself. Greed and covetousness can also rob you of true peace. There was a king in Israel called Ahab. This king was sullen and would not eat because a man called Naboth did not sell his piece of land to him to be used for vegetable garden (1 Kings 21).

> Ahab said to Naboth, "Let me have your vineyard to use for a vegetable garden, since it is close to my palace. In exchange I will give you a better vineyard or, if you prefer, I will pay you whatever it is worth. But Naboth replied, "The LORD forbid that I should give you the inheritance of my fathers. So Ahab went home, sullen and angry because Naboth the Jezreelite had said, "I will not give you the inheritance of my fathers." He lay on his bed sulking and refused to eat. His wife Jezebel came in and asked him, "Why are you so sullen? Why won't you eat? He answered her, "Because I said to Naboth the Jezreelite, 'Sell me your vineyard; or if you prefer, I will give you another vineyard in its place.' But he said, 'I will not give you my vineyard.' Jezebel his wife said, "Is this how you act as king over Israel? Get up and eat! Cheer up. I'll get you the vineyard of Naboth the Jezreelite (1 Kings 21:2-7).

This king would not eat because someone did not sell his piece of land to him. This is greediness! There are many people in our society like this king. They always want to have what belong to someone.

They want their friend's fiancée, or they want their colleague's role, or they want what their senior pastor has or is doing. Anytime you are restless, please find out what you have looking for in life.

Some people too are not at peace because they may have wronged someone. Another way to find personal peace is to learn to live at peace with everybody. This may involve forgiving those who will offend you, never take revenge, but leave revenge to God. Unforgiving attitude can keep you from moving forward in life and can even cause you to become bitter.

> Do not repay anyone evil for evil. Be careful to do what is right in the eyes of everybody. If it is possible, as far as it depends on you, live at peace with everyone. Do not take revenge, my friends, but leave room for God's wrath, for it is written: It is mine to avenge; I will repay, says the Lord. On the contrary: If your enemy is hungry, feed him; if he is thirsty, give him something to drink. In doing this, you will heap burning coals on his head. Do not be overcome by evil, but overcome evil with good (Romans 12:17-20).

I think it is time you forgive those who have wronged you. Forgiveness is one of keys to the attainment of personal peace. Sometimes those who offend you can distract and steal your peace if you are not careful because they can cause you to seek revenge which can drain your energy further. Christ Jesus, our saviour and the one we are to imitate prayed for those who drove the nails into his hands (Luke 23:34). Your offenders may think they are smart, but often they are acting in ignorance. Don't come down to their level by retaliating. Forgive them and let them go. This is another way to seek peace for yourself. Let us discuss the subject of peace further in the following paragraphs.

We drink water when we feel thirsty because we have been taught to drink water when we are thirsty. We eat food when we feel hungry because we have been taught to eat food when we are hungry. In the same way, we have been designed by our creator (God) with an inbuilt need and a desire to have a relationship with him. Our relationship with God can also give us peace. Unfortunately, many people have not been taught what to do when they desire God that is why many people are looking for somebody or something to call God or a 'higher being' or a 'supreme being'. It is possible that such people will wonder restlessly through life unless they come to know God and be filled with his holy spirit.

Those who have been taught how to seek God when they desire him know what to do: A song writer wrote this:

> As a deer longs for streams of water God, I long for you in the same way. I am thirsty for God. I am thirsty for the living God. When can I go and meet with him? (Psalm 42:1-2).

As the life of a deer depends upon water, so our lives depend upon God. Feeling separated from God, this psalmist wouldn't rest until he restored his relationship with God because he knew that his very life depended on it.

Many people thirst for God but they do not know that their desire or thirst is a spirit to spirit relationship with the God of the universe. God has inspired a desire for Himself in the heart of everyone. As observed by the writer of Ecclesiastes (3:11), in addition to all the abilities given to us by God: our innovations, creativity, and so forth, God has also set eternity in the heart of mankind and it is a feature of our time that people are looking for somebody or something beyond themselves that is why many people have turned to the practise of spirituality. Augustine of Hippo, also known as Saint Augustine or Saint Austin, was an early Christian theologian and philosopher whose writings were very influential in the development of Western Christianity and philosophy has this to say:

> You have made us for yourself and our heart is restless until it finds its rest in you (Augustus of Hippo).

One of the greatest insights of life is that our longing for God is something which is inspired by God and can only be fulfilled through His grace. This point is made clear in a famous prayer to Christ by Anselm of Canterbury (1033-1109).

> Give me what you have made me want. Grant that I may attain to love you as much as you command. I praise and thank you for the desire that you have inspired. Perfect what you have begun and grant me what you have made me long for.

These words express the fundamental point that our longing to know God or to be at peace with ourselves is a divine gift. As Anselm points out, prayer is an essential aspect of our quest for a better and peaceful world. We must ask God to perfect what he has begun, and to grant us more fully what he has caused us to desire. God has caused every person in this world to desire peace, joy and happiness. Such good qualities can only be received from the one who caused you to desire them. Why don't you turn to him in prayer for such blessings?

True peace and joy can only come from God. This is possible if only you ask God in prayer. God does not force people to acknowledge or pray to Him. This is a decision people must make for themselves. This however, does not mean that we will have or know all the answers to our questions, but we can trust Him and enjoy His good gifts in our place and time as we look forward to the time when He will unite the entire universe to bring about the peace and harmony that has eluded the cosmos for so long.

There are thousands of good and honest souls in today's world, who are outwardly prosperous yet inwardly bankrupt—hurting and wounded, but not knowing where to turn for personal healing. To people like that, the message of Jesus is simple. 'Come to me He says, all of you who are tired of carrying heavy load, and I will give you rest' (Matthew 11:18). For those who are honestly searching for spiritual meaning, personal transformation, inner healing and harmony with the world and its people, his call is irresistible today as it was then. And as millions will happily affirm—His power to change things through the work of the Holy Spirit is undiminished.

However God does not offer escape route from the harsh realities of everyday life. Even Jesus Christ, went through difficulties and sufferings. But because of his trust in the Father, He had hope and received divine grace to accomplish his mission on earth. Now through the ministry of Jesus Christ, God has shared the realities of human life and can transform even the darkest corner with the brilliance of his light as ordinary people are empowered by the Spirit of God to accomplish extraordinary things. For all genuine searchers after truth, this has to be good news—the best news of all.

3. Finding a sense of belonging or Interconnectedness

Another aspect of spirituality people seek is the 'interconnectedness or the relational dimension of life'. This is what Astin *et al.* research describes as Ecumenical world view. Ecumenical Worldview is another measure of spirituality people seek and this involves people's interest in different religious traditions, countries, cultures, a strong connection to all humanity, and a belief that all life is interconnected.

Finding a sense of belonging or Interconnectedness is a sense of unification with others that one experiences. We are created into relationships, in the home, in the church, at the recreation centre, or at the work place. In both the Old and New Testament, God urges his children to continue to meet together as often as possible. Hebrew 10:25 says 'let us not give up meeting together, as some are in the habit of doing, but let us encourage one another—and all the more as you see the day approaching. Meeting together foster the development of deep relationships and a sense of greater purpose, as life and culture exist in a web of interrelationships. In fact this is how God wants us to live, in relationship with one another:

Dear friends, let us love one another, for love comes from God. Everyone who loves has been born of God and knows God. Whoever does not love does not know God, because God is love. This is how God showed his love among us: He sent his one and only Son into the world that we might live through him (1 John 4:7-9).

4. The search for meaning to life

Everything in this world has a purpose, and many people are in search of meaningfulness of life. In the beginning, God created the earth, and he looked upon it in his cosmic loneliness and said, "Let Us make living creatures out of mud, so the mud can see what we have done." And God created every living creature that now moves, and one of the living creatures was mankind. Everyone has a reason for doing what they do. So it is with God. He has a reason for creating mankind. In this section we will be discovering the meaning of life. Someone has discovered this great mystery and has documented his findings in the Holy Scriptures for us. People should not worry themselves finding out the meaning of life anymore, this work has been done, and has been tested to be true in all generations.

This person is Solomon, the son of David, a king of Israel in Jerusalem. Having tried everything life has to offer, the Teacher circles back to this uncomplicated formula for making sense of our time on earth: He concluded his findings on the search for meaning to life this way:

> Now all has been heard; here is the conclusion of the matter: Fear God and keep his commandments, for this is the whole duty of man. God will bring every deed into judgment, including every hidden thing, whether it is good or evil (Ecclesiastes 12:13-14).

Someone may ask, how did he come to such conclusion? The author of Ecclesiastes had tasted just about everything life has to offer in order to find the meaning of life. Wealth? No one could exceed him in luxurious lifestyle (Ecclesiastes 2:4-9). Wisdom? His was world-renowned (Ecclesiastes. 1:13-18). Fame? He was king, the most famous man of his time (Ecclesiastes 1:12). Systematically, he sampled all of life's powers and pleasures, yet all ultimately disappointed him. All proved meaningless.

What is the point of life? He asked. You work hard, and someone else gets all the credit. You struggle to be good, and evil people take advantage of you. You accumulate money, and it just goes to spoiled heirs. You seek pleasure, and it turns sour on you. And everyone—rich or poor, good or evil—meets the same end. We all die. There is only one word that seems to describe this life, if you look at it on only one level apart from God: meaningless!

Ecclesiastes strikes a responsive chord in our age. Its words show up in folk songs and at presidential inaugurations. No century has seen such progress, and yet such despair. What is the purpose of life anyway? Is there any ultimate meaning? "Is that all there is?" asked one songwriter after listing life's pleasures. A key phrase in this book, "under the sun," describes the world lived on one level, apart from God and without any belief in the afterlife. If you live on that level, you may well conclude that life is meaningless.

Ecclesiastes gives some words of hope, including the final summary: "Fear God and keep his commandments, for this is the whole duty of man" (Ecclesiastes 12:13). That's the positive message, the "lesson" of Ecclesiastes. But such positive words are almost overwhelmed by the author's powerful negative example. You could summarize his whole life in Jesus' one statement, "What good will it be for a man if he gains the whole world, yet forfeits his soul?" (Matthew 16:26).

Questions about meaning of life can appear to be so difficult that some people think they are unanswerable. Rumour has it that Woody Allen, an American actor, filmmaker, comedian, musician, and playwright whose career spans more than 50 years was engaged in a philosophical discussion one evening at a dinner party when he was asked his opinion about the meaning of life. His response was equal to the occasion: "You ask me about the meaning of life? Good Lord, I don't even know my way around Chinatown!"

Some Philosophers, for example Paul Edwards deny that there is any point in asking the question, often on the grounds that the question itself is cognitively meaningless or that it would be impossible to know what an answer to the question would look like.[10] This is one reason many philosophers and scientists do not want to think about the meaning of life because to them, the answer to the question about the meaning of life must be empirically verifiable, testable by science, and so forth.

My suggesting in this book is that if people do not have any model or method(s) for finding answers to life's big questions such as the existence of God, who am I, and what is life about, then they should start inventing or looking at new ways of addressing these questions. They can turn to the Christian faith for answers to such questions because these questions won't go away. Your soul will continue to demand answers to these questions, and until you address them, it is possible that true peace and joy can elude you.

But things are changing now. Many academicians are researching on the meaning and purpose of life. A new study by University College of London, studied people with an average age of 65 and found that those who enjoyed "wellbeing" were likely to live longer. The researchers believe they may have unlocked the secret to a longer life – a sense of meaning and purpose. Professor Andrew Steptoe, director of the UCL Institute of Epidemiology and Health Care, who led the study, told Sky News: "We have previously found that happiness is associated with a lower risk of death." These analyses show that the meaningfulness and sense of purpose that older people have in their lives are also related to survival.

But what do we mean by asking the question 'what is the meaning of life'? The question is not asking whether or not people find life subjectively satisfying and of personal significance. Some people say 'I find a lot of significance and meaning in life by playing golf'. Others say they find significance and meaning in life when they watch a football match'. These are all subjective answers. People who think they can find meaning to life in just doing 'something' often end up

---

[10] See E.D. Klemke, ed., *The meaning of Life*, New York: Oxford University Press, 1981, pp.175–261

being disappointed because the very thing they thought will give them satisfaction ends up becoming the source of their woes.

There are some people who have concluded that life has no meaning at all and that nothing has any real value. Of course life has no meaning if you view it only at one level, without considering the after death life. Philosophers call this group of people Nihilist. Nihilism is a pessimistic philosophy of life and has been held by philosophers such as Friedrich Nietzsche and Albert Camus. According to Nihilism, life is absurd, there is no reason why the universe exists, there is no purpose towards which the cosmos is moving, and human history has no real goal or end. These people hold the view that human beings are not the favoured creation of a loving God, but are modified monkeys. Human beings are the chance product of random mutations, natural selection, and the struggle for survival. They hold the view that there is no life after death.

Fortunately, this view is not the truth. God created mankind in his own image and gave us abilities to take care of the creation. We are to reproduce and fill the earth. We are to live in constant relationship with him until He calls us home to paradise. There is life after death for mankind, a beautiful life indeed. The human soul is immortal and departs to either heaven or hell after death. Where do you think your soul will go to after death, heaven or hell? It is important that you do something about the final destination of your soul. Make sure you make it to heaven after death.

The question is, why will people believe in nihilism, which holds the view that life is meaningless? According to J.P. Moreland in his book, *scaling the Secular City*, two main reasons are often given for adopting nihilism. First, some nihilist argue that since God is dead (i.e., since the concept of God can no longer be believed and no longer holds sway for modern people) then life is absurd and values do not exist. 'If God is dead do whatever you' please, says the nihilist.

The truth is that God is not dead as these people claim. God cannot die, he lives forever. The human race cannot exist if God is dead.

First, as a matter of factual observation, the concept of God is not vanishing from western culture at all. Many people are replacing formal religion with spirituality, a trend which will continue way beyond the 21st century. For some time now, the evangelisation of the western world has not been as intense as it used to be centuries ago. Because of this, many people are seeking God by themselves; probably many western people are fed up with formal religious structures.

Secondly, the claim by nihilist that values do not exist is totally false. Value, is defined by the dictionary as *'the usefulness or the importance of something'*. Everything in this world has a meaning and a purpose. An automobile has a meaning and a purpose; why it was designed by its manufacturer. The same principle applies to human beings as well. There is a reason why the designer and the creator of the universe made you. When God said 'let us make mankind in our own image', he had a purpose for creating mankind.

God has a purpose for the cosmos and this purpose informs the purpose of human life in general and each individual life in particular. You have a purpose in this world. Your purpose in life is to live your life according to God's commandments. This will make you wise unto salvation in Christ Jesus. You do not need to experiment with your life in order to find meaning. This can be very costly, but build your life on God's principles; this will save you from a lot of problems and from a life of despair.

King Solomon has done this research for us and has documented his findings in the Bible in the book of Ecclesiastes. He was blessed with the resources from heaven to embark on this study. You don't need to repeat this research, it is not necessary. Many spiritual searchers are in search for the meaning of life. In the words of Solomon, 'to fear God and keep his commandment is the whole duty of mankind'. God has principles governing every aspect of your life.

Discover these principles in the Bible and build your life according to them; this will give you meaning to life.

5. Discovering yourself

Another thing modern spiritual searchers seek is discovering 'self'. Who am I? Knowing who you are; what you can do to become the person your soul desires to be, can be a very comforting experience and can bring joy and deep satisfaction in your life and this is one of the aims of this section. One of the benefits of building your life on the principles of God is that you will discover yourself and you will receive the needed grace to be transformed and empowered. But the process of discovering something in life may require exploration or investigation. The approaches adopted in this book to discover yourself are: discovering yourself through your unique SERVE profile, discovering yourself by looking into the Bible, and discovering yourself by an encounter with God.

But what does it mean to discover oneself? Who you are is what I call your '**persona**' in this book. Your persona is the way you behave, talk, and interact with other people and God that causes them to see you as a particular kind of person. Your persona has less to do with what you have acquired materially.

Before I discuss this subject further, I will like to state in plain language who you are, who am I, who he is, who she is! Every human being is made in the image of God (Genesis 1:26-27). But because of the transgression of the first parents, every human being is not able to reflect this image of God. So, in order to reflect this image of God, you need to be 'born again' where you receive a new spirit, a new mindset, a new resurrected body etc. The term born again will be explained in details later this section.

Someone may ask, in what ways are we made in the image of God? God obviously did not create us exactly like himself because God has no physical body. Instead, we are reflections of God's glory. Some feel that our reason, creativity, speech, or self-determination is the image of God. We will never be like God on this earth because he is our supreme creator. But he has given us the ability to reflect his character in our love, patience, forgiveness, kindness, reasoning, creativity, self-determination, faithfulness etc. It is these abilities that have been impaired due to the sinful nature we inherited from the first parents, but can be restored when one is born again. 'For those God foreknew he also predestined to be conformed to the likeness of his Son, that he might be the firstborn among many brothers (Romans 8:29).

Many people live their lives anyhow because they do not know how precious they are. Some even commit suicide because they think they are worthless. Knowing that we are made in the image of God, and thus share many of his characteristics provides a solid basis for self-worth. Many people want to discover themselves to know their worthiness or unworthiness. Human worth does not just depend on possessions, achievements, physical attractiveness, or public acclaim. Instead, it is based on being or made or remade in God's image.

Although we all have weaknesses, make wrong decisions, or fail to do the right things at times, these are not the only things God sees in us. God sees the possibility of us changing to become better people, fulfilling our destiny, and finally joining him in paradise. But not many people know this, so they give up on life easily when things are not working well.

Discovering oneself can also help to explain why we do what we do. As someone lamented, 'I do not understand what I do. For what I want to do I do not do, but what I hate I do' (Romans 5:17). It is very easy for people to deceive themselves into thinking that they are perfect until they find themselves in challenging situations. Many people are surprised to see themselves exhibiting some strange and sometimes disgraceful behavior. It is beneficial for one to know their strengths and weaknesses. This will help them to know which area in their personality they need to work on in order to improve themselves.

The acronym SERVE stands for: *S-Spiritual* gifts, *E-Experiences*, *R-Relational style*, *V-Vocational skills* and *E-Enthusiasm*. The SERVE profile can help you to discover yourself to some extent. The reason I chose to use the SERVE profile as one of the ways of discovering yourself is because everything we do in life is a service to God, service to ourselves, and service to our fellow human beings. Teachers serve student. Health workers serve sick people. Politicians serve the citizens. Pastors serve church members. Even Jesus Christ who is the Son of God and the soon coming King says ' even the Son of Man did not come to be served, but to serve, and to give his life as a ransom for many' (Mark 10:45). Your service to God, yourself, and others can help reveal some aspect of your personality.

Discovering yourself through your unique SERVE profile is not enough to give you a true picture of your persona, because sometimes your life experiences can overwhelm and blind you to see other aspects of yourself. The Bible, which is the word of God, can also give us a true image of ourselves because 'the word of God is living and active. Sharper than any double-edged sword, it penetrates even to dividing soul and spirit, joints and marrow; it judges the thoughts and attitudes of the heart' (Hebrews 4:12). Advances in technology—MRI tests, x-ray machines, CAT scans—make it possible for doctors to see inside the human body and judge what goes on there. But no one has yet devised a machine that can peer inside the brain to detect thoughts and attitudes. God has such ability: his word and an encounter with him.

Your SERVE profile cannot reveal your thoughts and the attitudes of your heart, but the word of God does. Lastly, discovering yourself by an encounter with God will also be looked at in this section. Our encounter with God can give as a sense of our own worthiness and unworthiness because who we are is plain before God.

Discovering yourself is not the same as fortune telling or enquiring about your future. The practice of enquiring about your future from a spiritualist or a fortune teller is an act of abomination to God

(Deuteronomy 18: 10-12). Let us start the journey of discovering ourselves in the next section.

1. Discovering yourself through your unique SERVE profile

A closer look at what you have experienced in life will reveal many things to you, some positive, some negative. You will need to work on your weakness, mistakes and any imperfections you may have as you discover them. This process can be very exciting and rewarding because you will become a better person in the end. You will also need to encourage yourself to continue to make good use of any virtue in you. You may have some gifts and talents you have not been using at all. You may have some ideas, or even a vision you have not worked on yet. It is time to put your ideas into action as you discover them in this book.

Your **S**piritual gifts, and your **E**nthusiasm, your **R**elational styles, your **V**ocational skills, and your life **E**xperiences are the elements which make up your SERVE Profile and these elements can help you to discover yourself, although not exhaustive. Let us study these elements one by one.

Spiritual gifts & natural talents: There is difference between spiritual gift and natural gift or talent. Spiritual gifts are only given to people who are born again through faith in Jesus Christ to empower them for service in the kingdom of God. Natural gift (talent) is a mixture of personality and skill. This can be acquired through hereditary, or from birth. Remember Saul, who later became Paul, had natural gift but lacked that of the Spirit of God until his conversion when he received spiritual gifts and became very useful to God. To receive God's grace of salvation is to receive God's gifts for service as well. Believers can have both spiritual gifts and natural gifts or talents. Unbelievers can only have natural gifts or talent. If you want to know who you are, take your time to identify your spiritual gift(s) and or your natural gifts or talents. Some of the spiritual gifts scripture mentions are:

> There are different kinds of gifts, but the same Spirit. There are different kinds of service, but the same Lord. There are different kinds of working, but the same God works all of them in all men. Now to each one the manifestation of the Spirit is given for the common good. To one there is given through the Spirit the message of wisdom, to another the message of knowledge by means of the same Spirit, to another faith by the same Spirit, to another gifts of healing by that one Spirit, to another miraculous powers, to another prophecy, to another distinguishing between spirits, to another speaking in different kinds of tongues, and to still another the interpretation of tongues. All these are the work of one and the same Spirit, and he gives them to each one, just as he determines (1 Corinthians 12:4-11).

There are many more spiritual gifts given by the Spirit of God. It must be said here that Satan can also give people false spiritual gifts or powers (Revelation 16:14). One can receive spiritual gift(s) from God upon being born again. The kind of spiritual gift you posses in some respect defines who you are. Let us look at the next element which can help you to discover yourself.

Your Enthusiasm: what are you passionate about in life or what have you been passionate about in the past? This element can help tell who you are. For the born again believer, this is the passion God puts in your heart for his work in his kingdom. For the unbeliever, this can be anything you are passionate about in life. Passion comes with a true calling; a person motivated by God's goal is always more enthusiastic than a person maintaining the status quo. Once we have humbled ourselves before God's call on our lives, that call in turn becomes the well-spring of passion that makes us true servants.

For the believer, your enthusiasm drains anytime you get off God's mission and focus on short-term goals rather than eternal purposes. Why was Jesus a passionate servant? How can you become a passionate servant? The fact that you feel passionate about something does not necessarily mean your passion or desire is good. Make sure you are passionate about things which are profitable and have a reward in this world, and in heaven. Let us see the next element which can help define who you are.

Your Relational styles: your relational style is another defining element of how God has moulded you into a unique person. There are four categories of relational styles; namely Dominance, Influencing, Conscientious, and Steadiness (DICS). These relational styles are ingrained in who we are. No one temperament is superior for service among God's people. We are all a blend of these four basic personality types, but most of us have one or two dominant styles. Our individual blends make us unique, like fingerprints. One of the best ways to improve our relationship is to bring a balance to any of our traits that we have neglectfully or subconsciously pushed to an extreme. You will need self-discipline in order to bring a balance to your life in relating to others in a better way.

Vocational skills: These are skills and abilities you have acquired through learning and training. Your skills and abilities can help define who you are and what you can do. Whatever vocational skills you have learnt can be invested wisely such as in the mission of the church, helping other people, or setting up a business. God also uses your vocational skills as raw material for service. For example, a woman called Lydia in the city of Philippi invested her business skills to support part of God's mission (Acts 16:11-15). Similarly, Aquila and Pricilla invested their tent making skills into Paul's mission. How are you investing your skills and abilities into the things of God? Let us look at the next element in our SERVE profile which can help you discover yourself.

Your Experience: what you have experienced in life, either positive or negative can also contribute to your identity. Someone who has given birth is called a mother because of the birth experience. A lot of people's personality has been affected because of their life experiences. My faith stance, based on the biblical record, is that God either allows or ordains events in our lives. I call this, God's permissible and God's perfect will respectively. God's permissible will is what he allows to happen to you based on what you have decided to do. With God's permissible will, he allows you to do whatever you want whether good or bad (1 Samuel 8:4–22).

God's perfect will is what God has originally planned for your life which is always a plan to prosper you and not to harm you, a plan to give you hope and a future (Jeremiah 29:11). This is another reason why you need to build your life on the principles of God. It is for your own benefit. God's Perfect plan for your life will satisfy all your needs according to His will: body, Spirit, and soul. 3 John 1:2 says 'Dear friend, I pray that you may enjoy good health and that all may go well with you, even as your soul is getting along well'.

Over and over again, scripture tells us that God will give you another chance and restore you to his original plan if you have missed His perfect will at some point in your life. All you need to do is to return to him with all your heart (read Deuteronomy 30:1–11). Your past life may not have been good or positive, but please come back to the Lord; He will restore you and give you a bright future. Let us now do a simple check to find out more about your experience in life. This can help you to identify your strengths and weakness and what needs to be done for a brighter future.

Your positive tendencies: these are things you have done which can be considered positive. Let us start to discover the positive tendencies in you first, and see how you can improve upon them to better your life and the people around you. This will bring glory to God, our Father in heaven. Some Christian theologians are hesitant to admit that someone can do positive things in life to some extent without being 'born again'. But life experiences and what we see around us can tell the fact that some people do 'some positive' things in life without necessarily being born again. Many reasons can be attributed to this.

What are some of the good things you have done in the past? Showing kindness to people, forgiving friends, relatives, and colleagues, giving to a charity, worshipping God, restraining yourself from harming someone either verbally or physically, making peace, remaining faithful to people, to your work, to your church, and remaining faithful to God. The list can be endless. If you have been doing all or some of these positive things, then people will be calling you a good person. Your good deeds can identify who you are.

Doing positive things in this world does not necessarily mean you will enter the kingdom of God. To enter the kingdom of God, one must be 'born again' and live their new life according to God's principles which include doing good deeds for people amongst other things. Scripture says 'it is by grace you have been saved, through faith—and this not from yourselves, it is the gift of God— not by works, so that no one can boast. For we are God's workmanship, created in Christ Jesus to do good works, which God prepared in advance for us to do'(Ephesians 2:8-10).

It is said that people do good things when they are inspired by either the Spirit of God or when they are inspired by someone who has the Spirit of God in themselves or when they see or hear something good. Leave someone in darkness, he can do nothing significant. But bring in light and you will see the difference. Scripture says 'For God, who said, let light shine out of darkness, made his light shine in our hearts to give us the light of the knowledge of the glory of God in the face of Christ (2 Corinthians 4:6). A little light from God can make a huge difference in your life. My prayer for you in this section is to receive light from heaven to fulfil your destiny on earth and to receive eternal life.

Your negative tendencies: these are things you have done which can be considered negative. Let us now discover some of the negative tendencies in you and see how you can help yourself to become a better person. Now, do a simple check, what about your morality, and the inner struggles? Are you perfect in everything you do or do you make mistakes. The unintentional insults you have meted out on people. Do you gossip, have you looked lustfully at a man or woman, have you engaged in any improper sexual conduct before, do you have hatred for someone, do you find it difficult to forgive people, do you have any addiction(s), do you gamble, do you get jealous, just to mention a few. James 3:2 says' we all stumble in many ways. If anyone is never at fault in what he says [or does], he is a perfect man, able to keep his whole body in check'.

Don't feel shy; you are not the only person with these negative tendencies. Read the following honest confessions by the apostle Paul. I believe you can identify yourself with his struggles:

> I do not understand what I do. For what I want to do I do not do, but what I hate I do. And if I do what I do not want to do, I agree that the law is good. As it is, it is no longer I myself who does it, but it is sin living in me. I know that nothing good lives in me, that is, in my sinful nature. For I have the desire to do what is good, but I cannot carry it out. For what I do is not the good I want to do; no, the evil I do not want to do—this I keep on doing. Now if I do what I do not want to do, it is no longer I who do it, but it is sin living in me that does it. So I find this law at work: When I want to do good, evil is right there with me. For in my inner being I delight in God's law; but I see another law at work in the members of my body, waging war against the law of my mind and making me a prisoner of the law of sin at work within my members. What a wretched man I am! Who will rescue me from this body of death (Romans 7:15-24).

This text tells a lot about our personality. The fact that all people, without exception, commit sin proves that we have sinful nature. We are lost in sin and cannot cure ourselves of this sin. Sometimes we do not understand our own actions, we become baffled and bewildered. We do not practice or accomplish what we wish for, we sometimes do the very things we loathe, which our moral instinct condemns. If you will be sincere with yourself, your instinct has been telling you that you are not the kind of person you wish for yourself. God, your creator also says the same: 'for all have sinned and fall short of the glory of God' (Romans 3:23). You don't need to look far to realise that you have fallen short of the glory of God. Check the condition of your life!

All these negative tendencies in our lives need to be worked on, if not they have the potential to damage us or the people around us. A lot of women and men manage to get their dream partners only to lose them because of their bad behaviour. Some couples also destroy their own relationship or marriage because of their bad behaviour. Many people end up in prison because they did not work on their rebellious attitude. Many people have lost positions of influence because of their bad behaviour. Some people are also jobless now because they were sacked as a result of their behaviour. Do you know that a lot of people will go to hell after death because they refused to allow Jesus Christ to forgive them their sins? The starting point of personal transformation starts from discovering the negative tendencies in yourself and mastering your will to seek help from God.

So far, we have looked at discovering yourself using the SERVE profile. What have you discovered about yourself? Write down ten things you have discovered about yourself and discuss these with your church pastor for help.

2. Discovering yourself via the Bible- God's word

In the previous section we used the SERVE profile to help in our discovery of self. In this section we will look into the Bible to see what God's word tells us about ourselves. The Bible is the word of God, from God written by human beings under the inspiration of God's Spirit. The Bible says 'what shall we say, then? Is the law [the word of God] sin? Certainly not! Indeed I would not have known what sin was except through the law. For I would not have known what coveting really was if the law had not said, do not covet (Romans 7:7). You can discover yourself through what God says about you and this information can be found in the Holy Bible.

In the Bible, God reveals who we are and what He will do to help us become better. For example, in Romans 3:23-24 God says ' for all have sinned and fall short of the glory of God, and are justified freely by his grace through the redemption that came by Christ Jesus'. We are sinners but we can be justified through Jesus' sacrifice if we believe in him. Sometimes, people try to hide their true personality from others especially if they have done something bad in the past. David, the second king of Israel was like that at some point in his kingship until God sent his word through the prophet Nathan to tell David what he David had been doing in secret. In this way, the word of God (either written or spoken) can be compared to an x-ray or MRI machines, exposing our inner self:

> For the word of God is living and active. Sharper than any double-edged sword, it penetrates even to dividing soul and spirit, joints and marrow; it judges the thoughts and attitudes of the heart. Nothing in all creation is hidden from God's sight. Everything is uncovered and laid bare before the eyes of him to whom we must give account (Hebrews 4:12-13).

How God sees us through His spoken or written word is what is important and helpful in discovering ourselves. God sees every aspect of your life. God is all seeing, all knowing, all powerful, and everywhere present. This revelation about how God sees us is written by King David in Psalm 139:1-12. The revelation is somewhat lengthy, but so profound I couldn't decide what to cut out. Enjoy.

> O LORD, you have searched me and you know me. You know when I sit and when I rise; you perceive my thoughts from afar. You discern my going out and my lying down; you are familiar with all my ways. Before a word is on my tongue you know it completely, O LORD. You hem me in—behind and before; you have laid your hand upon me. Such knowledge is too wonderful for me, too lofty for me to attain. Where can I go from your Spirit? Where can I flee from your presence? If I go up to the heavens, you are there; if I make my bed in the depths, you are there. If I rise on the wings of the dawn, if I settle on the far side of the sea, even there your hand will guide

me, your right hand will hold me fast. If I say, Surely the
darkness will hide me and the light become night around
me, even the darkness will not be dark to you; the night
will shine like the day, for darkness is as light to you.

Nothing can escape God's concern or attention, according to this
psalm—no person, no thought, no place, and no time.

King David[11] focused on his own desires so when temptation
came he could not resist. He sinned deliberately by sleeping with
someone's wife. The woman became pregnant. He committed
murder by killing the woman's husband to cover up. David himself
had become insensitive to his own sins so it was until a year later,
when God sent the prophet Nathan to confront David's multiple sin
of coveting, theft, adultery, and murder. It is sometimes very difficult
for someone to assess your behavior. Even the prophet Nathan could
not see David's wrong doing until God told the prophet what David
had done in secret.

David admitted his guilt when he was confronted, and the Lord
forgave him although God disciplined him later to teach him a lesson.
During the incident, David wrote Psalm 51 giving valuable insight
into his character and offering hope for us as well. David also wrote
Psalm 32 to express the joy he felt after he was forgiven:

Blessed is he whose transgressions are forgiven, whose sins
are covered. Blessed is the man whose sin the LORD does
not count against him and in whose spirit is no deceit.
When I kept silent, my bones wasted away through my
groaning all day long. For day and night your hand was
heavy upon me; my strength was sapped as in the heat
of summer. Then I acknowledged my sin to you and
did not cover up my iniquity. I said, "I will confess my
transgressions to the LORD"— and you forgave the guilt
of my sin.

---

[11] The story is recorded in 2 Samuel chapters 11-12

There is power in forgiveness. There is healing and restoration in forgiveness. No matter how miserable guilt makes you feel or how terrible you have sinned, you can pour your heart out to God and seek his forgiveness as David did. If we confess our sins God is faithful to forgive and to cleanse us from all unrighteousness.

So far we have looked at how God's word (either written or spoken) can help discover ourselves, especially our weaknesses. It was God's law that revealed David's true character to him as told by the prophet Nathan. David was not angry when he was told of his sins, but admitted it, and repented. When you hear a preacher man telling you of your sins, please don't get angry or don't say that he is judging you. No, he is only diagnosing your illness. He will also offer you a cure. Please allow God's word to help discover yourself so that you can receive the necessary help to change. Let us look at how encountering God can help us discover ourselves in the next section.

3. Discovering self through an encounter with God

Everybody will one day have an encounter with God, either in this life or on the judgment day. This is the main reason for writing this section to encourage you to begin to imagine how you will feel, if one day you stand before God. Hebrews 9:27 says 'People have to die once. After that, God will judge them'. No one can hide his or her true persona in God's presence. In God's presence, our true nature, worthiness, and unworthiness are revealed.

In this section, I will discuss two people who discovered themselves when they had an encounter with God: the prophet Isaiah (in Isaiah 6) and Paul of Tarsus (in Acts 9). I hope these two discussions will help you to assess yourself, whether you will be happy to see God or you will scream in his presence. I am looking forward to the day when I will stand before God in His holy temple and bow down and worship. This section will also help you to make the necessary adjustments to your life in case you are not standing right with God.

The prophet Isaiah experienced a dramatic call from God to become a prophet. His experience is recorded in the book named after him. It is worth quoting the entire revelation here:

> In the year that King Uzziah died, I saw the Lord seated on a throne, high and exalted, and the train of his robe filled the temple. Above him were seraphs, each with six wings: With two wings they covered their faces, with two they covered their feet, and with two they were flying. And they were calling to one another: Holy, holy, holy is the LORD Almighty; the whole earth is full of his glory. At the sound of their voices the doorposts and thresholds shook and the temple was filled with smoke. Woe to me! I cried. I am ruined! For I am a man of unclean lips, and I live among a people of unclean lips, and my eyes have seen the King, the LORD Almighty. Then one of the seraphs flew to me with a live coal in his hand, which he had taken with tongs from the altar. With it he touched my mouth and said, See, this has touched your lips; your guilt is taken away and your sin atoned for. Then I heard the voice of the Lord saying, Whom shall I send? And who will go for us? And I said, Here am I. Send me! (Isaiah 6:1-8).

In God's presence, the contrast between His holiness and our sin is magnified—not just to condemn or produce feelings of self-loathing, but to help us see our wrongdoing from His perspective so we'll confess, repent and receive help. Isaiah's view of God gives us some sense of God's greatness, mystery, and power. Seeing the Lord and listening to the praise of the angels, Isaiah realized that he was unclean before God. One of the results of an encounter with God is an immediate awareness of our own sinful condition. That's why Isaiah cried out, "Woe is me, for I am ruined!" (Isaiah. 6:5).

The sight of the Lord immediately reminded Isaiah of his own area of weakness: 'I am a man of unclean lips and I live among people of unclean lips' (Isaiah. 6:5). But when Isaiah lips were touched with a live burning coal, he was told that his sins were forgiven. Then he heard a voice saying 'who shall I send', and Isaiah said 'here am I send me'. The only time Isaiah felt comfortable was when he was told his sins were forgiven. In the same way, the only time people will feel comfortable in God's presence is when their sins are forgiven and cleansed. The process may be uncomfortable at the beginning, but please, go to God in prayer or in the church for his forgiveness so that a time of refreshing may come upon you.

It is very important to point out that, it wasn't the coal that cleans Isaiah of his sins, but God. The coal was only the prescribed means of cleansing Isaiah's sins. Just like, in the days of Moses, the blood of animals was the means by which people's sins were cleansed and forgiven. This is how God stated it:

> For the life of a creature is in the blood, and I have given
> it to you to make atonement for yourselves on the altar; it
> is the blood that makes atonement for one's life.

In our days, it is the blood of Jesus Christ which God has prescribed as the means by which our sins can be forgiven and cleansed. John says 'the blood of Jesus Christ, his own son purifies us from all sins' (1 John 1:7). Paul says in Roman 3:23-25 'for all have sinned and fall short of the glory of God, and are justified freely by his grace through the redemption that came by Christ Jesus. God presented him as a sacrifice of atonement, through faith in his blood'. Jesus Christ died for the sins of the whole world, but it is only those who will believe in him who will receive forgiveness of sin. All the prophets testify about him [Jesus] that everyone who believes in him receives forgiveness of sins through his name (Acts 10:43). The prophet Isaiah's true identity was exposed when he saw God on His throne. Although he was unclean, God changed his identity from rugs to riches in righteousness.

I am particularly interested in the conversion story of Paul of Tarsus formerly known as Saul which took place on his way to Damascus to persecute the early Christians. His conversion story teaches us many things in life. First, we will see how ignorant one can be even when he or she thinks he is doing good deeds in the name of God. Secondly, his story teaches us that, all those who persecute Christians or the church may be ignorant about the true God. The story is recorded in Acts chapter 9.

Damascus, is said to be the oldest continually occupied city in the world, and now is the capital city of present-day Syria. Saul undertook the 150-mile journey from Jerusalem in order to persecute Christians there.

> As he neared Damascus on his journey, suddenly a light from heaven flashed around him. He fell to the ground and heard a voice say to him, "Saul, Saul, why do you persecute me? Who are you, Lord?" Saul asked. I am Jesus, whom you are persecuting, he replied. Now get up and go into the city, and you will be told what you must do (Acts 9:3-6).

On the "Damascus Road" he had an encounter with Jesus, the son of God that changed his life forever. He was amazingly transformed by God from a persecutor of Christians to a preacher of Christ. As Paul was travelling to Damascus to persecute the Christians there, he was confronted by the risen Christ and brought face to face with the truth of the gospel. The gospel which is the word of God reveals our persona, and at the same time offers solution on how we can become better people.

Sometimes, until people have an encounter with God, they may think their actions are positive. Paul thought that by persecuting the early Christians he was doing God a service. He thought Christianity was a wrong religion, until he met the Lord who corrected him. People, who discourage others from worshipping God or going to church, are acting in ignorance. An encounter with God will change their perspective of life.

Sometimes God breaks into our lives in a spectacular manner, and other times conversion can be a quiet experience. The right way to come to faith in Jesus is whatever way God brings you in. There are many ways God can use to bring someone to faith. God can use a preacher man, a friend, a colleague, a believer, or an evangelist to tell you about the way of salvation. God can send an angel to tell you about the salvation message (see Revelation 14:6-7). This usually occurs in regions where missionaries cannot have access to preach the gospel because of severe persecution. But at the centre of this wonderful experience by Paul, was Jesus Christ himself. Paul acknowledged Jesus as Lord, confessed his own sins, surrendered his life to Christ, got baptized and resolved to obey him till death.

Before his conversion, Paul thought he was persecuting heretics. He later acknowledged that he acted in ignorance (1 Timothy 1:13). How many people do we have as friends, colleagues and relatives who are ignorant about God and his ways? Of course they may make claims that there is no God, or that Jesus Christ is not the only saviour or that they don't need God. The truth is that none of their opinions matter. It is what God says, that matters. I pray all such people will have an encounter with God through the church, God's servants, the Bible, or any means God may deem appropriate.

A call to action: our encounter with God also leads us to action in some unimaginable areas of service. When the Lord appeared to Isaiah, He asked, "Whom shall I send, and who will go for us?" (Isaiah. 6:8). He had a job for Isaiah, just as He has assignments for each of us. And sometimes, in order to move us in the right direction, God has to interrupt our lives with an overwhelming sense of His presence. That's what happened to Moses when he was tending sheep in the desert. Suddenly the Lord appeared to him in a burning bush and turned his life in an entirely different direction. Paul was on his way to persecute Christians when the Lord met him and helped him to change his course of action. Paul later became one of the greatest servants of God (Acts 9). There are many benefits one can enjoy for having an encounter with God.

The next question to be addressed is how can one redeem their true nature? How can one become, holy, pure, loving, and a person destined for good works?

How can one be a better person to fulfil their destiny?

So far we have looked at how you can discover yourself through the word of God, through taking a critical look at your life experiences and through an encounter with God. The obvious conclusion on our exploration so far is that human beings have fallen short of the glory of God. We are not the kind of beings God originally designed us to be. In this section we will look at how we can be better people in order to fulfil our destiny.

I once met a man in his sixties who said he wished his age could be reduced to thirty years because he now knows better. Please make sure you make good use of your time well. You cannot reduce your age. Ask anyone this question, what will they like to become and you will be surprised to hear all kinds of things people are desiring to become- a doctor, a lawyer, an artist, a celebrity, a footballer, a politician, a musician, a millionaire, or a model, just to mention a few. All these are professions or what people can do to earn some income. They are not the real you.

I believe in order to answer the question, what kind of person do I want to become; it will be helpful to first look at the question 'what am I supposed to be originally that I am not? This is because, it is a common practice for people to define how their lives should be only to realise later on that their world view has been very narrow or sometimes misleading. For example, someone may decide to define the kind of person they want to become as getting education, start working after university, getting married, and having children. Someone else may decide to focus their lives on working for money and spending their income the way they like. These lifestyles are good, but they are not good enough because these are not all that human beings were originally created to be. In the paragraphs which follow, I will be discussing what the creator originally created you to be.

Righteousness is the word the prophets often used to describe the state every human being is supposed to attain in life. This is what

God demands from his people, if they want to become who they were originally created to be. We are to reflect his image. It is the character of God that demands this state of righteousness from his people because God is Holy (Isaiah 1:4), different, and so his people must be different and holy too, because 'without holiness no one can see God' (Hebrews 12:14). A problem is posed: because we are not righteous, we don't naturally do what is really right (Romans 3:9–18). Two possibilities follow: If humanity can do nothing to produce the righteousness God demands, and if God does nothing to make us righteous then punishment is inevitable (Isaiah 6:5), and that is bad news because our righteous acts are like 'filthy rags' so far as God is concerned (Isaiah 64:6).

The character of God is lit up again at this point by the news that God does deal with our problem of sin, how? The servant of the Lord comes and He suffers for our transgressions, our sins, our iniquities (Isaiah 53:5). 'The Christian church says this suffering servant passage (Isaiah 52:13-53:12) refer to Jesus Christ'. John the Baptist refers to Jesus Christ as the Lamb of God who takes away the sins of the world (John 1:29). So the prophet Isaiah strikes home with his picture of a holy God who makes impossible demands of righteousness from us, and then He Himself makes a way of salvation available to us. And that is the sheer grace of God. Because of this, Paul could say 'God made Jesus who had no sin to become sin offering for us, so that in him we might become the righteousness of God (2 Corinthians 5:21).

If anyone desires to become the kind of person he or she want to become, then I believe on the basis of the fact that we have fallen short of God's glory, there is a need for a Cure. Paul's message in the book of Romans is the great news about God's amazing grace: a complete cure is available to all, so that you can become the kind of person you want to become. But people won't seek a cure until they know they are ill. Thus, the book of Romans begins with one of the darkest descriptions in the Bible. Paul concludes, 'There is no one righteous, not even one.' The entire world is doomed to spiritual death unless a cure can be found. This cure is found in Jesus Christ. Accept him today into your life for forgiveness of sins and eternal life.

Personal transformation is one of the benefits people get from building their lives on the principles of God. This subject has been thoroughly discussed in chapter five of this book. Please read that chapter on how you can become the person you were created to be. What I will say in this section regarding how one can be changed is that through God's help people can change from any bad situation they find themselves; from being a sinner to becoming a saint; from the kingdom of darkness to the kingdom of light, from condemnation to justification, from hell fire to heaven.

Personal transformation or personal holiness is the process whereby you allow God to restore you to the most glorious state in life where you become free from sin and any bad habits or attitudes (Roman 3:21-24). It is a glorious state indeed, because you become pure, your soul or your inner man is cleansed from any sin or guilt. A person who has allowed himself to be transformed by God does not need any alcohol or cigarette or any substance to calm themselves when they are stressed or under duress, because God's spirit which will live in them will give them peace and joy in such difficult times (Romans 15:14). Those who have been transformed by God rejoice when they see good things, they shun evil, and give themselves to good course.

Why are you on earth? This is the subject matter in the next section.

6. Discovering your purpose in Life

The dictionary defines purpose as the reason why something is done or used: the aim or intention of something. So, when we talk about one's purpose in this book, we mean the reason for your existence. Your purpose in life can only be made plain to you by the one who created you. You are God's workmanship created in Christ Jesus which God prepared in advanced for you to do (Ephesians

2:10). This is your purpose in life. God created you to worship him, live abundant life on earth, and to help him build his kingdom with your talents, spiritual gifts, profession, skills, your love, and all your strength. That is why Jesus says 'seek the kingdom of God first and all other things will be added to you' (Luke 12:22-24).

The starting point of discovering and pursing your purpose in life is to be born again, and then making a contribution to this world and the future world, the kingdom of God (John 3:3-9). Don't worry if you have already read the subject of being 'born again' elsewhere in this book. You will understand why this is so important in a moment. John 6:28-29 says' **and the people asked Jesus, "What must we do to do the works God requires?" Jesus answered, "The work of God is this: to believe in the one he has sent**. Many people want to do things for God without a relationship with him. To be born again is the same as to believe in Jesus as your Lord and savior in order to receive the new birth which involves repentance, baptism, and a godly lifestyle.

In this section, we will also look at some of the benefits of making a contribution to our future world. Secondly, we will look at some theories about the nature of our future world and finally, we will look at what we can do to help create a better world for ourselves. Whatever you do must help make this world and the world to come a better one.

Astin *et al.* research findings indicate that global citizenship has positive effects on people's satisfaction with life, academic performance, leadership development, interest in further studies as a means of positioning oneself to make a difference in the world. Global citizenship also enhances students' [people] interest in self-rated ability to get along with other races and cultures, and commitment to promoting racial understanding.

Astin *et al.* define Global citizenship as a spirituality measure that combines items such as Ethic Caring (caring about others), charitable involvement (caring for others) and Ecumenical worldviews (a sense of connectedness to all beings). Global citizenship also reflects people's concern about helping others and one's identification with the global community. It can also include items such as trying to change things that are unfair in the world, reducing pain and suffering in the world, and a feeling of strong connection to humanity. This sense of interconnectedness clearly addresses the notion of interdependence, suggesting that "what we do to others, we do to ourselves". This is what Astin *et al.* research describes as *Charitable Involvement* which can include activities such as participating in community service, donating money to charity, helping friends with personal problems.

Caring for others and caring about others is therefore very much an expression of one's spirituality. As one interviewee said, "I feel most spiritually alive when I am working with the community and when I am learning about their issues, and how I can help them, and trying to be in solidarity with them." There are a lot of benefits for making a contribution to our future world, depending on how one sees this future world. Scripture says in 1 Corinthians 15:58 'Therefore, my dear brothers, stand firm. Let nothing move you. Always give yourselves fully to the work of the Lord, because you know that your labor in the Lord is not in vain'. There is reward for those who make positive contributions to this world according to God's plan. Their labor is never in vain. The Bible summarizes everyone's purpose in Ephesians 2:10 as:

> For we are God's workmanship, created in Christ Jesus
> to do good works, which God prepared in advance for
> us to do.

Going by this revelation, you are God's workmanship. Meaning, you are to work for God in doing good things in this world which God prepared before you were born.

The phrase '*created in Christ* Jesus', means your original image which was impaired in Adam, but now could be restored back through the process of the new birth or being born again. This means that before anyone can discover their purpose in life, they must be born again– they must be created anew in Christ. The starting point of discovering your true purpose in life is to be 'born again':

> In reply Jesus declared, "I tell you the truth, no one can see the kingdom of God unless he is born again. "How can a man be born when he is old?" Nicodemus asked. "Surely he cannot enter a second time into his mother's womb to be born! Jesus answered, "I tell you the truth, no one can enter the kingdom of God unless he is born of water and the Spirit. Flesh gives birth to flesh, but the Spirit gives birth to spirit (John 3:3-6).

From this text it is clear that no one can go to heaven unless they are born again. I will explain what it means to be born again in a moment. But let me explain some doubts someone may have about doing good deeds without being born again. It is true that there are a lot of people who seem to be doing various acts of kindness in this world although most of these people are not born again in the Christian sense. Does it mean these people will not go to heaven, someone may ask? Does it mean that these people's acts of kindness to their fellow human beings are not appreciated by God to merit them eternal life?

The natural person's answer to these questions could be that if one does good deeds enough they will go to heaven. But God's answer to this question is that every man and woman needs to be born again before they can make it to his kingdom. There are many examples in the holy scriptures of men and women who were considered to be 'good, nice and kind people'[12] but had to be born again or receive the new birth. Let us look at two examples in the next paragraphs.

Dr Luke reports in the book of Acts chapter ten that, 'At Caesarea there was a man named Cornelius, a centurion in what was known as the Italian Regiment. He and all his family were devout and God-fearing; he gave generously to those in need and prayed to God regularly'. One day at about three in the afternoon he had a

---

[12] According to Jesus' words in Mark 10:18, 'no one is good except God alone'.

vision. He distinctly saw an angel of God, who came to him and said, "Cornelius! Cornelius stared at him in fear. "What is it, Lord? he asked. The angel answered, "Your prayers and gifts to the poor have come up as a memorial offering before God. Now send men to Joppa to bring back a man named Simon who is called Peter'. And so through a series of divine appointments, Peter came to the house of this noble man. But the bible says 'While Peter was still speaking these words, the Holy Spirit came on all who heard the message'. Then Peter said, Can anyone keep these people from being baptized with water? They have received the Holy Spirit just as we have. So he ordered that they be baptized in the name of Jesus'.

The lesson here is that, although this man was considered a good man who regularly gave to the poor and even prayed to the God, he had to be born again. He had to believe the gospel, accept Jesus into his life, and had to be baptized. Everyone has to be born again before they go to heaven. A drug dealer, criminal, a prostitute, politicians, health workers, lawyers, pop stars, footballers, celebrities all need to be born again.

But what does it mean to be born again in order to discover our true purpose in life? 'How can someone be born when he is old?" Nicodemus asked. "Surely he cannot enter a second time into his mother's womb to be born' (John 3:4). The phrase '*born again*' literally means born from above by the spirit of God where you receive everything new; A new heart, a new spirit, a new family, a new attitude, a new life, a spiritual transformation, and a new name in heaven.

The New birth, or being born again, is the work of God whereby eternal life is imparted to the person who believes in Jesus Christ as their Lord and saviour, repents from their old lifestyle, get baptised and starts living a godly life. This is how someone can be born again. In my previous book, *The Final Destination of the Human Soul*, I described these four steps to be born again as the four requirements for the salvation of the human soul.

Once someone is born again, it means that person has been *created in Christ Jesus* to do good works towards making this world a better place according to God's plans. This is the starting point of discovering and pursing your purpose in life which is the subject matter of this section.

Different Views about our future world: There have been many attempts to define what our world should be in future. You may have heard of the 'New World order'. As a conspiracy theory[13], the term *New World Order* or *NWO* refers to the emergence of a totalitarian world government.

According to *Wikipedia*, the Free online dictionary, 'The common theme in conspiracy theories about the New World Order is that a secretive power elite with a globalist agenda is conspiring to eventually rule the world through an authoritarian world government—which will replace sovereign nation-states. Numerous historical and current events are seen as steps in an ongoing plot to achieve world domination through secret political gatherings and decision-making processes'.

Sometimes, things done in secret or in disguise cannot be trusted, and can be very diabolic. The fact that this New World Order agenda is not taught or discussed openly in the public space raises a lot of concern. The Inter Faith Movement or dialogue, which works to promote understanding, cooperation and good relations between organisations and persons of different faiths, can easily become one of the many movements in the 21st century which will be promoting the aims of this New World Order. Christians who participate in these Inter Faith Dialogue should be cautious else they may out of ignorance promote things contrary to the will of God. Religious and political movements which hold the view that there is not only one way, but that there are many ways' to God may be promoting

---

[13] A **conspiracy theory** is an explanatory proposition that accuses two or more persons, a group, or an organization of having caused or covered up, through secret planning and deliberate action, an illegal or harmful event or situation

this New World Order. This means that nobody can dare to present Jesus as 'the way, the truth and the life... the only way to the Father (John 14:6).' To do so would be considered divisive and contrary to the ideal of 'one community.

Christian evangelism does not fit this utopian vision, because to Christians, Jesus is the way, the truth and life. This can offend people of other faiths. This threatens the religious leaders who have built their platform on secular standards rather than the Bible. Those who share the UN vision of a 21st Century community...seek a global village of peace and social equality, not by faith in the Biblical God, but by faith in human leadership without God and a pluralistic god-spirit operating in and through each person. Such a movement flies in the face of the Gospel message that Jesus is the Saviour of the world, the one mediator between God and humanity. For Christians it means joining the God who created us and redeemed us through faith in the Lord Jesus Christ from all other gods which the Bible declares to be idols which cannot save us (Psalm 96:5, Isaiah 45:18-23).

The reader is encouraged to find out more about this New World Order before making any contribution towards its establishment. Can this New World Order be satanically inspired? Yes! This movement ties in with the picture of the woman riding the beast (false religion in alliance with the political power) which we have in Revelation 17. This New world order does not come from God. It is inspired by the human desire to do things without God. I call this 'human ambition without God'. Some people are ambitious—they want to succeed without God. This is not the first time humanity has attempted to do things without God's approval on a global scale. The Book of Genesis portrays human beings as so ambitious that they try to compete with God, rather than to serve God. This was Adam and Eve's sin (Genesis 3:5; 22), and at Babel the people were at it again, in a citywide effort to build a tower to reach heaven. God frustrated their plans by confusing their language (Genesis 11).

In the same way, this New World Order will be frustrated, and destroyed by God according to Biblical prophecy (Revelation 16:10-16; 18). There is not enough space in this book to describe how these events will unfold. The reader is encouraged to read the book of Revelation in the Bible for details.

Our aim in this section is to look at the different views people have about the future of this world. It is possible that many people do not know how this world is supposed to be ideally according to God's plan. Some people are of the view that we should start thinking of moving to a different planet to inhabit there. In his book, *The Bible Phenomenon: Its significance in the world of Science and New Age spirituality*, John Drane defines what sort of world we should dream of:

> The cosmos must be under= where it is, in the hand of its loving divine creator and sustainer, where everything occupies their God-appointed place in an idyllic scene, where each part of the cosmos can function as it was intended, and reach its own potential in the process.

This is a glimpse of the new heaven and the new earth. Let us read this view in the Bible as well:

> Then I saw a new heaven and a new earth, for the first heaven and the first earth had passed away, and there was no longer any sea. I saw the Holy City, the New Jerusalem, coming down out of heaven from God, prepared as a bride beautifully dressed for her husband. And I heard a loud voice from the throne saying, "Now the dwelling of God is with men, and he will live with them. They will be his people, and God himself will be with them and be their God. He will wipe every tear from their eyes. There will be no more death or mourning or crying or pain, for the old order of things has passed away." He who was seated on the throne said, "I am making everything new!" Then he said, "Write this down, for these words are trustworthy and true (Revelation 21:1-5).

We are trying to define what sort of world we want to help create in discovering and pursuing our purpose in this world, and this is what God says it is. Read the text again carefully and you will see that this is the kind of world we are all longing for, consciously or unconsciously. Have you wondered what eternity will be like? The Holy City, the New Jerusalem is described as the place where God will wipe every tear from our eyes. It will be the perfect place for human habitation where there will be no more sickness, pain nor suffering because Satan will be cast out from the city. We do not know as much as we would like, but it is enough to know that eternity with God will be more wonderful than we could ever imagine.

What can you do to help create this new world? If we are to have meaning and satisfaction in all our endeavours, then certainly whatever we do should be a contribution towards this New World we all desire to have else all our efforts may be considered to be in vain. So what can we do? To help answer this question, let us first look at the features of this dream world. In this dream world, there will be no wicked people, no sickness, crying or pain, everything is new. Even the human personality has to be born again.

All of us make hundreds of choices every day. I believe some of the things we can do is to help other people turn from their wicked ways because wicked people will not be allowed into this New Heaven and New Earth. 'Nothing impure will ever enter it, nor will anyone who does what is shameful or deceitful, but only those whose names are written in the Lamb's book of life.[14] We must do things which can help ourselves to be at our best in helping others by any genuine means to know God for themselves and to be born again. We call this, witnessing Christ to people or evangelism.

'After John was put in prison Jesus went into Galilee, proclaiming the good news of God. The time has come, he said. The kingdom of God is near. Repent and believe the good news! (Mark 1:14-15).

---

[14] Revelation 21:23-27

We must tell people to make a clean break from their sin. God says turn away from all your offenses; then sin will not be your downfall. Rid yourselves of all the offenses you have committed, and get a new heart and a new spirit. Why should you perish? For I take no pleasure in the destruction of anyone, repent and live, says God! (Read Ezekiel 18:30-32; & 1 Timothy 2:3-4). We should also remember the poor and the disadvantaged in the society, but more importantly we should not neglect to tell them about the gospel of salvation. Go ahead and pursue your career, build your own family and buy your possessions, but don't forget to be born again yourself, and don't forget to tell people to be born again and to come to the Lord. This is what it means to discover your purpose in life and to pursue it.

In this section, we have looked at the fact that building your life on God's principles can provide answers to life's big Questions: Who am I? What is my purpose in life? Your purpose in life is to make a contribution to the betterment of this world using your spiritual gifts, talents, and the opportunities that come your way. What kind of person do I want to become? As discussed in this section, God wants you to reflect his image, to be conformed to the image of his Son Jesus Christ, through a process called ' born again' and finally make it to heaven when your number of days on this earth is over. The new heaven and the new earth is the sort of world you must dream to be part of.

In this chapter, we have been discussing the subject of spirituality. Let us lastly look at some of the dangers in 21st century spirituality and how people can avoid them.

7. Avoiding the dangers in spirituality

Since the practice of spirituality involves an interaction between one's spirit and some divine spirit, my main concern has been the type of spirit people expose themselves to. There are good spirit(s), and there are also bad spirits. Which spirit have you exposed yourself to? Bad spirits ultimately bring misfortunes into the lives of those who consult them or operate with them. God's Spirit ultimately brings blessings to those who are led by them, here and the life after.

There are two main types of spirits. The Holy Spirit which is the Spirit of God, and Satan's spirit, sometimes called unclean spirit or evil spirit. My aim in this section is to advice people to be careful which type of spirit they interact with or operate with.

Spirituality is the search for what cannot be seen. This search for the unknown can be both rewarding and at the same time perilous especially if not guided properly. In this section I will be discussing some of the dangers involved in spirituality and how people can avoid them. The main reason for discussing these dangers is not to discourage spiritual searchers but rather to help them discover some of the potholes on their journey. Some of these dangers are: (1) the practice of spirituality can be confusing and uncertain; (2) spiritual searchers may end up being connected to evil spirits or Satan himself if not guided properly.

First of all, one of the dangers in spirituality is that, any spirituality that does not lead to true religion can be very confusing if not guided correctly according to research:

> Research has suggested "spiritual" people may suffer worse mental health than conventionally religious people...[15]

It is not difficult to realise that people who classify themselves as spiritual but not religious can suffer worse mental health than religious people. Spirituality, mainly involves a search for 'something'. The question is how long can one continue to search for that very particular 'thing' if you are not making any success? You can become frustrated, leading to confusion and possibly mental disturbances as some research have suggested.

It seems to me that people who call themselves spiritual but not religious will continue to be in the searching stage of life because

---

[15] By Tom de Castella, *BBC News Magazine*, 13 January, 2013.

they may keep on changing their minds on what they think is the truth. But scripture provides absolute truth. If you are looking for gold according to your own description of what the colour of gold should be like, it is possible that you may find a gold which does not meet your description, but that does not mean what you discovered is not gold. Probably your description of gold is wrong. In the same way, many people have their own projection of God, instead of seeking God according to the knowledge He has given us about himself in scripture. God will definitely reveal himself to those who are seeking a connection with the 'higher being'. People should learn to accept the form God will reveal himself to them. I know a lot of people have a problem with worshipping a God they cannot see. God is spirit, and his worshippers must worship him in spirit and in truth (John 4:24).

Let us briefly discuss how spiritual searchers can find what they are frantically looking for so that they will not continue to seek in a perpetual cycle. The Bible says 'everyone who asks receives; he who seeks finds; and to him who knocks, the door will be opened' (Matthew 7:8). The 'parable of the hidden treasure' and the 'parable of the pearl' in Matthew 13: 44-46 can describe the two main ways seekers can find what they are looking for:

> The kingdom of heaven is like treasure hidden in a field. When a man found it, he hid it again, and then in his joy went and sold all he had and bought that field. "Again, the kingdom of heaven is like a merchant looking for fine pearls. When he found one of great value, he went away and sold everything he had and bought it.

Naturally we don't look for the best things in life. Best things in life are most of the time accidentally discovered. What these parables teach spiritual seekers is that, in their search for a meaning to life or a connection to 'the higher being' they may accidently discover God and his kingdom which is more valuable than anything else. They must then be willing to give up everything to have a relationship with God and be part of his kingdom. The ultimate aim of spirituality in my opinion is to have a relationship with the God and the Father of the universe, and this parable teaches us one of the ways people can meet God so that they can stop the searching and enjoy a spirit to spirit relationship with Him where they can draw strength, joy, hope, encouragement. The kingdom of heaven which can be defined as the rule of God in the heart and life of people in this age and in the age to come is more valuable than anything else we can imagine or think of. People must be willing to give up everything to obtain it.

A spiritual searcher who is not guided properly may find himself or herself in the company of evil spirits or even meet the devil himself. This is the second danger in the practice of spirituality without proper guidance. There are evil spirits in this world. It is not a wise thing for one to deny their existence. Those who want to have a connection with a 'higher being' without proper guidance may be surprised to find themselves engaging with evil spirits or bowing to a false god or Satan himself.

To illustrate the dangers in spirituality without a proper guide, Richard Brink, pastor and state coordinator for the US Strategic Prayer Network in Maine, shares the following story:

> In 1997, reports came out of New Brunswick, Canada, that the tenth teenager had just committed suicide at Big Cove, a Micmac First Nation reserve. Over the next five years, our church did various outreaches and prayer projects there. We found that besides unemployment and substance abuse, there was something more sinister behind some of the suicide. A local witch doctor was leading many of the teens into the sweat lodges and teaching them how to talk to the spirits. The suicides increased soon afterward. We had the opportunity to share Jesus with this witch doctor and also to go on the reservation and pray against this situation. When we returned last year, we found that there had been no documented suicide since 1997 and that the government was no longer funding the witch doctor's

sweat lodges. God showed his mighty power and love to the wonderful Micmac people[16].

Young people were committing suicide because a witch doctor had taught them how to communicate with evil spirits. These evil spirits, including Satan himself primary purpose is to steal, kill, and destroy. Spiritual seekers who are not guided by good spiritual guides or shepherds may find themselves engaging with evil spirits or demons, and sometimes with Satan himself.

How can spiritual searchers avoid the problem of having an encounter with evil spirits or a witch doctor? The suggestion I am offering in this book is for one to build their spirituality on Jesus Christ, the Son of God. John describes Jesus as the word of God who became man and made his dwelling amongst us (John 1:14). Look for someone who will lead you to Jesus Christ as your saviour. Jesus Christ is the way, the truth and the life. No one can go to the Father except through him (John 14:6). For God so loved the world that he gave his one and only Son, that whoever believes in him shall not perish but have eternal life. For God did not send his Son into the world to condemn the world, but to save the world through him. Whoever believes in him is not condemned, but whoever does not believe stands condemned already (John 3:16-17).

Turning to Jesus Christ as your saviour can help you find answers to life's big questions such as: where did I come from? Where am I going to? What is this world about? Where did it come from? Where is it going? The Christian community or the church has systems of beliefs centering on God, which I think spiritual searchers may find helpful in their quest. The church provides forms of relationship and social support which research suggests are missing from the lives of many people who commit suicide. There is some research evidence to suggest that people with religious beliefs and an active involvement in religious communities are less likely to commit suicide because they have hope of eternal life in Christ Jesus. They

---

[16] Authority in Prayer by Dutch Sheets, 2006, page 70

know that weeping may come in the night but joy will come in the morning (Psalm 30:5). They are sure that their God will renew their strength although they may grow weary and tired (Isaiah 40:28-31). The problem is that, many spiritual seekers are less likely to access all these benefits available within the Christian faith.

Selfishness and Robbery in Spirituality

The word 'private' comes from the Latin word *privation* which means robbery. Therefore in spirituality once something becomes private, that thing becomes a robbery. Any benefit we derive from the practice of spirituality or life in general must be shared with other people and God himself.

Within many societies, the spiritual dimension of one's life has traditionally been regarded as intensely personal and private, an innermost component of who one is that lies outside the realm of socially acceptable public discourse or concern. There are many reasons why this is so. As one writer shared in her book; 'people are probably scared to reveal their spirituality for fear that they are stepping on people's rights, or not being inclusive' enough. However in an era characterised by 'spiritual poverty', there has been a growing societal hunger for what crisis management consultant expert Ian Mitroff, and organisation consultant Elisabeth Denton have described as ' nonreligious, nondenominational ways of fostering spirituality'.

But no matter the reason people give for regarding spirituality as a private affair, I see this attitude as selfish. The ultimate aim of spirituality is to be empowered to go into the real world to live and serve people and God. The parable of the Good Samaritan in Luke 10:25-37 presents a balanced spirituality between being co-workers with God in ministering spiritually, socially, politically, and economically. This makes the parable of the Good Samaritan a measure of all spirituality, because all spirituality should have implications for politics, economics, and social arrangements out of reverence for God.

So far in this chapter we have discussed the subject of spirituality, its popularity in the twenty first century, its benefits in the field of education, health, leadership, social care, at the work place, and the individual's life. The conclusion I am coming to in this chapter is that people should choose Jesus Christ as their Lord and saviour upon which to build their spirituality because Jesus is the saviour of the world, he has the supremacy over all creation and he is inviting people to come to him for rest. In Christ, God has provided everything humanity needs for good life and godliness. Our duty is to ask, seek and knock. Scripture or the Bible is the best source we should turn to, to find guidance.

Let us look at some of the benefits couples and those in relationship will enjoy for building their lives on the principles of God in the next chapter.

Chapter 4

Guidance for Relationships & family Life

God instituted marriage as one of the means by which couples could help each other to achieve their God given assignment on earth. The woman needs something that only the man has, and the man also needs something that only the woman has. God favours those who get married (Proverbs 18:22). Marriage is good for a secured companionship (Ecclesiastes 4:9-11; Genesis 2:18-24); for healthy sexual life style- (1 Corinthians 6:18; 7:9); marriage provides a homely environment for raising godly children (Malachi 2:14-15).

Marriage or relationship between a man and a woman is a journey. And this journey requires direction; there are a lot of unknowns on the road; the marriage will need refuelling because the love the couple started with will need to be rekindled with time. Marriage also needs maintenance because the couple will experience burn out as they journey on, and there are many obstacles on the road to overcome. Because of all these challenges, it is suggested in this book that every couple should seek divine help, help from God because 'with God all things are possible'. In this chapter, we will look at how scripture can help men, women, and children find help especially when it comes to relationships or family life.

Many couples do not prepare themselves before and during the marriage and so they end in the middle of the road exhausted, discouraged, and 'run out of fuel'. A lot of women and men manage to get their dream partners only to lose them because of their bad behaviour, inexperience, or ignorance. Some people also do not know how to go about the marriage process when they meet the right person they want to marry, so they end up losing that person. Many beautiful marriages and relationships have ended on the rock because the couples did not know how to solve their problems. Many parents do not know how to bring their children up to become good adults in the future. Because of this, many children are confused and do not know what to do in life. Some parents have also lost their children to either the social services or to gangsters, because perhaps they were not in a better position to take care of their own children properly. These are some of the reasons why I believe every man, woman, and child should 'groom' themselves in the Lord in order to enjoy their relationship and family life.

To Understand what marriage is, the purpose of marriage, and how to manage it well, I believe we need to go back and practice God's guidelines for marriage and all other issues of life. This is because God is the author of marriage, and He alone has the best guidelines for family life (Psalm 68:6, Genesis 2: 18). Secondly, modern attempt to redefine marriage and family life has failed many couples because the redefinition of marriage did not come with any viable ways or guidelines on how couples should live. Because of this, many couples do not know how to marry or take care of themselves. Thirdly, because scripture is God's 'own word', God will see to it that what you put into practice will work. God watches over his word to perform according to Jeremiah 1:12. He will come to your aid in times of trouble because you are obeying his word about marriage.

In this chapter, we will also look at how scripture can help groom a man so that he can become a better husband to his wife, a better father to his children, a responsible man to God, and a happy person in the relationship. In the same way, we will look at how scripture can groom a woman to become a better wife to her husband, a good mother to her children, a responsible woman to God, and a happy woman in the relationship. The children are our future strength in the sense that they are the ones to inherit us. How do we prepare them for the future? In this chapter we will also look at how scripture can help parents to prepare their children for a better future.

Every relationship or marriage will face some challenges. Domestic abuse, unfaithfulness and financial problems appear to be some of the main problems facing couples in this century. According to scripture, marriage can also blind the couples from preparing for the second coming of Jesus if care is not taken:

> For in the days before the flood, people were eating and drinking, marrying and giving in marriage, up to the day Noah entered the ark; and they knew nothing about what would happen until the flood came and took them all away. That is how it will be at the coming of the Son of Man (Matthew 24:38-39).

Matthew 24 records one of Jesus' longest statements about the future. Jesus gives direct clues to events that will precede his second coming. But, notably, almost half the chapter consists of warnings that no one can predict the precise time of his coming. So, although marriage is good, we should not make it the ultimate thing in life, else we will miss heaven. Marriage should help us to serve God well, fulfilling our destinies on earth. Men and women should turn to the word of God and build their relationships and family lives on it.

I once visited a couple who were going through marital crisis and I asked the woman how she wanted her man to treat her. Her answer was "I want my husband to respect me, not to be harsh on me". I then opened 1 Peter 3:7 which says "Husbands, in the same way be considerate as you live with your wives, and treat them with respect..." I turned and asked the man how he wanted his woman to treat him. His answer was "I want my wife to respect me and to take my opinions serious". Again, I opened 1 Peter 3:7 which says "Wives, in the same way wives be submissive to your husband's..."

God commands men not to be harsh on their wives, and women to be submissive.

Many of the domestic abuse cases can be prevented if couples will build their relationships on the word of God. These couple had been together for more than ten years but only got wedded after I gave them guidelines on relationships and marriage using scripture. I believe many people will not go through some problems in life if they have been guided properly using the word of God. God says, 'because of lack of knowledge my people perish'.

Ask any woman what she expects from her husband or her partner in terms of conduct and attitudes, and you will find that the most common answer is 'I want a man who is caring, understanding and someone who will be there for me always'. Who does not like good things in life? And this is exactly what God wants every woman to have in a relationship or marriage. God knows the deepest needs of women, he commands the men to love the women and to treat them with respect as the following sections will explain. God is the one who made the woman and so he knows the physiological make up of the woman and what she truly needs to make her happy and complete (Genesis 2:21-24).

I have identified some of the areas any woman or man in a relationship or marriage may need to work on using the word of God in order to make themselves attractive and useful to their partner. The following are some of the areas couples need to work on: the ability to solve problems in the marriage, communication, sex in marriage, proper child care, inner beauty, outward appearance, good home management, and cooking skills.

4.1 Grooming the man

Many men find it difficult to attract the right woman for marriage. There are many reasons why this is so. Women have some qualities they look for in men before they decide to settle down with them. Some of these qualities are good communication skills, a sense of humour, caring, generosity, purposeful, godliness, hardworking, good morals, faithfulness, good hygiene practice, and sometimes romance just to mention a few. If a man can take his time to prepare himself to acquire these skills, it will be easier for him to find the right woman for life. This is one of the reasons for writing this section on grooming men.

In this book, I used the term 'grooming' to describe the kind of preparation a man or a woman needs in order to become a suitable partner. If you are a woman and you think your husband or partner is not up to the standard you want in terms of behaviour, outlook, spirituality, career, romance etc, nothing stops you from helping your man to become the best.

Just as people need driving lessons with a pass before they are allowed to drive a motor vehicle, so do I believe men need some kind of training or coaching or counselling before they should be allowed to marry. Women are more important than cars. If the government finds it unsafe for untrained person to drive a car, so do I believe it is unsafe for a man to be in a relationship with a woman without any training on how to take care of the woman! It is possible the relationship may end in disaster if the man is not qualified to handle the woman. When accident occurs, it is not only the car which damages, the passengers can also be injured or even lose their lives. In the same way, a lot of men and women have lost a lot in life because they entered into a relationship or a marriage they were not properly counselled or trained for.

So what are some of the things men should know and do in a relationship? The man should first learn his duty towards God as the head of the family. The man should also learn his duty towards the woman and the children. God has provided a set of time tested guidelines on how men should groom themselves for marriage. Let us discuss these guidelines in the following paragraphs.

The duty of the man towards God

Everything the man does in the relationship must be seen within the context of God's expectation. The man must fear and love God, work on his own salvation, and make sure he goes to heaven after death. When God saw that the first man Adam was alone, he made a suitable helper for him (Genesis 2:18). So the man should always bear in mind that God has a hand and an interest in the marriage. God wants the marriage to succeed that is why he made the institution of marriage in the first place (Genesis 1:27-28; Proverbs 18:22). It is the duty of the man as the head to make sure everything in the family is going well. The man must know that he is accountable to God. This means the man should constantly maintain a good relationship with God so that he can draw strength and wisdom from heaven to take care of the family. A man, who fears God will respect and love his wife, because God commands him to do so. He will endeavour to remain faithful to the wife out of obedience to God. Because of this, I will urge the women to encourage their men to be godly.

The duty of the man towards the woman in a relationship

Every man has a personal duty towards his woman. The man is to love the woman as his own body just as Christ love the church (Ephesians 5: 25-30). To love the woman means the man should seek the best in life for the woman; physically, emotionally, and spiritually. The command 'to love' is from God that is why I will encourage every woman to make sure her man is God fearing. If your husband is God fearing he will obey God and this is good for you the woman. St. Peter urges the men this:

> Husbands, in the same way be considerate as you live with your wives, and treat them with respect as the weaker partner and as heirs with you of the gracious gift of life, so that nothing will hinder your prayers (1 Peter 3:7).

Many women are abused by their husbands these days. This trend may be due to the fact that a lot of men do not have good relationship with God and so they have not been groomed or be commanded to be considerate as they live with their wives and to treat them with respect. It is out of order for the man to beat or mistreat his wife (1 Peter 3:7). According to scripture, a man's prayers or blessings can be hindered if he does not treat his wife with respect and love (see 1 Peter 3:7). Could this be a reason why most men are suffering? It is possible! God will bless any man who treats his wife well.

The man should also take his time to study the woman so that he can understand her unique and personal need. Many marriages are not working well due to lack of good sex and effective communication. Communication and sex is very very very important in the marriage. If the man does not know how to perform sex to satisfy the wife, then he should be willing to seek help. One cannot give what he does not have. The man should not feel shy to seek help. The same applies to the woman. Providing food and daily necessities for the family should also be the concern of the man although women these days are willing to help in these areas. The man must protect the wife in all things.

Since, the man is the head or the leader of the family, it is expected that he provides vision for the family and leave a godly legacy (Proverbs 13:22). The man should have a plan for the family to follow. This will make the marriage more fulfilling. These are all some of the duties of the man, including raising a godly family. Men who do not encourage their wives to attend church services are hurting themselves. After all, if your wife is godly, who benefits? The man! On the other hand if the woman is ungodly, rude, promiscuous, the man loses. The man must make sure his wife is godly.

The duty of the man towards the children

One of the commonest problems destroying families in recent times is men who run away from their responsibilities towards the family, especially towards the children. Sadly, research and experience have shown that men who run away from their responsibilities towards the family suffer later in life, some even end up as homeless, and some also die as paupers. The world is designed by the creator such that those who help build families, churches, or nations are always resourceful, while those who are irresponsible become weaker and weaker. The father or the man of the family is to bring the children up in the way of the Lord:

Fathers, do not exasperate your children; instead, bring them up in the training and instruction of the Lord (Ephesians 6:4).

Children are to be taught good from evil. Children need instructions on every aspect of life. Children must be taught how to respect the elderly, must be taught about God, and must be taught how to take care of their parents in their old age. If the father refuses to train the children, it is possible that the children will be trained by gangsters or in some cases the children may receive their training from their friends. This is one of the main reasons why the youth of today lacks moral integrity. If you want your children to grow up to be responsible, then train them.

Many parents limit this training to just providing food, clothing, entertainment, vacation, and accommodation for the children. There is the need for parents to sit with their children and teach them the principles of God in every aspect of life so that when they grow up they will not depart from it (Proverbs 4:10-13). This training may sometimes involves discipline:

He who spares the rod [discipline] hates his son, but he who loves him is careful to discipline him (Proverbs 13:24).

Heaven endorses the discipline of children, but not the abuse of children. Heaven also respects and blesses parents who will instruct their children in the things of God. We can see this example in the life of Abraham, the father faith (Genesis 18:16-19). In this text, the angel of the Lord was going to destroy Sodom because of their perversion. But because Abraham will instruct his children and household to keep the way of the Lord, God could not hide his agenda from him. Parents who train their children will be blessed by God. Let us look at another duty of the man towards the children in the next section.

The Man should try to leave inheritance for the children

The man of the house is to seek the best welfare of the children and try to live some kind of inheritance for them:

> A good man leaves an inheritance for his children's children, but a sinner's wealth is stored up for the righteous (Proverbs 13:22).

The man of the house should purpose in his heart to live some inheritance for the children. Such decision alone will attract blessings from heaven. As you read this book it is my prayer that you will be able to live a good life leaving inheritance for your children's children. Amen.

In this section we have looked at some of the duties of the man towards God, the woman and the children. This is how a man should groom himself for the marriage, in doing so he is building his family on the principles of God, the solid foundation.

4.2 Grooming the woman

A well groomed woman will easily attract the right man if she is single. If she is married, she will receive praise from her husband and the children, and in fact from the society and God himself. She herself will be happy because she will be well spoken of. How the woman can groom herself to become a better woman to the husband, a better mother to the children, a responsible woman to God, and a happy person for herself is the subject matter of this section. The mother or the woman in the family has unique roles and duties in the family. The woman becomes more fulfilled as she discharges these duties. The word of God can help any woman who wants to become a good woman to her man and the children. Before we discuss some of the duties of the woman, let us first study some of the qualities a woman should seek to attain:

> A wife of noble character who can find? She is worth far more than rubies. Her husband has full confidence in

her and lacks nothing of value. She brings him good, not harm, all the days of her life. She selects wool and flax and works with eager hands. She is like the merchant ships, bringing her food from afar. She gets up while it is still dark; she provides food for her family and portions for her servant girls. She considers a field and buys it; out of her earnings she plants a vineyard. She sets about her work vigorously; her arms are strong for her tasks. She sees that her trading is profitable, and her lamp does not go out at night. In her hand she holds the distaff and grasps the spindle with her fingers. She opens her arms to the poor and extends her hands to the needy. When it snows, she has no fear for her household; for all of them are clothed in scarlet. She makes coverings for her bed; she is clothed in fine linen and purple. Her husband is respected at the city gate, where he takes his seat among the elders of the land. She makes linen garments and sells them, and supplies the merchants with sashes. She is clothed with strength and dignity; she can laugh at the days to come. She speaks with wisdom, and faithful instruction is on her tongue. She watches over the affairs of her household and does not eat the bread of idleness. Her children arise and call her blessed; her husband also, and he praises her: Many women do noble things, but you surpass them all. Charm is deceptive, and beauty is fleeting; but a woman who fears the LORD is to be praised (Proverbs 31:10–31).

The woman described in this text has outstanding abilities. Her family's social standing is high. But the truth is, your days are not long enough to do everything she does! See her instead as an inspiration to be all you can be. We can't just be like her, but you can learn from her industry, integrity, spirituality and resourcefulness.

The book of Proverbs is very practical for our day because it shows us how to become wise, make good decisions, and how to live according to God's ideal. The book of Proverbs begins with the command to fear the Lord (Proverbs 1:7) and ends with a picture of a woman who fulfils this command. Her qualities are mentioned throughout the book: hard work, the fear of God, respect for spouse, foresight, encourager, care for others, concern for the poor, and wisdom in handling money. These qualities when coupled with the fear of God, lead to enjoyment, success, honour, and worth. Women who desire to be happy in life should aim to attain these qualities.

How a single woman can groom herself to attract the right man

Many single women make the mistake of falling in love with the wrong man only to be disappointed. How can single women attract the right men? One way is for them to groom themselves, prepare themselves so that only the serious guys can approach them. Single women should learn how to dress modestly, how to cook, how to communicate politely with men, they should work on any behavioural problem they may have, and to train themselves to be godly.

My final advice for single women on how to fall for the right man is that they should not only follow their heart, or their preferences, but rather they should only agree to marry a man who is interested in them. You can be interested in the man, but he may not be interested in you that much. Give your heart to a man who is ready to love you back; who will have your welfare at heart; who is ready to care for you and be there for you, and not just someone who can just make you happy. Unfortunately, many women go in for guys who entertain them during courtship. Experience has shown that the fun loving guys do not become good husbands, there may be exceptions though.

The duty of the woman towards God

The woman, like the man has a personal responsibility towards God because, like the man, we will all appear before the judgement seat of God to give an account. It is therefore important that the woman takes her role seriously. The woman must fear and love God, work on her own salvation, and make sure she goes to heaven after death. After all, the importance of marriage is to help us fulfil our destiny, not to bring us down or not to lead us to hell. Unfortunately, some women once they get married relegate God to a secondary level. This should not be the case. We must always seek the kingdom of God first and all other things will be added to us (Luke 12:22–34). We must put God first in everything we do because He is our Father in heaven. He is the great God, and deserves the best place in our lives. Families which put God first, are always blessed.

The duty of the woman towards her man as expected by God

Every woman must put up her best behaviour so that her husband will be pleased with her. Many women are wonderful during the courting period; but once they get married they stop being kind, hardworking and caring. Some women even stop keeping themselves tidy and attractive once they get married. This is not a good practice. This can tempt the man to start looking at other women. Beautiful women attract the men because most men are moved by what they see. A wife must always make herself attractive to her man whether at home or outside the home.

Most men like sex even more than food. Most men see sex as something more important than anything else in the relationship although they may not say it. A woman who will deprive her man of sex may be inviting trouble upon herself. Most men commit adultery because their women do not satisfy them sexually. Women should therefore learn to satisfy their men sexually and vice versa. Godly women and men should heed the advice in 1 Corinthians 7:5:

> Do not deprive each other [sexually] except by mutual consent and for a time, so that you may devote yourselves to prayer. Then come together again so that Satan will not tempt you because of your lack of self-control.

God knows that men and women have to satisfy their biological needs. Husbands and wife should not deprive each other sexually unnecessarily.

The single women who are yet to meet their partners should train themselves to be godly; they should start learning how to take care of a man, how to cook and serve in the home, and how to manage a home. These are all skills men look at when deciding on whom to marry. Many single women only focus on their outward appearance, attending parties and social gathering with the aim of meeting a man. This can be frustrating sometimes. If a woman is well groomed, the men will look out for her; not just to have fun with her, but to make a home with her. Men naturally do not like to settle down in life with party women. To some men, party women are for fun. Most men look for godly women when they are ready to settle down. Single women, please wise up!

God's principle for a successful family life, is husband loving the wife, the wife submitting to her husband, and the children obeying their parents (Ephesians 5: 22-24; 1 Peter 3:1-6). The man is to love the wife, and the wife is to submit to the husband. Submission makes a woman beautiful. It does not mean the woman is inferior at all. Women who find it difficult to submit to their husbands may end up not having any man to love them. It is to the benefit of the woman to submit to the man; else she may have to play the role of the man in the relationship. This is the reason why many women have assumed the role of the man in the family. Many women have lost good husbands because they were not submissive. Most men cannot stand a woman who is not submissive. If you are a woman and you want to keep your man, then learn how to be submissive.

In Ephesians 5:22-30, God commands the woman to submit to the man, and commands the man to love the woman. I believe it is worth finding out why God did not command the woman to love the man, but instead commanded the woman to submit to the man and the man to love the woman. The popular explanation normally given to this order of command from God is that, it is easier for a woman to love a man than for a woman to submit to a man. In the same way it can be very difficult for a man to love the woman that is why God commanded the man to love the woman and the woman to submit to the man. God sometimes tells us what he knows we will find difficult to do although such action is good for us. Secondly, in every team work, one has to submit to the leader. The leader should care for the one doing the submission. Without this arrangement, nothing can be achieved in any relationship or team. So one of the duties of the woman towards the man is to submit to the man because the man and the woman with or without the children form a team:

> Wives, submit to your husband as to the Lord. For the husband is the head of the wife as Christ is the head of the church, his body, of which he is the Savoir. Now as the church submits to Christ, so also wives should submit to their husbands in everything (Ephesians 5:22-24).

Saint Peter also adds his voice to this order of arrangement this way:

> Wives, in the same way be submissive to your husbands so that, if any of them do not believe the word, they may be won over without words by the behaviour of their wives (1 Peter 3:1-2).

What is the meaning of the word submission? The Key to Submission can be found in Ephesians 5:21:

> Submit to one another out of reverence for Christ.

This simple sentence sets the tone for all that follows: we are to submit to others in the proper context because of our reverence for Christ. In other words, in any human relationship one has to do the submission—between a husband and a wife, the wife does the submission, between a child and the parent, the child does the submission, between a slave and the master, the slave does the submission. Paul urges us to conduct those relationships in light of Christ's own spirit. So submission by the woman to the man is a voluntary arrangement out of respect to God but the men should not take advantage of that to abuse the woman. This is an order from God.

The duty of the woman towards the children as expected by God

The woman has a unique duty towards the children just like the man as discussed in the previous section. The woman must train the children properly in the way of the Lord. Women have been endowed with special grace to run the family. Although the man is the head of the family, the stability of every family to some extent depends on the woman. If the woman is ok, the family will survive any crisis. God bless our women for the good work they are doing.

The woman must cooperate and agree with the man on how to raise the children up. Many couples split up on how to raise up their children. In some cases, you will see the father doing his own thing with the children different from what the woman does with the children. Many children do not receive the best from their parents because of this problem.

4.3 Grooming the children for a better tomorrow

Sons are a heritage [gift] from the LORD, children a reward from him (Psalm 127:3).

Children are a blessing from God to the parents. And as such, parents are to groom their children in order to become responsible when they grow up. In life, nothing happens by chance. If you want your child to become a responsible grown up then you must show them the right way. Children who are not well brought up in most cases bring disgrace to the parents:

> The rod of correction imparts wisdom, but a child left to himself disgraces his mother...correct your son, and he will give you rest; yes, he will give delight to your heart (Proverbs 29:15–17).

God also expect parents to dedicate their children to him in the church:

> On the eighth day, when it was time to circumcise him, he was named Jesus, the name the angel had given him before he had been conceived. When the time of their purification according to the Law of Moses had been completed, Joseph and Mary took him to Jerusalem to present him to the Lord (Luke 2:21-22).

Although this very practice sounds like an Old Testament practice, it is recommended that every child be dedicated to God. Dedicating your child to God is a sign of appreciation to God for giving you that child. It is also a declaration of the parent's intentions to bring the child up in a godly way. Finally, dedication of children to God in the church is like entrusting the child into God's care. God will definitely take care of all the children dedicated to him. Parents are to teach the children about God and his word, morality, respect for the elderly, and obedience to societal rules and regulations.

The duty of the child towards the parents as expected by God

Every matured child has a duty towards God. A child who can distinguish good from evil is expected to be obedient to their parents and must stay away from evil. Such children must behave in a good way so that their parents can be proud of them. If a child pleases their parents, their parents in turn will bless them and bestow gifts on them. Every child has a duty from God towards their parents:

> Children, obey your parents in the Lord, for this is right. Honor your father and mother"—which is the first commandment with a promise— that it may go well with you and that you may enjoy long life on the earth (Ephesians 6:1-3).

Children should honour their parents even if the demands of the parents seem unfair. Obeying your parents comes with special blessings of long life. Parent should also care gently for their children, even if the children are disobedient and difficult. Children also have the duty to care for their parents in their old age as well.

4.4 Managing Crisis in relationship or in the family

> In every marriage or relationship more than a week old,
> there are grounds for separation or divorce. The solution
> is to find, and continue to find grounds for marriage ¬
> ROBERT ANDERSON.

Human beings are both "the scum and glory of the universe," said Blaise Pascal, the 17th-century mathematician and philosopher. The Bible, too, paints a realistic picture of people as definite mixtures of good and bad. Apart from Jesus, no one is so good as to be flawless, but rarely is anyone portrayed as all bad. There are many crises in families and in all relationships. A crisis is a difficult or dangerous situation that needs serious attention. Problems in a relationship can come from the influence of friends, in-laws, and other family members. Lack of communication and bad behaviour by the couple can also cause problems. But there is a solution to every problem. Couples need to develop an attitude of solving problems in the relationships in love, with respect, and with the help of God.

In this section I will only discuss how the word of God can help people deal with three of these crises in families and relationships: cheating/adultery, financial problems, and domestic violence will be looked at. It is my personal belief that when God comes to live in our families, our families become heaven no matter the problems in the family especially as the family does things according to the word of God.

1. Managing cheating or adultery in relationships

Adultery has destroyed many beautiful families. Many prominent men and woman have also lost wonderful partners and positions of influence in the church, in the society and at the work place because of adultery. Cheating or the act of adultery is very dangerous because it can lead to divorce. It is a sin against God. It always hurt someone else in addition to the sinner. People who commit adultery should repent and ask for forgiveness from the Lord.

Many people do not know the consequences of adultery because the society does not teach these values any more. Nevertheless when one commits adultery, the law allows the other partner to seek divorce. But scripture always teaches us what to do so that we will not get ourselves into trouble. Scripture also provides us with guidelines on what to do to make amends in case we sin. This is one of the many reasons why people should turn to the word of God and begin to build their lives on it.

In any love relationship between a man and a woman, cheating can be defined as one partner having another love affair outside the relationship. The Bible uses the word adultery (anglicised from Latin *adulterium*) – to describe the extramarital sex that is considered objectionable on social, religious, moral or legal grounds. According to Jesus teachings, cheating or adultery can occur in various forms:

> But I tell you that anyone who looks at a woman [or a man] lustfully has already committed adultery with her in his heart (Matthew 5:28).

According to this text, Jesus is saying that the desire to have sex with someone other than your spouse is mental adultery and thus sin. Here, Jesus is emphasizing that if the act is wrong then, so the intention. To be faithful to your spouse with your body but not your mind is to break the trust so vital to a strong marriage. In this text, Jesus is not condemning natural interest in the opposite sex or even healthy sexual desire, but the deliberate and repeated filling of one's mind with fantasies that would be evil if acted out. Someone will say that if sinful desire is sin then I must go ahead to do the act. We must understand that sinful act is always dangerous than sinful desire.

Why do people cheat on their partners in a relationship? Some people argue that they cheat because they are not able to resist when they are tempted to do so. Others also say they cheat because their partners are not able to satisfy them sexually. Others also do not see cheating as a sin; they are of the opinion that cheating is normal. Cheating or adultery is a sin against God and your partner. But what is the way out? How can scripture help couples not to commit adultery? 1 Corinthians 7:2-5 provides helpful guidelines:

> But since there is so much immorality, each man should have his own wife and each woman her own husband. The husband should fulfill his marital duty to his wife, and likewise the wife to her husband. The wife's body does not belong to her alone but also to her husband. In the same way, the husband's body does not belong to him alone but also to his wife. Do not deprive each other except by mutual consent and for a time, so that you may devote yourselves to prayer. Then come together again so that Satan will not tempt you because of your lack of self-control.

Sometimes, sexual temptations can be difficult to withstand because they appeal to the normal and natural desires that God has given us. Marriage provides God's way to satisfy these natural desires and to strengthen the partners against temptation. Married couples have the responsibilities to care for each other; therefore husbands and wives should not withhold themselves sexually from one another, but should fulfill each other's sexual needs and desires. A lot of women deny their husbands sex. This sexual denial can compel the man to go out there to look for another woman. Some men's greatest need in a relationship is sex. The women should take note of this fact! If you want to keep your man, then don't deny him sex unnecessarily. The men are to follow the same advice.

But what should single people do? They are encouraged to get married than to burn with passion:

> Now to the unmarried and the widows I say: It is good for them to stay unmarried, as I am. But if they cannot control themselves, they should marry, for it is better to marry than to burn with passion (1 Corinthians 7:8).

I always advice single people to look for a faithful partner, undergo godly counseling so that they can settle down with one person. It is not good in the sight of God for single people to be sleeping around with different partners. This is called fornication. Fornicators are to seek repentance from the Lord; they should aim to settle down with one partner in marriage else they will not inherit the kingdom of God if they die as fornicators (1 Corinthians 6:9). Some people also carry bad lack, so if you happen to have sex with them, they may transfer their bad lack into your life to cause havoc to you:

> Do you not know that he who unites himself with a prostitute is one with her in body? For it is said, "The two will become one flesh. But he who unites himself with the Lord is one with him in spirit. Flee from sexual immorality. All other sins a man commits are outside his body, but he who sins sexually sins against his own body (Corinthians 6:16-18).

Those who cheat on their partners are harming themselves. Adultery is one of the problems in marriages these days. And in this section, we have seen some of the guidance scripture provides on what singles and married couples should do.

2. Managing Financial problems

Financial problems have the tendency to break families, and even cause divorce. There are a lot of families going through financial difficulties; there are many reasons for this trend. Some couples overspend, and so they are always in debt. In some cases too, lack of transparency and accountability can also result in financial dispute between couples. Unfortunately, many couples only fight over money instead of putting systems in place to help solve the problem. Guidelines should be set up by couples to manage the finances of the family.

There are three main types of guidelines when it comes to how couples can handle their finances in the family. I will explain all the three here. It is the duty of the couples to choose which of these three will work well for them, taking into consideration their unique situation because every family is different.

The first financial practice in most families is the situation whereby each of the couple keeps their income to themselves; the bills in the house are shared equally between the man and the woman. The disadvantage of this practice is that if one of them loses his or her job, the other party has to bear all the bills and expenses in the house. This can put extra stress on the couple who will be paying all the bills, because she or he may not be used to that. The second disadvantage is that this practice creates too much independence in the marriage. When this happens, it becomes easy for the marriage to end in divorce; at the slightest opportunity.

The second type of financial practices in families is the situation whereby the man pays all the bills, and allows the woman to make a small or no financial contribution towards the running of the family. This is commonly practiced in marriages whereby the man is very rich, and the woman is a housewife. If the man is not very rich and the woman is not a housewife, then this practice can cause a lot of financial problems in the marriage, leading to a possible divorce. I strongly recommend the third type of financial practices in situations where both the man and the woman are working or have some sources of income.

The third type of financial practice in families is a situation whereby the man and the woman bring their income together, and do everything together. They have common savings, common projects, they do everything in common. This is the ideal way families should do things or handle their finances.

> Two are better than one, because they have a good return for their work: If one falls down, his friend can help him up. But pity the man who falls and has no one to help him up (Ecclesiastes 4:9-10).

The family that prays together and does all things together lives together. Families which do things together are always united because they have a lot of things in common.

3 Managing Domestic abuse or Violence

The main reason for writing a section on domestic abuse or violence is because of its destructive nature and the rate at which many people are suffering abuse these days especially in marriages and other healthy and unhealthy relationships. It is estimated that there are more than 250,000 officially reported cases of domestic abuses in UK alone. According to Women's Aid's view, domestic violence is physical, sexual, psychological or financial violence that takes place within an intimate or family-type relationship and that forms a pattern of coercive and controlling behaviour.

Domestic abuse can result in low self esteem, personality disorders, mental illness, and domestic abuse can even cost you your life either as victim or the abuser. The abuser can end up in jail or may lose his or her family. Domestic abuse can affect the children in the family. A growing child may think that abuse is a normal way of life because may be he or she has seen the parents abusing each other. Many young people have been abused sexually and are carrying the guilt and the pain in their heart. May heaven's constant benedictions touch these victims and restore peace in their hearts.

In this chapter, I will be discussing what domestic violence is and how victims can be comforted and receive help to overcome this problem in marriages and relationships. An attempt will also be made to offer help from different sources to help perpetrators of domestic abuse to change from being abusive partners to becoming loving partners.

One of the questions we cannot avoid asking about domestic violence is, why on earth will two people who have consented to love each other become enemies to the extent of harming themselves through insults and sometimes through beatings? Is there a silent unseen enemy between the man and the woman responsible for this problem? There are many reasons why couples behave strangely in the relationships or marriages resulting in domestic violence or abuse. Some of these reasons are; family conflict due to monetary issues, demands for sex, jealousy, anger problem, cheating, lying, and other behavioural influence. Of course, there could be a spiritual dimension to domestic abuse, and this cannot be overlooked. Someone will ask how this is possible!

It is believed in most cultures that spirit beings (demons) tend to marry women or men spirituality. When this happens, the spirit who has married the man or the woman can cause that man or that woman to behave in a way which will provoke conflict, resulting in a possible domestic abuse.

A lady I counselled years ago told me that she could not have normal relationship with men because she was married to an 'old man' (a demon) spiritually. Any man who married her could not have erection, let alone have intimacy with her because that spirit caused the men not to have erection anytime they came near the lady. The lady suffered a lot of marital problems because of this old man (evil spirit) who married her spiritually. This evil spirit was jealous, for any normal man to come near this lady. This lady was always sad and depressed.

The question is how can people be delivered from such predicament? This lady for example, could have been set free from her predicament by giving her life to Jesus Christ as her Lord and saviour, repented from her old lifestyles, be baptised and to start to live a godly life which will involve praying to God, reading the bible, doing good deeds to people, attending church meetings regularly etc. Many men and women have been set free from spiritual problems this way. Sometimes, people who are going through domestic abuse problems may need spiritual help.

Before we define what domestic abuse is, let us first look at how one psychologist has described this problem.

The Cycle of Domestic Violence – (by Lenore Walker, 1979)

Lenore Walker, who conducted a study on domestic violence years ago, says domestic violence normally occurs in three phases: the tension building phase, the acute battering episode and the honey moon phase. According to the research, the tension building phase can occur as a result of "basic domestic" issues like finance, children, sexual demands, lack of communication, jobs etc. The tension phase can get to a situation where physical abuse begins. This is the acute battering episode or phase and this can be triggered by anything at all or by the abuser's emotional state. Some people believe that in some cases the victim may provoke the abuser consciously or unconsciously. The honeymoon phase begins when the abuser becomes ashamed of what he or she has done. The abuser will apologise for his or her actions and start to show love, care, and support. This loving and contrite behaviour strengthens the bond between the partners and will probably convince the victim that, leaving the relationship is not necessary.

According to Lenore Walker, "This cycle continues over and over, and may help explain why victims stay in abusive relationships. The abuse may be terrible, but the promises and generosity of the honeymoon phase give the victim the false belief that everything will be all right".

From this research, we can define domestic abuse or violence as a violent or aggressive behaviour within the home, typically involving the violent abuse of a spouse, partner or a child. The UK Home Office has broadened the definition of domestic violence as "Any incident or pattern of incidents of controlling, coercive or threatening behaviour, violence or abuse between those aged 16 or over who are or have been intimate partners or family members regardless of gender or sexuality. This can encompass but is not limited to the following types of abuse: psychological, physical, sexual, financial or emotional. Domestic violence may include a range of abusive behaviours, not all of which are in themselves inherently 'violent'. Domestic violence can take different forms, from insults using abusive words to physical beatings and sometimes abuse in sex.

Let us now look at how victims of domestic abuse can be helped in the next section.

3.1.1 Help for victims of abuse

Victims of domestic violence or abuse in general are usually vulnerable, weak or are at a disadvantage compared to their abusers. In this section, I will suggest some of the assistance available to victims of domestic violence; and secondly help victims of abuse to become stronger so that their abusers cannot take advantage of them. I recommend two ways people can receive help when they are being abused: help from professionals and other agencies, and secondly practicing faith in God as a means to solve domestic problems.

A. Help from professionals, government and private bodies

If you are suffering an abuse of any kind, please don't keep silent, seek help. Find out from your local council, churches, or your community leaders the kind of assistance available to you. On the other hand, if you have been abusing your partner, please seek help; else the law will deal with you. You may end up losing your partner as well. In the United Kingdom for example, there are many government agencies, churches and voluntary organization that assist people suffering from any kind of abuse. If you know someone who has tried all sorts of help and still their situation is not improving, then please encourage them to turn their life to God. Tell them to give it a try! The next section explains how people can overcome an abuse by building their lives on the principles of God.

B. How faith in God can help victims of abuse

Many people suffer from domestic abuse or any kind of abuse because they appear weaker, vulnerable and at a disadvantage compared to their abusers. One of the best ways for sufferers of abuse is to practice faith in God and to improve on their spiritual life. Someone may ask, how can people putting their faith in God be able to overcome the abuse? Faith in God can turn your weakness into strength because God strengthens those who put their faith in him. Before I discuss this further, let us first look at God's concern for those who are weak or disadvantaged:

> Do you not know? Have you not heard? The LORD is the everlasting God, the Creator of the ends of the earth. He will not grow tired or weary, and his understanding no one can fathom. He gives strength to the weary and increases the power of the weak. Even youths grow tired and weary, and young men stumble and fall; but those who hope in the LORD will renew their strength. They will soar on wings like eagles; they will run and not grow weary, they will walk and not be faint (Isaiah 40:28–31).

God is very much concerned about the plight of those who are weak, but only those who hope in God can receive such help from Him in such times. How can one practically practice faith in God in order to receive strength? The following guidelines will help:

Prayer: this is the practice of acknowledging your need for help and asking God to help you. Ask the Lord for help in prayers. Even unbelievers pray to God or something else. There are certain things in life that only prayer can do especially spiritual problems. **Spiritual problems demands spiritual solutions.** Some people are abusers because they are possessed by an evil spirit. A man brought his demon possessed son to Jesus' disciples to heal him but the disciples couldn't drive the spirit out. This spirit has robbed the boy of speech. Whenever it seizes him, it throws him to the ground. He foams at the mouth, gnashes his teeth and becomes rigid. When Jesus appeared on the scene, He rebuked the evil spirit to come out of the boy. Later Jesus' disciples went to ask him, "Why couldn't we drive it out?" Jesus replied, "This kind can come out only by prayer" (Mark 9:17–29). Some things can only be overcome by prayer. That is why God encourages us to ask, seek, and knock

(Matthew 7:7). God told the prophet Jeremiah 'Call to me and I will answer you and tell you great and unsearchable things you do not know' (Jeremiah 33:3). Victims of domestic abuse should pray to God for help.

Reading the Bible for wisdom and guidance can also help victims of domestic abuse on how to deal with the situation. Psalm 119:130 says' The entrance of your words gives light; it gives understanding to the simple'. There are many men and women in the Bible who were victims of abuse, but were able to overcome their predicaments with the help of God. Their stories are recorded in the Bible as lessons.

Church fellowship can also help victims to receive counselling from the leaders. In fellowship we draw strength and encouragement from the Lord and from one another. Victims of domestic abuse can get advice from other members of the fellowship. They don't have to suffer in silence. Living wisely and a godly lifestyle can help victims to come out of any abusive relationship. Often times, either the victim or the abuser or both are ungodly. **Sometimes, living a godly live creates an atmosphere of peace and respect in your home.** Godly home will attract the angels of God to your home. Ungodly home may attract bad spirits who can cause troubles in the family. Please let Christ Jesus be at the centre of your marriage and everything you do. The reader is also encouraged to read the chapter on 'Help in times of Personal crisis' in this book for further guidelines on how victims of domestic abuse can help themselves.

Restoring people's dignity- How abusers can change

Abusers in any relationship or position of authority are rather supposed to help their victims, but because of their behavioural problems, they end up becoming abusers. It is obvious that abusers have behavioural problems, there is definitely something wrong with someone who abuses people. For example, a husband or the man in the relationship is supposed to help and love the wife or the woman, but what do we see in an abusive relationship? It is sometimes even shameful to hear what some couples do to each other and even to their own children! How can abusers change to become loving and helpful partners? There is a lot of information in the next chapter to help abusers to be transformed.

Chapter 5

Personal Transformation & Salvation of the soul

In life, one can only give what he or she has and it seems unfair to me, sometimes for people to expect good behaviour from someone who does not have such qualities or the grace to deliver such good behaviour. We must rather help people to become what we expect them to be through training, counselling or coaching. A husband or wife who does not have the virtue of love cannot give love to the spouse. Please don't fight your spouse when he or she is not acting in love but rather encourage your spouse to acquire love from God to be equipped with an eternal love for you. If your husband is abusing you, what is needed is change. If your wife is not acting appropriately, she may need to change. Behavioural change is good, not only good but also very rewarding. Nonetheless, with every good thing in life, discomfort is not absent in the midst of change. Many people have lost their dream partners because of their bad behaviour. Some have also lost their dream jobs because they did not have the right attitude. As you read this chapter, open your heart and mind unto the Lord to change you for good.

In this chapter we will look at three types of personal transformation namely, Personal transformation by the Power of God; Religious Personal Transformation (without the prescribed relationship with God); and Trinitarian Personal Transformation.

Sometimes it is very helpful not to approach subjects like these as an academic piece of work, but rather the message you read in this book should evoke a response and stir up something within you both in belief and in conduct. This is what it means to build your life on the word of God–putting into practice what God says.

What is transformation? The verb 'transform' from which we get the word transformation is defined by the Merriam-Webster dictionary *as a change in form, function or nature.* Looking at this definition, I think it is obvious that we all need this personal transformation or change. The only constant thing in life is the process of change. Either you are changing to become a better person or you are changing to become a bad person. Either your relationship or marriage is strengthening or it is worsening. Either your financial situation is getting better or your financial situation is deteriorating. Either your health is getting better or it is getting worse. Either you are on your way to heaven or you are on your way to hell.

Do you know why some employers spend thousands of pounds on their employees to acquire certain skills? Think for a moment! The answer is simple; employers know they will demand certain skills from their employees which they may not have; hence the huge budget on personnel development at the work place. Jesus said something very profound regarding the need for people to change or to become better people in Matthew 12:33:

> Make a tree good and its fruit will be good, or make a
> tree bad and its fruit will be bad, for a tree is recognized
> by its fruit.

This is the main objective of this chapter. How people can be changed or transformed to become good people so that they can give goodness back to God and their fellow human beings.

In scriptures, human beings are sometimes referred to as trees bearing fruit (see Matthew 7:16-20; Luke 6:43-45). In this text, Jesus is saying that, make a person good, and what will come from him or her will be good, or make a person bad and what will come from him will be bad. Jesus says similar thing elsewhere:

> No good tree bears bad fruit, nor does a bad tree bear good fruit. Each tree is recognized by its own fruit. People do not pick figs from thorn bushes, or grapes from briers. The good man brings good things out of the good stored up in his heart, and the evil man brings evil things out of the evil stored up in his heart. For out of the overflow of his heart his mouth speaks (Luke 6:43-45).

Personal transformation or personal change is one of the many benefits you get when you build your life on the principles of God. This is the situation whereby you allow God to restore you to the most glorious state in life where you become free 'from sin' and any bad habits, addictions or attitudes (Roman 3:21-24). It is a glorious state indeed, because you become purer, your soul or your inner being is cleansed from any sin or guilt.

A person who has allowed himself or herself to be transformed by God does not need any alcohol or cigarette or any substance to calm themselves when they are stressed or under duress, because God's Spirit, which will live in them, will give them peace and joy in such difficult times (Romans 8:26-27). Those who have been transformed by God rejoice when they see good things, they shun evil, and give themselves to good causes, and they receive their reward in heaven. These are all benefits of personal transformation as a result of one building their life on the word of God.

There are certain blessings God will not give to people who are not mature or transformed. Personal transformation helps people to become mature so that precious things can be entrusted to their care. You have to change to become a responsible person before you can receive certain things in life. This is also true in spiritual matters.

But who are those who need a change or transformation? The words of Jesus in Luke 5:31-32 gives us the answer: Jesus said 'It is not the healthy who need a doctor, but the sick'. I have not come to call the righteous, but sinners to repentance' (Luke 5:31-32). Anyone who knows they have sinned before can be considered a sick person in spiritual terms; such a person is welcome into the kingdom of God because Jesus Christ came to save such people. Jesus Christ came to die for sinners, so that they will become righteous as his blood cleanses and removes their guilt. This acknowledgement of personal sin and the need for a saviour is the beginning of personal transformation.

Many people are offended when they are told they are sinners by the preacher man. Let us not forget, the preacher man was sick once too! But He was shown mercy when he acknowledged his sinful state. His job now is to point people to Jesus for forgiveness of their sins (1 Timothy 1:12-16). A sick person is not offended when told of his or her sickness by the health worker. In the same way, a sinner should not be offended either when the preacher man tells them. Both the sick person and the sinner need a cure. Unless you know your sickness, you would not accept the cure. In the same way, unless you know you are a sinner you won't accept and appreciate the cure for your sins. Sin is very dangerous. It can rob you of good life, happiness, and eternal life if it is not dealt with on time. Jesus Christ offers cure for sin (1 Jon 2:2).

Some people think that they need to stop all their bad habits before they can come to God for a change. If you are one of these people, please, take a moment to take in what is coming next. This is a very vital point; people must come to God with all their problems and bad habits for God to change them (Matthew 11:28-30). There can be no transformation outside the presence of God. What this means is that **you cannot change yourself without the help of God.** Can the Ethiopian change his skin or the leopard its spots? Neither can you do good who are accustomed to doing evil (Jeremiah 13:23). One cannot change one's own nature. That is why God wants us to be born again in order to receive a new nature, a regeneration of body spirit and soul.

You can only manage your bad behaviour, at best, but real change is from God. So if you think you have to change before coming to God, then I think you are delaying. If today you hear God's voice through any means whether on radio, TV or even as you read this book do not hardened your heart (Hebrews 4:7). Be willing and allow God to warm your heart as I take you through what it means to be changed and how possible this change is.

Life is full of changes, because of this I believe it is a very wise thing to decide to change for the better. Else, the pressures of life can drag you to a worse or difficult situation. You either influence your life positively or you allow life situations to bring you down. Those who build their lives according to God's word will enjoy a glorious life with Him because they can relate to Him as a result of their new state in life. You cannot enjoy glorious life with God and the angels without Holiness. Scripture says, 'without holiness no one can see God' (Hebrews 12:14). So, either we do something to make ourselves holy so that we can relate to God, or God does something to help us become holy, righteous so that we can relate to him. God did the latter. He sent Jesus Christ to be a sin offering for us, so that by accepting this gift from God, we can become holy and righteous (2 Corinthians 5:21). The blood of Jesus will wash all your sins away and present you righteous to God if, and only if, you accept this gift from God. Scripture says:

> But if we walk in the light, as he is in the light, we have
> fellowship with one another, and the blood of Jesus, his
> Son, purifies us from all sin (1 John 1:7).

It is not enough to hear God's word; you must believe, and ask God for mercy in order to benefit from His offer of cleansing and forgiveness.

If you are not holy, Satan may accuse and deprive you of many blessings, unless God grants you mercy (Zachariah 3:1-7). The story is told about Moses and the angel Michael in Jude 1:9. God sent the angel Michael to go for the body of Moses, because Moses was not buried when he died. According to the account, Satan disputed with the angel Michael about the body of Moses. Satan brought forth an accusation saying that the body of Moses belongs to him, because when Moses was alive, he murdered someone. Can you believe this? Satan claiming the body of Moses because he says Moses murdered someone. Someone may ask what right has Satan got to claim the body or the life of someone? You see, Satan is the father of lies and the originator of every evil thing in this world. So when you do anything bad, it means you are championing the course of Satan. This gives Satan the legal right to make a claim on you:

> You belong to your father, the devil, and you want to carry out your father's desire. He was a murderer from the beginning, not holding to the truth, for there is no truth in him. When he lies, he speaks his native language, for he is a liar and the father of lies (see John 8:44).

If you have done anything wrong, or show any of the characteristics of Satan and if you have not asked for forgiveness nor changed your lifestyle, then know that Satan can claim ownership of you when you die or even while you are still alive.

Personal Holiness is also very good for your health because anytime you do bad things, the evil things you do can make you unhappy, they can wage war with your soul, you may not feel comfortable, you may even attract negative things to yourself (1 Peter 2:11). How peaceful it is to be freed from addictions and bad behaviours such as anger, immorality, drugs, alcohol addictions etc! Many people are miserable in life because they are loaded with guilt from their past lifestyles. Some even end up committing suicide because of the torment they go through. Forgiveness and cleansing from guilt can heal you and restore joy into your life. Turn to God today for forgiveness:

> Come now, let us reason together, says the LORD. Though your sins are like scarlet, they shall be as white as snow; though they are red as crimson, they shall be like wool. If you are willing and obedient, you will eat the

best from the land; but if you resist and rebel, you will be devoured by the sword, for the mouth of the LORD has spoken (Isaiah 1:18-20).

The ultimate aim of personal transformation is to become holy unto God, where your nature is changed to conform to the image of God and his Son Jesus Christ (Romans 8:29-30). Transformation by God can also take place in every aspect of your life where positive change is needed, in the body, in your spirit and in your soul (1 Thessalonians 5:23). This work of grace in transformation can also be extended to your economic situation, your social life and your spiritual life (3 John 2). True Personal transformation is entirely the work of God's grace bestowed upon people who will accept this gift. God's grace is defined as God's unmerited favour towards people who need help (2 Corinthians 6:1-2). Depending on where you need a change, God in his river of mercy will provide you with the resources you need to change.

Let us look at these various ways people can change in the following sections.

5.1 Personal transformation by the Power of God

This type of transformation involves the power of God coming upon a person to effect a change in any situation the person may find himself or herself. The result of this type of transformation could be healing, or deliverance from the grip of satanic powers or some sort of miracle, just to name a few here. There are only two necessary conditions for this type of transformation to be experienced; namely belief (faith) in God and sometimes prayer.

There are certain habits or problems that can only be overcome by the power of God. To understand this, it is important for the reader to begin to think for moment, that there are evil spirits in our world which are responsible for certain bad behaviours or infirmities in the lives of many people (read Ephesians 2:1-2). For example, there was a young boy who could not speak because of demon possession, but when Jesus rebuked the demon by the power of God, the demon left and the boy was able to speak (read Mark 9:17–30; Luke 11:14;20).

There are certain behaviours which can only be changed by the power of God because these behaviours are caused by evil spirits. Sadly, people who do not believe in God sometimes become ignorant of these things to their own detriment. How can one allow the power of God to change their situation? Jesus said to the man whose son could not speak:

> Everything is possible for him who believes." Immediately the boy's father exclaimed, I do believe; help me overcome my unbelief (Mark 9:24–25).

All things are possible for the one who believes. If you want the power of God to change your life from any situation you don't like, the first step is to believe in God that He is able to help you. One of the principles of life is that you will benefit from whatever you believe in. If what you believe in has some virtue, you will benefit from it. Sadly many people do not even know what they believe in. Believe in God today, because he has blessings for you.

The second thing you can do for a change in your life is to pray to God.

> After Jesus had gone indoors, his disciples asked him privately, "Why couldn't we drive it out?" He replied, "This kind can come out only by prayer (Mark 9:28–19).

Prayer is one of the means to communicate to God for him to release his power to effect a change in your situation. You can pray to God yourself or you can ask your church leaders to help you in prayers when necessary (James 5: 13–16). The latter is usually recommended when you are helpless to pray by yourself. I believe this is one of the main reasons why you should belong to a local church and attend service regularly so that in times of trouble you can call upon the church leaders to help you.

The power of God and prayer can also help you to experience the salvation of your soul. Scriptures says 'I am not ashamed of the gospel, because it is the power of God for the salvation of everyone who believes: first for the Jew, then for the Gentile (Romans 1:16). But this type of personal transformation (salvation of your soul) will require repentance, baptism, and godly lifestyle in addition to faith. This type of transformation is what I call Trinitarian personal Transformation in this book, which will be discussed in the next two sections in this chapter.

So far we have looked at how believing in God and prayer can make it possible for the power of God to transform you for from any bad situation- from, sickness to health, poverty to provision. Please don't settle for this type of transformation, there is more, aim for eternity. Let us now look at the second type of personal transformation in the next section.

5.2 Religious approach to Personal Transformation

Religious approach to personal transformation mainly involves obeying certain beliefs and abstaining from certain lifestyles. Religion is an attempt by humanity to relate to God according to people's own set of derived rules and regulations. Trinitarian Personal Transformation which will be discussed in the next section is the opposite of religious Personal transformation. Religiosity says, do this and don't do that without any divine help or grace from heaven. People can be transformed to some extent in their outward behaviour through religion. This type of transformation may involve giving gifts or money for charitable purpose, abstaining from certain foods and drinks, learning to say the right thing, using the right words at the right time. This type of transformational approach is not good enough to effect the best change the human personality needs. Colossians 2:21-23 says:

> Do not handle! Do not taste! Do not touch! These are
> all destined to perish with use, because they are based on

human commands and teachings. Such regulations indeed have an appearance of wisdom, with their self-imposed worship, their false humility and their harsh treatment of the body, but they lack any value in restraining sensual indulgence.

Scripture says religious activities which are based on human commands without a true relationship with God have no lasting effect in restraining people from doing evil. This explains why a lot of people do evil in the name of religion. Religious transformational approach is mainly outwardly, the inner self remains the same. Let no man therefore judge you'.—That is, impose his own laws upon you because it will not help, unless such teachings will lead you to Jesus Christ:

> Therefore do not let anyone judge you by what you eat or drink, or with regard to a religious festival, a New Moon celebration or a Sabbath day. These are a shadow of the things that were to come; the reality, however, is found in Christ (Colossians 2:16).

Legalism in ancient days concerned such issues as diet, festival days, and religious ceremony. Such rules although may appear "spiritual" can actually lead a person away from true devotion to God. The Old Testament Law like any other religious law had a shadow of good things to come, but not the very image (or, substance) of the things (Hebrews 10:1). When Saint Paul deals with the legal and coercive aspect of the Old Testament Law in Galatians 3:24, he calls it "the schoolmaster. ' So the law was put in charge to lead us to Christ that we might be justified by faith'. Religious instructions are good if only they will lead people to Jesus Christ for them to experience the salvation of their soul and to live according to Christ commandments. All true religion will lead people to Christ as their saviour if the followers will be ready to accept him as their Messiah. Jesus says:

> No one can come to me [Jesus] unless the Father who sent me draws him, and I will raise him up at the last day. It is

written in the Prophets: 'They will all be taught by God.'
Everyone who listens to the Father and learns from him
comes to me [Jesus] (John 6:44-45).

If religion is seen as an attempt by mankind to relate to God, then
definitely God will draw genuine religious people to Jesus Christ
for their salvation. We see and hear this notion from missionary's
testimonies of religious men and women who eventually came to
put their faith in Jesus Christ for their salvation.

Scripture also records a good number of such real life experiences
with the risen Lord. Acts 8:26-40, is the account of a religious
Ethiopian official, an important official in charge of all the treasury
of Candace, queen of the Ethiopians who was graced with the
opportunity to give his life to Jesus. This man had gone to Jerusalem
to worship and was on his way back to his country reading the Holy
Scriptures but could not understand it. Scripture says, the Spirit
of God told Philip to go to this man and to explain the scriptures
to him. The man accepted the message, and had himself baptized,
when they came to a source of river. Scripture says, the man went
home rejoicing. The modern Christian church in Ethiopia claims an
uninterrupted descent from the conversion of this man described in
Acts 8:26-40.

In a similar incident recorded in Acts 10, scripture describes a man
called Cornelius as 'devout and God-fearing; who gave generously
to those in need and prayed to God regularly'. In short, this man
had a sterling character. When an angel told him where to seek help,
Cornelius responded immediately. He sent for Peter, the leader of
the group of believers at that time. This man had enough faith to
assemble friends and relatives in his home in expectation of Peter's
arrival for the message God had for him. Scripture says 'While Peter
was still speaking these words, the Holy Spirit came on all who heard
the message. So Peter ordered that they be baptized in the name of
Jesus Christ. Then they asked Peter to stay with them for a few days'.
Peter, who probably had never stepped inside a non-Jewish house
before, was stunned. He quickly grasped the point: "I most certainly

understand now that God does not show partiality, but accept people from every nation who fears Him and does what is right".

I have met many people who say, they are religious; they give to the poor and so God must be pleased with them. This is not the whole truth, I would not want you to be misled. Those who do good deeds in the name of God or religion should go a step further by accepting God's offer of salvation through faith in Jesus Christ, repenting of their sins, get baptized and continue to live a godly lifestyle until the time of their death. Someone may ask, "Will God not consider me for the good things I have done for people and grant me access to heaven without me accepting the way of salvation?" God's message to such people can be found in John 3:16-18:

> For God so loved the world that he gave his one and only Son, that whoever believes in him shall not perish but have eternal life. For God did not send his Son into the world to condemn the world, but to save the world through him. Whoever believes in him is not condemned, but whoever does not believe stands condemned already because he has not believed in the name of God's one and only Son.

Continue to do good deeds to people, but don't forget to accept God's way of salvation, else you will be condemned on the judgment day for not accepting Jesus Christ. There are many people in and outside the church who think that going to church on Sundays and giving money to the poor is enough. Cornelius was like that but God sent his servant to tell him what to do next. Acts 16:11-16 is also an account of a rich woman named Lydia whom scripture described as a 'worshipper of God'. Scripture says 'The Lord opened her heart to respond to Paul's message. When she and the members of her household were baptized, she invited Paul and his missionary team to her home'. Are you a religious person? Then please do the next thing by accepting God's way of salvation through faith in Jesus Christ, repent of your sins, get baptized and start to live a godly life..

In this section we have looked at what I called Religious Personal transformation (without a relationship with God). This involves obeying a set of rules and regulations set out by the sect or the group. This type of transformation however, only produces outward change. One of the main points that I am making in this section is that God will reveal himself and his way of salvation to all true religious people or spiritual seekers. It is up to them to accept God's way of salvation. Let us look at the last approach to personal transformation in this chapter.

5.3 Trinitarian approach to personal transformation

In this section, we will look at Trinitarian approach to personal transformation. The word Trinity from which we have the word Trinitarian, is the three persons of the Christian Godhead; Father, Son, and Holy Spirit. Trinitarian approach to personal transformation involves the work of God the Father, the Son Jesus Christ and the Holy Spirit (1 Peter 1:1-2). The result of this kind of personal transformation is the salvation of your soul and eternal life where you begin to change gradually until you meet God in heaven. It is sometimes very important that you understand how you can be saved. So, let us discuss the roles of the trinity in this section.

1. The role of God the Father: God chooses those who are ready to hear the message of the gospel. According scriptures, 'the eyes of the LORD ranges throughout the earth to strengthen those whose hearts are fully committed to him' (2 Chronicles 16:9). If your heart is fully committed to the Lord, God will locate you with his blessings, including the salvation of your soul irrespective of your religious affiliation, gender, tribe, or nationality.

2. The role Jesus Christ- Jesus Christ is the sacrificial lamb for our sins. Jesus has made his blood available to be sprinkled on people for forgiveness because, 'without the shedding of blood there is no forgiveness of sins' (2 Corinthians 5:21; Hebrews 9:22; Acts 10:42-43). There are many things we can say about Jesus, but we will only limit it to his atoning role in our salvation and sanctification in this section.

3.The role of the Holy Spirit; The Holy Spirit sets up the appointments for you to meet someone who will share God's message of salvation with you; and also to help you understand the gospel message (John 16:7-9). For example, in Acts 8:26-40, we see the Spirit of God directing Phillip to locate the man who needed salvation. The Spirit of God is involved in your salvation from the beginning to the end. There are two more personalities who are also involved in your salvation.

4. The role of the messenger: the fourth person involved in your salvation is the person who will share God's message with you. This person is a vessel of God bringing you the good news. He or she carries blessings specifically meant for you. Even if you are not ready for the message he or she is bringing you, please don't abuse the messenger but treat him or her with respect. What many people don't know is that the messenger has been given authority from the Lord to either put the peace of God upon you or not to bless you. Read this in Matthew 10:12-15:

> As you enter the home, give it your greeting. If the home is deserving, let your peace rest on it; if it is not, let your peace return to you. If anyone will not welcome you or listen to your words, shake the dust off your feet when you leave that home or town. I tell you the truth; it will be more bearable for Sodom and Gomorrah on the Day of Judgment than for that town.

The question is, why did Jesus tell his disciples to shake the dust off their feet if a city or a home would not welcome them? In Jesus' days, when leaving non-Jewish cities, pious Jews often shook the dust from their feet to show their separation from non-Jews practices. And so, this gesture was to show the people that they were making a wrong choice- that the opportunity to choose Christ might not present itself again. Are you receptive to teachings from God through his servants? If you ignore the preacher's message, you may not get another chance.

Encouragement & Caution to preachers: Messengers of God need both encouragement and caution. Messengers of God do a good work and a wonderful job. God bless you richly, including the author of this book. We need encouragement to continue to share the word of God with people. The apostle Paul in his days, at some point was so discouraged to the point of giving up his missionary work but the Lord appeared to him and encouraged him:

> One night the Lord spoke to Paul in a vision:"Do not be afraid; keep on speaking, do not be silent. For I am with you, and no one is going to attack and harm you, because I have many people in this city. So Paul stayed for a year and a half, teaching them the word of God (Acts 18:9-11).

May the Almighty God, in His own way encourage all preachers and teachers of his word, amen.'

But preachers and teachers of God's word also need caution. Jesus says:

> He who speaks on his own does so to gain honor for himself, but he who works for the honor of the one who sent him is a man of truth; there is nothing false about him (John 7:18).

Preachers of the gospel are not to preach with the aim of becoming popular or to please themselves. We should not forget that we are only messengers, sent to deliver a particular message to the world. What is this message, someone may ask? Paul writing to his Roman readers said:

> I am not ashamed of the gospel, because it is the power of God for the salvation of everyone who believes: first for the Jew, then for the Gentile. For in the gospel a righteousness from God is revealed, a righteousness that is by faith from first to last, just as it is written: The righteous will live by faith (Romans 1:16-17).

God is reconciling people through the preaching of the gospel; forgiving them of their sins by the blood of Jesus; giving them His

Holy Spirit to live the Christian life of holiness, love, and service. What people should do is repent from their sins, be baptised, and live a godly life. Preachers are not to make the acquisition of material things a priority, but rather preachers and all other believers are to seek the kingdom of God first, and all other things will be added to them as well Luke 12:29-34). Unfortunately, many preachers have subtly and mistakenly focused more on the 'all other things' instead of focusing on God's kingdom. Because of this, the apostle Paul warned Timothy, his disciple and fellow worker in the Lord as follows:

> Watch your life and doctrine closely. Persevere in them, because if you do, you will save both yourself and your hearers (1 Timothy 4:16).

Preachers and messengers of God are to watch their life style and what they tell others in order not to harm the people they preach to. Let us look at the fifth person involve in your salvation or Trinitarian transformation.

5. The fifth person involve in your salvation is you: you have a personal responsibility either to accept or reject the message the preacher man will give you. Remember that you have free will, and God respects your choices (Genesis 2:15-17; Mark 16:15).

So far in this section, we have been looking at the Trinitarian approach to personal transformation involving the Father, the Son, and the Holy Spirit. We have also looked at the fact that there are two more personalities involved in this redemptive work: the messenger and the receiver of the message. The end result of this approach of personal transformation is the salvation of the body, Spirit and soul where the Lord gives the beneficiary a new spirit, a new body (to be given at the resurrection of the dead) and a saved soul which is going to heaven after death.

We can see this pattern of Trinitarian transformation in both especially in the New Testament. In the New Testament, we have Philip and the Ethiopian Eunuch in Acts chapter 8, Peter and

Cornelius in Acts chapter 10, Paul and Lydia in Acts 16:13-15. My duty as a servant of God is to present the gospel message faithfully to you and to tell you what to do in order to be saved. It is up to you to act on what you will read in this book. It is my wish that you give your life completely to the Lord and allow him to change you and to grant you eternal life in Christ Jesus.

Those who will experience the Trinitarian transformation will go to heaven when they die. Where do you stand, will you go to heaven when you die? I believe the subject of heaven and what happens after death should be something that you must attend to alongside other vital issues of life, because death is inevitable and believe it or not, the day of judgment is drawing near (Hebrews 9:27). Heaven is a beautiful place; make it your ambition to be there. Give yourself a good treat, how can you ignore heaven and end up in hell!

What should people do? There are four main requirements one has to satisfy in order to *experience* the Trinitarian transformation. These are faith in God through Jesus Christ, repentance, baptism and the practice of a godly lifestyle until you die or until the second coming of Jesus. Let us now briefly discuss these four requirements in the following paragraphs, please follow me through.

Requirement number one: Faith in God through Jesus Christ

The first requirement to experience salvation of your soul or total transformation is a belief in God which will lead to faith in Jesus Christ for the forgiveness of your sins (John 6:45). Someone may ask "why I should put my faith in God through Jesus and not in God alone!" Let us look at it this way, if you want to go and see the Queen of England, there are some personalities you will meet first before you can see the queen. The queen has entrusted some responsibilities to these people. In the same way God who is in heaven has entrusted the salvation of the human soul to Jesus Christ, that is why Jesus could say *that I am the way the truth and the life, no one goes to the father except through me* (John 14:6). Those who claim to believe in God and yet find it difficult to put their faith in Jesus should know that unless the Father draws them to Jesus it is not possible for them to believe in Jesus for the salvation of their soul. According to scriptures those who genuinely believe in God will come to Jesus for forgiveness of sins (read John 6:43-44). To believe in Jesus Christ is the first requirement for the salvation of your soul or the end result of Trinitarian transformation.

Requirement number two: Repentance

Repentance is a willing change of mind and lifestyle *towards God* and your *personal sin*. Repentance is more than being sorry for your sins. In practical terms, I have broken down what repentance means as follows:

- Repentance means you are willing and have chosen to live your life the way God wants. You are ready to live for God.

- Repentance means you are ready to allow God to forgive you your sins, so that you can become holy unto Him, because without holiness no one can see God (Hebrews 12:14; Revelation 22:14-15).

- Repentance means you are ready to say good bye to all of your known sins with the help of God e.g. gossiping, sexual immorality, witchcraft, hatred, anger, jealousy, drunkenness, idolatry and more (see Galatians 5:19-21).

Repentance is good for you, because through repentance you can change for the better, whereby you are able to throw away all of your bad habits. Repentance can also bring a time of refreshing into your life. Acts 3:19 says: 'Repent, then, and turn to God, so that your sins may be wiped out, that time of refreshing may come from the Lord'. Guilt feeling can be dangerous to your wellbeing and sin can be a source to your downfall in life. So, if you know you have done something wrong to somebody or God, why don't you repent and seek forgiveness so that times of refreshing may come to your life.

Someone once asked the question, how many times can we be forgiven by the Lord or by someone we have sinned against! The answer to this question can be found in Luke 17:3-4:

> So watch yourselves. If your brother sins, rebuke him, and if he repents, forgive him. If he sins against you seven times in a day, and seven times comes back to you and says, 'I repent,' forgive him.

We are to forgive people who sin against us if they come to ask for forgiveness. It is not necessary going round looking for people who have sinned against you to forgive them. It is their duty to go and look for the person they have sinned against and ask for forgiveness. In the same way, God will not be chasing you to forgive you of your sins. It is your duty to go to God in prayers, confess your sins and ask for forgiveness:

> If we claim to be without sin, we deceive ourselves and the truth is not in us. If we confess our sins, he is faithful and just and will forgive us our sins and purify us from all unrighteousness. If we claim we have not sinned, we make him out to be a liar and his word has no place in our lives. My dear children, I write this to you so that you will not sin. But if anybody does sin, we have one who speaks to the Father in our defense—Jesus Christ, the Righteous One. He is the atoning sacrifice for our sins, and not only for ours but also for the sins of the whole world (1 John 1:8-2:2).

Someone once asked, is it right to continue to sin and keep asking for forgiveness all the time? The apostle Paul put the same question this way: What shall we say, then? Shall we go on sinning so that grace may increase' (Romans 6:1)? On one of our radio programs a caller put the same question this way: 'what, if you are saved but you continue to sin can you be re-saved?' The Russian monk Rasputin, for example, concluded, "I will sin more to earn more forgiveness." He lived a bizarre life of immorality because of this ideology.

The more you commit a particular sin regularly you may end up becoming a 'slave' to that bad habit (read Romans 6:11-14). Therefore ask God to help you to stop any habitual sin. You may also need to make the effort yourself to stop that particular sin. For example, if you continuously commit sexual sin, it may be advisable to get your own wife or husband. If you continue a particular sin for a long time, you may become discouraged in yourself, and start condemning yourself to hell fire. This attitude can also make your sanctification or maturation process very difficult if you are a believer and this can also make you unfruitful in life. In some cases, you can be snatched from hell fire if heaven continues to look on you with favour or if you have not committed any of the unpardonable sins. Some sins cannot be forgiven, so watch out!

> If anyone sees his brother commit a sin that does not lead to death, he should pray and God will give him life. I refer to those whose sin does not lead to death. There is a sin that leads to death. I am not saying that he should pray about that (1 John 5:16).

Biblical scholars and commentators differ widely in their thoughts about what this sin that leads to death is, and whether the death it causes is physical or spiritual death. Paul wrote that some Christians had died because they took the Holy communion in an 'unworthy manner' (1 Corinthians 11:27-30). Ananias and Sapphira were struck dead because they lied to God (Acts 5:1-11). Blasphemy against the Holy Spirit results in spiritual death, and cannot be forgiven (Mark 3:29), and the book of Hebrews describes the spiritual death of a person who turns against Christ (Hebrews 6:4-6). If one rejects Christ as Lord and saviour, and dies in that state, he or she will not receive forgiveness on the Day of Judgment.

Death is separation. A physical death is the separation of the soul from the body. Spiritual death, which has severe consequences, is the separation of the soul from God. Those who die spiritually will not make it to heaven. In Genesis 2:17, God tells Adam that in the day he eats of the forbidden fruit he will "surely die." Adam did fall, but his physical death did not occur immediately; God must have had another type of death in mind—spiritual death. This separation from God is exactly what we see in Genesis 3:8. When Adam and Eve heard the voice of the Lord, they "hid themselves from the presence of the LORD God." The fellowship had been broken. They were spiritually dead.

New Year's resolutions have helped many people make significant changes in the way they live. But New Year's resolutions do not go far enough, as compared to the act of repentance, because repentance is a regular daily practice, where you keep amending and changing anything negative and sinful in your life immediately you discover them. Let us now look at the third requirement for Trinitarian personal transformation, water baptism.

Requirement number three: Baptism

I have had many people come to me asking whether water baptism is important or not, what is your opinion? There is another group of people who say they were baptised when they were young, should they be baptised again. There is also an ongoing debate whether baptism should be by immersion or by sprinkling. I am happy to address all of these concerns in this section, but let's first look at the meaning of baptism.

Water Baptism is a Christian rite where a person who has believed in God through faith in Jesus Christ as their saviour is immersed in water as a sign of his/her conversion. It is also a sign of surrendering, dying and rising up with Christ (read Romans. 6:3-8). To resolve all the questions about baptism, let us take a look at the following scripture concerning the baptism of Jesus Christ:

> Jesus came from Galilee to the Jordan River. He wanted to be baptized by John. But John tried to stop him. He told Jesus, "I need to be baptized by you. So why do you come to me?" Jesus replied, "Let it be this way for now. It is right for us to do this. It carries out God's holy plan." Then John agreed. As soon as Jesus was baptized, he came

up out of the water. At that moment heaven was opened. Jesus saw the Spirit of God coming down on him like a dove. A voice from heaven said, "This is my Son, and I love him. I am very pleased with him (Matthew 3:13-17).

We can deduce the following from the scripture just read concerning the baptism of Jesus Christ.

1. If even Jesus Christ, who is the Son of God, got himself baptized because of his humanity, then who are we to say baptism is not important? Baptism is very important, anyone who says he or she believes in God must undergo water baptism.

2. In the same way, Jesus has command his church to baptize those who will believe in the good news: 'whoever believes and is baptized will be save' (Mark 16:15-16). In Acts 8:26-40, the religious Ethiopian Eunuch, after believing in Jesus Christ was baptized. In Acts 9:1-19, Paul was baptized after his conversion. In Acts 10:1-48, the godly Italian centurion was also baptized. In Acts 16:11-15, a woman, a worshipper of God was baptized after believing in the gospel message. In Acts 16: 25-36, the prison officer also got baptized the very night he put his faith in the Lord. We can therefore conclude that everyone who has put their faith in Jesus Christ needs to be baptized. Have you done your water baptism? Is it a decision you made yourself or your parents decided to baptize you?

3. It is also clear that Jesus' baptism was by immersion, which agrees with the Greek word for baptism, *baptizo,* which means to be dipped into and also corresponds to the surrendering, dying and rising up with Christ (Romans 6:3-8).

4. It is also clear from the scripture read, that Jesus got baptized, when He reached the age of awareness and accountability. We can therefore conclude that Jesus was not baptized as an infant, but was dedicated to the Lord in the temple by His

mother when he was eight days old (Luke 2:21-24), and was later baptized when He was old enough (Matthew 3:13-17). From this we can say that, the right time for someone to be baptized is when the person is old enough to decide for themselves whether they are ready to live the Christian faith or not. Although some churches baptize infants, I believe these differences should not bring division among Christians.

5. It is also clear from what we read in the text that Jesus was baptized by a human being, John the Baptist. At this juncture, I would like to bring to your attention that there are four main types of baptism, namely water baptism which we are discussing, Holy Spirit baptism, baptism by fire and baptism into the body of Christ.

Water baptism is done by a human being for the forgiveness of sins: John the Baptist said 'I baptize you with water for repentance. But after me will come one who is more powerful than I, whose sandals I am not fit to carry. He [Jesus] will baptize you with the Holy Spirit and with fire. (Matthew 3:11). The Holy Spirit baptism is done by Jesus Christ, where the believer is filled with God's Spirit for power, self-discipline, love and wisdom (Acts 1:8; 2 Timothy 1:7). Baptism by fire is also done by Jesus Christ (Matthew 3:11). This is the situation where by Jesus allows the believer to go through a bit of uncomfortable life situations in order to make them mature and strong. Both Peter and James wrote on the need for believers to endure hardship, which they say will result in good:

> Though now for a little while you may have had to suffer grief in all kinds of trials. These have come so that your faith—of greater worth than gold, which perishes even though refined by fire—may be proved genuine and may result in praise, glory and honor when Jesus Christ is revealed (1 Peter 1:6-7).

> Consider it pure joy, my brothers, whenever you face trials of many kinds, [Jas] because you know that the testing of your faith develops perseverance. Perseverance must

finish its work so that you may be mature and complete, not lacking anything (James 1:2-4).

God, sometimes allows believers to go through suffering a little bit in order to purify them; just as the refiner refines gold (Malachi 3:3). We can only become better and stronger when we go through some challenging times provided we do not give up.

Baptism into the body of Christ is another type of baptism and it is done by God the father himself. With this type of baptism, God through His own divine arrangements places a believer to join a particular local church, for their spiritual nourishment, maturity, and service (Galatians 3:26-27; 1 Corinthians 12:12-27). When you join any local church make sure you are faithful there and serve God with all your energy, knowing that you are not in that church by accident, but that it is God who has put you there.

Before I conclude the discussion on the subject of baptism, I would like to throw a bit of light on the issue of whether someone can do water baptism more than once. The answer to this question is yes and no depending on the validity of the previous baptism: the time and the mode of the previous baptism. I believe the following scripture can help you to understand this very well. In this passage of scripture the apostle Paul had to re-baptise a group of people, Acts 19:1-7:

> While Apollos was at Corinth, Paul took the road through the interior and arrived at Ephesus. There he found some disciples and asked them, did you receive the Holy Spirit when you believed? They answered, No, we have not even heard that there is a Holy Spirit. So Paul asked, "Then what baptism did you receive? John's baptism, they replied. Paul said, John's baptism was a baptism of repentance. He told the people to believe in the one coming after him, that is, in Jesus. On hearing this, they were baptized into the name of the Lord Jesus. When Paul placed his hands on them, the Holy Spirit came on them, and they spoke in tongues and prophesied. There were about twelve men in all.

From the scripture just read, it is clear that you can be baptised twice. For example if you think your first baptism was not done properly or if you think you were not fully ready for the Lord when you had your first baptism, or even if you think you were too young or did not understand the reason why you did your first baptism. Let us now discuss the fourth and the last requirement for Trinitarian approach to personal transformation or the salvation of the soul.

Requirement number 4: Godly lifestyle

The fourth requirement for the salvation of your soul, or to be changed completely body, Spirit, and soul is a continuous godly lifestyle. This is because the Trinitarian approach to personal transformation is both an instantaneous event and at the same time a gradual process. No one can become perfect in a day or a week or even a month or even a year. You will not have all your problems solved in a single day or month as you believe in God; this may take some time, sometimes. This is because before you came to God for a change, a lot of things might have gone wrong in your life. For example when someone loses their job for a year; this can affect the person's finances, relationships, health, etc. And so if this person gets a new job let's say a year later, it will take some time before that person will be able to sort out his life completely, this is how spiritual things also works.

It is important to realise that when someone believes in God, repent and is baptised, that person becomes a new person (2 Corinthians 5: 17), and so there is the need for the person to live a new lifestyle. For example if you were homeless and someone helped you to resettle, you are likely to become homeless again if you don't change from the old lifestyle which made you homeless. This is also true regarding the salvation of your soul. Jesus says:

> When an evil spirit comes out of a man, it goes through arid places seeking rest and does not find it. Then it says, 'I will return to the house I left. When it arrives, it finds the house swept clean and put in order. Then it goes and

takes seven other spirits more wicked than itself, and they
go in and live there. And the final condition of that man
is worse than the first (Luke 11:24-26).

In this text, Jesus was illustrating an unfortunate human tendency-
our desire to reform often does not last long. It is not enough to be
emptied of evil; we must then be filled with a new life in the power
of the Holy Spirit to accomplish God's purpose in our lives. Many
people are not ready to change their lifestyles, even after putting their
faith in Jesus Christ, and undergoing baptism and so they are always
in trouble. This change in life style begins with the renewing of your
mind, in the case of personal salvation; you renew your mind with
the word of God (Romans 12:1-2).

> Therefore, I urge you, brothers, in view of God's mercy,
> to offer your bodies as living sacrifices, holy and pleasing
> to God—this is your spiritual act of worship. Do not
> conform any longer to the pattern of this world, but be
> transformed by the renewing of your mind. Then you will
> be able to test and approve what God's will is—his good,
> pleasing and perfect will (Romans 12:1-2).

To live a godly life is a decision and begins with renewing of your
mind after the Lord has been gracious to you. To be saved is a gift
from God. The appropriate response is to willingly offer yourself as
a living sacrifice to God. Scripture says 'When you were slaves to
sin, you were free from the control of righteousness. What benefit
did you reap at that time from the things you are now ashamed of?
Those things result in death! But now that you have been set free
from sin and have become slaves to God, the benefit you reap leads
to holiness, and the result is eternal life (Romans 6:20-22).

In this chapter, we have looked at how we can change to become
good people who will inherit eternal life in Christ Jesus. We looked
at the three main approaches to personal transformation namely;
transformation by the power of God; religious transformation; and
Trinitarian transformation. Let us now discuss how the principles of
God can help the younger generation in the next chapter.

Chapter 6

Guidance for Young people

To be young is great but it comes with its own challenges. Thankfully, Scripture provides helpful guidelines on how young people can build their lives in a more productive way. Young people today have identity problems, they have low self- esteem, at times they are unsure of themselves, they seek acceptance but from the wrong sources. Scripture can help them find their identity- for them to know that they are fearfully and wonderfully made by the God of the universe right from the time their mothers conceived them. God has a good plan for everyone before conception. God has planned some to be prophets, world leaders, and all kinds of great people. David expressed this notion in this way:

> For you created my inmost being; you knit me together
> in my mother's womb. I praise you because I am fearfully
> and wonderfully made; your works are wonderful, I know
> that full well (Psalm 139:13-14).

Young people who have knowledge about their identity, who they are, are always content with themselves. Scripture can help young people in discovering who they are.

> The word of the LORD came to me, saying, "Before I
> formed you in the womb I knew you, before you were
> born I set you apart; I appointed you as a prophet to the
> nations (Jeremiah 1:4-5).

Jeremiah was appointed by God as a prophet to the nation. God has a purpose for each person, some people are appointed by God for specific kinds of work. The young people can know more about their destiny as, and if they draw closer to God.

In this chapter we will discuss how the word of God can guide young people to receive the vision or mantle from the older generation. We will also look at how scripture can help younger people become wise; and also how scripture can help them in their character formation. Our society has become very anti-God to the extent that knowledge about good and wrong, guidelines for making good decisions which used to be 'common sense' decades ago, have to be paid for in order to acquire them in modern times.

The young people today are the future leaders. They have a lot to offer towards the betterment of this world. They can do it if they are guided properly. But I think today's young people face a lot of challenges, probably more than the previous generation. Teenage pregnancy is not something new, but the rate of teenage pregnancies is on the increase at an alarming rate. Self-harm and suicides are also found to be more common among young people than in the older people in this era. Our systems are well developed to the point where most young people, especially those in the West, do not see themselves making any significant contribution to our world. But the young people are the future leaders; they are the future of this world. How can we help them?

6.1 How young people can receive the vision from the older generation

Scripture encourages young people to learn to receive the torch or the mantle from the older generation so that they can continue or better the vision of their parents or the older generation. In life, most things are passed on, or handed down from the older generation to the next generation. This can be a business, a trade, a ministry, inheritance, advice, life experiences, money, or even anointing for service in the kingdom of God. Your mother or father may have something positive they can pass on to you. Young people should learn from their parents or the older people in the community. They are to show interest in their lives, to respect them, and to be submissive in order to receive from them.

Life is full of receiving and giving. There is nothing wrong with parents or grandparents receiving assistance from the children in their old age or in times of need if the children can be of such help. In fact God is pleased when children give to their parents especially in times of need. This is another reason why parents should bless their children; so that in their old age the children will be in a position to offer help to their parents or the older people in the community.

In scripture, we see Abraham passing on the mantle to his son Isaac; Isaac to Jacob; Jacob to his twelve children specifically to Joseph who helped the family in times of famine, and Judah through whom the Messiah, Jesus Christ came. Unfortunately, many young people do not know how to receive the vision from the older generation. Many reasons can be attributed to this problem. First, it is possible that young people have not been taught how to receive the 'mantle' or the vision from the older generation. Another reason could also be that some young people are not humble or reliable enough for the older generation to pass on certain blessings to them.

Every four years the world watches an ancient ritual unfold: the passing of the Olympic torch. The spectacular pageantry of the opening ceremonies cannot begin until the final carrier of the torch arrives in the stadium. The torch symbolically links the modern Olympic Games to their 2,700-year history.

"Passing the torch" has become a familiar phrase, used when the president of General Motors introduces his successor to the public, or, when an esteemed orchestra conductor hands over his baton, or a great sports figure tutors his or her replacement. Often the retiring person delivers an emotional farewell speech. He or she has finished the work; the time has come to pass the torch to another.

Scripture encourages the older generation to pass on their faith as follows:

> And the things you have heard me say in the presence of many witnesses entrust to reliable men who will also be qualified to teach others (2 Timothy 2:2).

If the church is to constantly follow this advice, it would expand geometrically as well-taught believers would teach others and commission them. Our work is not done until new believers are able to make disciples of others.

When a prophet like Elijah leaves the scene, who will dare to take his place? As time came to choose a successor, Elijah looked to someone out of a different mold. He settled on his most faithful companion, a young farmer named Elisha:

> When they had crossed, Elijah said to Elisha, "Tell me, what can I do for you before I am taken from you?" "Let me inherit a double portion of your spirit," Elisha replied. 2 Kings 2:9

In 2 Kings 2:11-14, passing on of the mantle from Elijah the prophet, to Elisha, his successor, symbolizes the passing of prophetic authority:

> "You have asked a difficult thing," Elijah said, "yet if you see me when I am taken from you, it will be yours— otherwise not." As they were walking along and talking together, suddenly a chariot of fire and horses of fire appeared and separated the two of them, and Elijah went up to heaven in a whirlwind. [2Ki 2:12] Elisha saw this and cried out, "My father! My father! The chariots and horsemen of Israel!" And Elisha saw him no more. Then he took hold of his own clothes and tore them apart. He picked up the cloak that had fallen from Elijah and went back and stood on the bank of the Jordan. Then he took the cloak that had fallen from him and struck the water with it. "Where now is the LORD, the God of Elijah?" he asked. When he struck the water, it divided to the right and to the left, and he crossed over. The company of the prophets from

Jericho, who were watching, said, "The spirit of Elijah is resting on Elisha." And they went to meet him and bowed to the ground before him (2 King 2:10-15).

And so Elisha received a double portion of the anointing on his master. How beautiful! For young people to receive the mantle or the vision from the older generation, wisdom and good character is required. Let us look at how the word of God can help young people to become wise in the next section.

6.2 Wisdom to deal with Life issues

The word of God can impart wisdom for godly living if people will seek the face of God with all their heart. The following people whom scripture considers wise can be helpful models in our own pursuit of wisdom. Joseph, who is referenced in Acts 7:10 and elsewhere in scripture is considered as a wise leader who prepared for a major famine and helped ruled Egypt. Abigail who is referenced in 1 Samuel 25:3 is considered a wise wife who managed her family sensibly in spite of a surly and a mean husband. Young women can learn lessons from her. David is referenced in 2 Samuel 14:20, he is also considered a wise leader who never allowed his failures keep him from the source of wisdom- reverence for God. Bezalel, a wise artist designed and supervised the construction of the tabernacle and its utensils for God (Exodus 31:1-5). Stephen a wise man who organised the distribution of food to widows, and preached the gospel (Acts 6:8-10). The magi are considered wise learners who not only received special knowledge of God visiting the earth but checked it out personally (Matthew 2:1-12). Jesus Christ became a wise youth (Luke 2; 40; 52), a wise saviour, the wisdom of God (1 Corinthians 1:20-24), not only lived a perfect life but died on the cross to save us and make God's wise plan of eternal life available to humanity. All these men and women are God's people we can learn from in the Bible.

Let us now look at the meaning of wisdom. Wisdom is an application of knowledge. If wisdom is the application of knowledge, then right knowledge or information is essential in order for someone to act wisely in any given situation. Wisdom and folly (foolishness) are rival enemies each preparing a feast and inviting people to it. Wisdom appeals first to the mind, while folly appeals first to the senses. The youth today have access to all kinds of knowledge; some are very helpful others too are very dangerous. People who have bad knowledge will obviously end up doing bad things if they choose to do so. On the other hand, people who have good knowledge will end up doing good deeds if they choose to do so. If wisdom is the application of knowledge, then people need to be exposed to or have access to the right information or knowledge. This is where scripture provides assistance. Scripture provides us with the right kind of knowledge so that we can apply them accordingly. Scripture also, through the inspiration of the Holy Spirit, will lead God's children to all truth (John 16:12-13).

There are two types of wisdom, godly wisdom and non-godly wisdom. Scripture provides godly source of wisdom for young people and the older generation alike. James 3:17 describes godly wisdom as: 'The wisdom that comes from heaven is first of all pure; then peace-loving, considerate, submissive, full of mercy and good fruit, impartial and sincere'. This is how James 3:13-16 describes non godly wisdom; 'Who is wise and understanding among you? Let him show it by his good life, by deeds done in the humility that comes from wisdom. But if you harbor bitter, envy and selfish ambition in your hearts, do not boast about it or deny the truth. Such "wisdom" does not come down from heaven but is earthly, unspiritual, of the devil. For where you have envy and selfish ambition, there you find disorder and every evil practice'. Godly wisdom produces peace, good fruit, humility, self-control etc. I believe the youth of today need godly wisdom badly.

How can people obtain godly wisdom? According to scripture:

> The fear of the LORD is the beginning of knowledge, but
> fools despise wisdom and discipline (Proverbs 1:7).

To receive godly wisdom, one needs godly knowledge or information and scripture is full of godly information. Anytime you encounter the word 'knowledge' in scripture, it usually refers to knowledge about God unless otherwise qualified. For examples, we can see this in Hosea 4:6:'my people are destroyed from lack of knowledge. Because you have rejected knowledge, I also reject you as my priests'. The word 'knowledge' here, is knowledge about God. The people in Hosea's day rejected the knowledge about God, and so they ended up prostituting themselves to their own detriment. When we choose God's way, he grants us wisdom. His word, the Bible, leads us to live right, have right relationships, and make right decisions.

Knowledge about God is good, but a vast difference stands between 'knowledge' (having the facts about God) and 'wisdom' (applying those facts to life). We may amass knowledge about God, but without correct application our knowledge is useless. We must learn how to live out what we know about God.

The apostle Paul encouraged young Timothy to continue to live according to God's word because of its benefits:

> But as for you [Timothy], continue in what you have
> learned and have become convinced of, because you know
> those from whom you learned it, and how from infancy
> you have known the holy Scriptures, which are able to
> make you wise for salvation through faith in Christ Jesus
> All Scripture is God-breathed and is useful for teaching,
> rebuking, correcting and training in righteousness, so that
> the man of God may be thoroughly equipped for every
> good work (2 Timothy 14-17).

The young Timothy benefited a lot from scripture, because from infancy his parents taught him the word of God and this helped him to become wise, even to the point of receiving Jesus Christ for his personal salvation. Parents have the duty to teach their children the word of God like how Timothy's parents taught him.

In scripture, Jesus Christ is portrayed as the wisdom and the power of God 1 Corinthians 1:20-24. Our society worships power, influence and wealth. Jesus came as a humble, poor servant, and he offers his kingdom to those who have faith. This looks foolish to the world, but Christ is our power, the only way people can be saved. Knowing Christ personally is the greatest wisdom anyone could have.

Let us look at how scripture can help young people build a good character in the next section.

6.3 Character Formation

> Character cannot be developed in ease and quiet, only through experience of trial and suffering can the soul be strengthened, ambition inspired, and success achieved.
> **Helen Keller**

Character is defined as the mental and moral qualities distinctive to an individual. Your character can define who you are and this can either have a positive or a negative effect on your life. Many people have lost good relationships, marriage, friends, and professions because of their character. On the other hand, some people have also been promoted at their work place, married their dream partners because they had the right character to attract and maintain what they received. We are all partly responsible for our own character. The full development of character is not something automatic; it requires rational decisions.

In this chapter, we will look at two ways of character building or character formation using scripture. These two main ways are "being born again" and the modelling of good mental and moral qualities. One other benefit of scripture in character formation is how it can help people, especially the young to distinguishing what is good from what is bad. Some of these good virtues to model are love, faithfulness, respect, self-control, perseverance, forgiveness, hard-working (Galatians 5:22-23). Some of the bad character traits, which the Bible calls the works of the sinful nature to avoid are, sexual immorality, impurity and debauchery; idolatry and witchcraft; hatred, discord, jealousy, fits of rage, selfish ambition, dissensions, factions, and envy; drunkenness, orgies, and the like (Galatians 5:19-21).

We all love people with good character. There are many more reasons why people should exhibit good character. Proverbs 3:3-4 says 'those who have good character will win favour and earn good name in the sight of God and man'. Secondly without good character it is possible that you may not make it to heaven (see Revelation 21:6-8). Why do people exhibit bad character? Many reasons can be attributed to this: Some people cannot exhibit good character because of the Adamic nature which has rendered all humanity sinners (see Jeremiah 13:23; Matthew 7:17-20). There are some people who can show good behaviour but they will not, especially those who have received the new birth or those who have been "born again" (2 Timothy 3:5).

The Psalmist once asked this question and answered it himself in Psalm 119:9-11 the question:

> How can a young man keep his way pure? By living according to your word. I seek you with all my heart; do not let me stray from your commands. I have hidden your word in my heart that I might not sin against you.

One of the best ways for young people to keep their lives pure is to live according to the word of God. The word of God tells right from wrong and the reward for living a good life and the punishment for living a bad life. For example, King Solomon warns young people in Ecclesiastes 11:9 this way:

> Be happy, young man, while you are young, and let your heart give you joy in the days of your youth. Follow the

ways of your heart and whatever your eyes see, but know
that for all these things God will bring you to judgment.

Young people should live a happy life, but they must remember
that God will ask them to give an account of whatever they will do
in this world. I believe this advice can be a helpful guide to young
people to be careful of how they live. If they spend their energy on
good things, they will be rewarded; if they spend their energy on
bad things they will receive punishment.

A man reaps what he sows. If you do good deeds, goodness will
follow you; if you do bad things misfortune will follow you sooner
or later. Our society today expects people to behave well, forgetting
that most people, especially the youth of today have not had the
chance to be trained to become godly. Our interest in this chapter
is to encourage young people especially to become or acquire the
mental and moral qualities needed for proper behaviour.

Even king Solomon, a man who possessed brilliant powers of
wisdom and observation, had to conclude that some things are
beyond understanding. Failing in his attempt to "figure out" life, he
fell back on simple advice: fear God and obey him, no matter how
things seem to you. In essence, he concluded in favor of a life of faith.
For him, an old man, much of life had already passed; in eloquent
poetry he describes the decay that was already at work in his body
(Ecclesiastes 12:1-7). Thus he stressed, "Remember your Creator in
the days of your youth" before the days of trouble comes and the
years approach when you will say I find no pleasure in seeking God
(12:1). Young people are to make the worship of God a priority.
Many people wait till they become old before they seek God, this is
not a good practice.

Let us continue our discussion on character formation. Aristotle, a
Greek philosopher and scientist from the Macedonian city of Stagirus
claims that character develops over time as one acquires habits from
parents and community, first through reward and punishment. But
I think this way of character formation is not the best because if for

example a person finds himself in a bad community; then that person may turn out to have a character which is shaped by such community. Fortunately, scripture provides principles that can guide people to acquire the mental and moral qualities necessary for responsible behaviour irrespective of which community he or she comes from, whether good or bad.

1. Character formation through modelling or copying good traits

One way of character building is to model or to copy good character traits. For example, if you are not virtuous, you may sometimes act like a virtuous person. This is what I called 'copying, but this can lead to pretence if the motive is not right. Most people live two lives: what people see outside and what is really going on inside. In school, some students learn what outward signs of attention will please the teacher. At the work place they learn to "put up a good front" whenever the boss happens to stroll by. As if donning masks, they style their hair, choose their clothes, and use body language to impress those around them. Over time, they learn to excel at hiding truly serious problems and character flaws. People tend to judge by outward appearances and so can easily be fooled. Sometimes, acquaintances are often shocked when a mass-murderer is arrested. Most people fail to act properly because they do not have what it takes to act in a decent manner. "He seemed like such a nice man!" they insist. The outside appearance did not match the inside reality. Jesus says in Luke 6:43-45:

> No good tree bears bad fruit, nor does a bad tree bear good fruit. Each tree is recognized by its own fruit. People do not pick figs from thorn bushes, or grapes from briers. The good man brings good things out of the good stored up in his heart, and the evil man brings evil things out of the evil stored up in his heart. For out of the overflow of his heart his mouth speaks.

In scripture, a tree can refer to people. Good people will bear or produce good deeds. Likewise bad people will bear or produce bad deeds. A bad person must not just model or copy good behavior but must be "born again" in order to acquire the mental, spiritual and moral qualities needed for a good life. One cannot give what he or she does not have. What should people do? This will be looked at in the next section.

2. Character Formation through the 'New Birth'

Being "born again" is the same as receiving the new birth where you receive a new spirit, a new mindset, a new nature different from what you were born with. The term "born again" was first used in John 3:3-6:

> In reply Jesus declared, "I tell you the truth, no one can see the kingdom of God unless he is born again. How can a man be born when he is old? Nicodemus asked. Surely he cannot enter a second time into his mother's womb to be born! Jesus answered, I tell you the truth no one can enter the kingdom of God unless he is born of water and the Spirit. Flesh gives birth to flesh, but the Spirit gives birth to spirit.

Here Jesus was explaining the importance of a spiritual rebirth, saying that people would not enter the kingdom of God unless they are spiritually born. Being "born with water and Spirit" refer to (1) the contrast between physical birth (water) and spiritual birth (Spirit), (2) being regenerated by the Spirit and signifying that rebirth by water baptism. The water also signifies the cleansing action of God's Spirit.

After being born again, one can then train themselves to grow or imitate good traits because the person now has the abilities to do so. Scripture says:

> Train yourself to be godly. For physical training is of some value, but godliness has value for all things, holding promise for both the present life and the life to come. 1 Tim. 4:7-8.

Young people are to be born again and to train themselves to be godly. To be born again is a gift from God to us as promised in Ezekiel 36:25-25. This gift is not given to all people automatic. Those who want this gift are to ask God in prayers and accept the means to be born again. This involves faith in Jesus as Lord and savior, repentance, baptism, and the desire to live a godly life. In fact to be saved, is the same as being born again.

But like an army personnel, unless those who are recruited train themselves, they will not be fit to do their job well. In the same way unless a born again person trains himself or herself, they may not have developed the mental and moral abilities necessary for good behavior.

How can "born again" people train themselves to become mature? Scripture offers many guidelines. 1 Peter2:1-2 says 'Therefore, rid yourselves of all malice and all deceit, hypocrisy, envy, and slander of every kind. Like newborn babies, crave pure spiritual milk, so that by it you may grow up in your salvation, now that you have tasted that the Lord is good'. When you become born again, you are like a new born baby; you will need milk, the word of God and training or discipleship in order to grow well. You need to belong to a local church, to learn how to become mature spiritually in order to behave as a child of God. Paul uses another term 'work out your salvation' in Philippians 1:12 after he has exalted the people to imitate Christ humility.

Romans 12: 1-2 says ' Therefore, I urge you, brothers, in view of God's mercy, to offer your bodies as living sacrifices, holy and pleasing to God—this is your spiritual act of worship. Do not conform any longer to the pattern of this world, but be transformed by the renewing of your mind. Then you will be able to test and approve what God's will is—his good, pleasing and perfect will'. Romans 6:11-13 says' in the same way, count yourselves dead to sin but alive to God in Christ Jesus. Therefore do not let sin reign in your mortal body so that you obey its evil desires. Do not offer the parts of your body to sin, as instruments of wickedness, but rather offer yourselves to God, as those who have been brought from death to life; and offer the parts of your body to him as instruments of righteousness'.

Ephesians 4:22–5:2' You were taught, with regard to your former way of life, to put off your old self, which is being corrupted by its deceitful desires; to be made new in the attitude of your minds; and to put on the new self, created to be like God in true righteousness and holiness. Therefore each of you must put off falsehood and speak truthfully to his neighbor, for we are all members of one body. In your anger do not sin": Do not let the sun go down while you are still angry, and do not give the devil a foothold. He who has been stealing must steal no longer, but must work, doing something useful with his own hands, that he may have something to share with those in need. Do not let any unwholesome talk come out of your mouths, but only what is helpful for building others up according to their needs, that it may benefit those who listen. And do not grieve the Holy Spirit of God, with whom you were sealed for the day of redemption. Get rid of all bitterness, rage and anger, brawling and slander, along with every form of malice. Be kind and compassionate to one another, forgiving each other, just as in Christ God forgave you. Be imitators of God, therefore, as dearly loved children and live a life of love, just as Christ loved us and gave himself up for us as a fragrant offering and sacrifice to God.

So far in this chapter, we have looked at how scripture can provide guidance for young people on how they can acquire wisdom; guidance on character formation, and how they can receive the mantle from the older generation. Let us now look at how scripture can provide guidance for the older generation in the next chapter.

Chapter 7

Guidance for the older generation

In general, we think of a generation of being 25-30 years- from the birth of a parent to the birth of a child. In this chapter, we will look at how Scripture provides guidance for the older generation on how they can live the rest of their lives peacefully till death and even beyond without regret. This is the main aim of this chapter.

7.1 The Well done stage in life!

The older generation, irrespective of their age, must see themselves as having achieved something in life no matter how minute or great their achievements may be. I called this the 'well done stage'. Whatever you have been able to do in life at any age is 'good'. There may be some setbacks, failures, mistakes, disappointments, and regrets, but, congratulate yourself and move on. Younger people should tell their parents and the older people around them not to be discouraged. Once they have life there is hope. There is a lot they can still do, until God calls you home peacefully. Where necessary, the older generation should learn from their mistakes and change their ways.

Many older people feel sorry for themselves for not being able to achieve certain things in life. The fact that you have a dream does not mean the dream must come to fruition in your lifetime. Sometimes the next generation will pick up the dream and make it a reality.

7.2 Passing on to the younger generation

There are many things the older generation can pass onto the next generation. There are many things fathers and mothers can pass on to their children. In this section we will look at three categories of things they can pass on, namely, life experience, the knowledge of God and material blessings.

❖ Passing on life experience

Certainly, the older generation have been around longer than the younger generation and as a result of that, they may have more life experience than the younger generation. These experiences can be in the area of relationships and marriage, career and job experience, success and failures, good times and bad times, or spiritual development and faith matters. All of these experiences are treasures and if passed on to the next generation, will help raise godly parents, good citizens, good employees and employers, promote healthy relationships, and produce good servants of God.

Parents are to share their life experiences, both the good ones and the bad one with their children and grandchildren. This will help the next generation to avoid some of the mistakes their parents may have made. A parent who did not have a successful marriage should point out their mistakes to the children so that they will not go the same path. It is very common to see children repeating the mistakes of their parents. There are many reasons why this happens. In some cases it could be a generational curse, which can only be broken by the power of God. If you are going through what any of your parents or grandparents went through, then I think you need to seek help from your pastor or someone higher in spiritual authority in the church for guidance.

The success story of the parents can also serve as a guide and a ladder for the children to climb to their heights in their generation. Parents who share their life experiences with their children will also benefit from these children later on in life, especially in their old age.

This same principle is also needed at the workplace. The older generation at the workplace must be willing to share their work experience with the up and coming ones instead of fighting or intimidating them. This will enhance unity, productivity, and continuity at the work place. Employers have special interest in older employees who mentor the up and coming new employees.

The same principle is expected to be implemented in the house of God. Here, the older church members are expected to pass on their experiences onto the new church members. In Titus 2:2-5 scripture advises older men and women as follows:

> Teach the older men to be temperate, worthy of respect, self-controlled, and sound in faith, in love and in endurance. Likewise, teach the older women to be reverent in the way they live, not to be slanderers or addicted to much wine, but to teach what is good. Then they can train the younger women to love their husbands and children, to be self-controlled and pure, to be busy at home, to be kind, and to be subject to their husbands, so that no one will malign the word of God.

The older women in the church are admonished to live a respected life, staying away from anything that will defame their character. In the church Paul wrote this letter to, it seems that, some of the women were slanderers and addicted to too much wine. What is the common problem caused by the older women in your church? The older women have been given the responsibilities to train the up and coming young women on how to run a godly family, how to live a pure life, and how to respect and be submissive to their husbands.

The older men in the church are to carry themselves in a worthy manner, so that they can win the respect of the younger men in the church. This will also make it easier for the younger men to approach them for advice and guidance since the older men have a lot of real life experience both in the church and outside the church. This will all count towards their rewards in heaven.

Some people are of the opinion that the reason most marriages are not successful these days is because most young people do not know how to marry or how to keep their partners. Older men and women, please teach the young ones. Don't take your experiences to the grave without leaving it behind to impact the next generation. Older men and women who share their lives with the young or who mentor the younger generation will always be occupied and will not feel much loneliness.

The church of today needs more young missionaries and pastors to do God's work. Older ministers of the gospel should be willing to pass on the mantle to the young ones and to encourage them to launch out. What we normally see these days is that the older and experienced ministers either use the young ones to build their own empires instead of training them unto the harvest field. In some cases the older ministers neglect the young and inexperienced ministers to struggle on their own. Paul passed the ministry onto Timothy and Titus who were also instructed to pass on what they learnt from Paul onto reliable men who will also pass it on to others (2 Timothy 2:2). This is God's strategy of recruiting men and women to work in his kingdom.

❖ Passing on material blessings

Older generations are expected to pass on their material blessings to the younger generations. Parents are naturally expected to pass on their material blessings to their children. This is also a commandment from God.

> Houses and wealth are inherited from parents, but a prudent wife is from the LORD (Proverbs 19:14)

The apostle Paul also made a reference to this principle when he wrote to the church at Corinth:

> After all, children should not have to save up for their parents, but parents for their children (2 Corinthians 12:14b).

There are many reasons why some parents do not pass on their inheritance to their children. Whatever the reason may be, it is expected that parents save up for their children no matter how small the inheritance may be. If a parent decides in their life time to leave an inheritance to their children, God in his mercies will grant that parent abundant blessings. God sometimes blesses us according to our good intentions.

7.3 Older generation receiving help from the younger generation

Life is full of receiving and giving. There is nothing wrong for parents or grandparents receiving from their children in their old age or in times of need if the children can be of such help. In fact God is pleased when children give to their parents especially in times of need. We can read this in 1 Timothy 5:4:

> But if a widow has children or grandchildren, these should learn first of all to put their religion into practice by caring for their own family and so repaying their parents and grandparents, for this is pleasing to God.

There comes a time when older people will need to depend on the younger generation for livelihood. But this is one of the things most seniors are not good at; how they can receive help, ideas, and encouragement from young people. There are some older generations who also swing the pendulum to the extreme by making too much demand from either their children or the young people around them. Thank God, scripture encourages these benevolent acts and services from young people to older people and the necessary guidance on how such services are to be administered.

The story of Jacob and his eleventh son Joseph in the Bible is a good example of how older people can receive help from their children or the young people. In this story, Joseph became the Prime Minister in Egypt and through a series of divine arrangements; Jacob himself, his children, his in-laws and his grandchildren came to live and depend on Joseph until the time of the exodus when Moses was sent to take the descendant of Jacob (Israel) from Egypt. The story is told in Genesis 39–48.

The older generation should learn to encourage the younger generation to excel in life, not to compete with them, so that they can also benefit from them. A mother should not compete or fight with her daughter. A father should not compete or fight with his son. Parents should teach their children the importance of taking care of them in their old age. The Bible says, 'train a child in the way he should go, and when he is old he will not turn from it' (Proverbs 22:6). Let us look at some of the guidance scripture provides the older generation on how they can prepare for eternity in the next section.

7.4 Preparing to depart to eternity

Death is one of the inevitable things that will happen to everybody. People have different reasons for being afraid of death. When I was growing up, one of the things that scared me most was the thought of the death of my parents. I loved my parents especially my mother so much that I was always afraid to lose them. I think part of the reason was due to the fact that I did not understand the nature of death and what life has in store for those who die in the Lord. One of the things that helped me to overcome this fear was the fact that I started looking at life from God's perspective, because he is the creator of the world, and he alone has the master plan. Human beings are limited in many ways, but God is eternal so it is important that we listen to God or see life from God's point of view, so that we can have a comprehensive understanding of the world we live in.

Everyone will die one day except those who will be raptured at the second coming of Jesus Christ. Corazon Aquino once said:

I would rather die a meaningful death than to live a meaningless life.

We can only die a meaningful death if we plan to die instead of allowing death to take us unexpectedly.

In this chapter, we have already looked at the need for the older generation to leave an inheritance for the next generation; this is one way of preparing for eternity. The other vital point worth considering here is the final destination of the human soul. Where will your soul go after death?

We are made up of body, spirit and soul. At death, the spirit returns to God who gave it to you. The body decays or is burnt depending on the type of burial method. There are two main destinations the human soul could go after death; heaven or hell. It is important that you make sure your soul will go to heaven before you die. This should be part of your preparation for eternity. Many people do not really bother themselves about where their soul will go after death. James Jacob Prasch in his book *Grain for the Famine,* says this:

"Rabbi Yohanan ben Zaccai was known as the "Mighty Hammer". At the end of his life, when he was on his deathbed, his disciples came and found him weeping. They asked him why he was weeping and he replied, "I am about to meet *Ha Shem,* blessed be His name, and there are two roads before me – one to paradise and one to Gehenna [hell]. And I do not know to which of these two roads he will sentence me. That is why I'm weeping." The founder of Rabbinic Judaism said he had no assurance of salvation when he died". But his classmate, Rabbi Sha'ul [Paul] of Tarsus said:

> For I am already being poured out like a drink offering, and the time has come for my departure. I have fought the good fight, I have finished the race, and I have kept the faith. Now there is in store for me the crown of righteousness, which the Lord, the righteous Judge, will

award to me on that day—and not only to me, but also to
all who have longed for his appearing (2 Timothy 4:6-8).

These two men both had the chance to prepare for their future
homeland. Paul of Tarsus made the right choice by accepting the way
of the Lord. At the end of his life, he knew where his soul would
depart to. He had the assurance of salvation. To be saved, and go to
heaven requires four main things: faith in Jesus as Lord and saviour,
repentance, baptism, and godly lifestyle till death. I have discussed
these four requirements in details in my previous book; *'The Final
Destination of the Human Soul'*. Please get a copy from your local book
store or from the Amazon website.

So far in this chapter we have looked at how scripture can provide
guidance to older generations on how they can live the rest of their
lives productively. Let us now look at another benefit people can get
for building their lives on the word of God in the next chapter.

Chapter 8

Guidance for Protection from bad people, evil spirits & Satan

The world we live in is a dangerous place; it is made up of good people, bad people, bad spirits & Satan himself. That is why Jesus taught us to pray to God to 'protect us from the evil one' in Matthew 6: 13. St Peter says, 'be self-controlled and alert, your enemy the devil prowls around like a roaring lion looking for someone to devour' (1 Peter 5:8). Someone may argue that if God loves us why doesn't He protect us automatically or remove evil from this world including Satan? I will give two answers to this very question in this chapter.

First, although Satan is the father or the original source of evil (Ezekiel 28:14–18), many people love to do evil to their fellow human beings. In fact you yourself, you have done badly something to hurt someone before. So, if God has to remove evil and those who do evil from this world, you won't be alive now. So, God in his mercy grants time to all people who do evil to repent or change their ways. This is one of the reasons why we see evil people in our society, God is given them time to repent. Secondly, God will remove evil people and Satan from this world at the appropriate time (Revelation 20:7–10).

Without discussing the genesis of evil further, what can be said here is that there are bad people in this world, there are evil spirits in this world (Luke 4:33-37; Revelation 16:13-14), and there is the devil himself in this world (Revelation 12:7-11). I am not saying this to scare you, I am only informing you. God has not promised a world free of danger, but He does promise His help to those who will call upon him whenever they face danger. This is the main aim of this chapter, how scripture provides guidance for protection from bad people, evil spirits & Satan.

Psalm 91 describes the security benefits for the person who dwells in the secret place of God. Because of the richness and depth of this psalm, I have quoted the entire revelation as follows:

> He who dwells in the shelter of the Most High will rest in the shadow of the Almighty. I will say of the LORD, He is my refuge and my fortress, my God, in whom I trust. Surely He will save you from the fowler's snare and from the deadly pestilence. He will cover you with His feathers, and under His wings you will find refuge; His faithfulness will be your shield and rampart. You will not fear the terror of night, nor the arrow that flies by day, nor the pestilence that stalks in the darkness, nor the plague that destroys at midday. A thousand may fall at your side, ten thousand at your right hand, but it will not come near you. You will only observe with your eyes and see the punishment of the wicked. If you make the Most High your dwelling— even the LORD, who is my refuge then no harm will befall you, no disaster will come near your tent. For He will command His angels concerning you to guard you in all your ways; they will lift you up in their hands, so that you will not strike your foot against a stone. You will tread upon the lion and the cobra; you will trample the great lion and the serpent. Because he loves me, says the LORD, I will rescue him; I will protect him, for he acknowledges my name. He will call upon me, and I will answer him; I will be with him in trouble; I will

> deliver him and honor him. With long life will I satisfy
> him and show him My salvation (Psalm 91:1-16).

Those who want God to protect them from evil are to learn how to dwell in the secret place of God and how to put Him first in everything they do. Many people have a casual relationship with God. This level of relationship is not good enough to receive protection from Him. From the text just read, God says 'because he loves me, says the LORD, I will rescue him; I will protect him, for he acknowledges my name. He will call upon me, and I will answer him; I will be with him in trouble; I will deliver him and honor him. With long life will I satisfy him and show him my salvation'.

God works with covenants, so those who want God to protect them must have a covenant loving relationship with God, they must love God. This involves accepting Jesus Christ as your Lord and saviour for the forgiveness of your sins, repenting from any known sin, being baptised and living a godly lifestyle. The godly lifestyle involves reading your bible, praying to God, attending church service regularly to worship, sharing God's word with other people, doing good deeds to other people and staying away from evil.

8.1 Protection from your personal enemies & bad people

Life is such that whether you like it or not you will have enemies at some point in your life. Sometimes, your enemies can be people who are jealous of you because maybe you are prospering. Sometimes buying a new car, or a new house, or securing a new job or meeting your dream partner can make people envious of you. Those who have God as their refuge will be kept safe from their enemies. What should our attitude towards those who hate us be? What should you do when being hated? Scripture answers this question in Romans 12:17-21 as follows:

> Do not repay anyone evil for evil. Be careful to do what
> is right in the eyes of everybody. If it is possible, as far as

it depends on you, live at peace with everyone. Do not take revenge, my friends, but leave room for God's wrath, for it is written: "It is mine to avenge; I will repay," says the Lord. On the contrary: "If your enemy is hungry, feed him; if he is thirsty, give him something to drink. In doing this, you will heap burning coals on his head."

If someone hates you without you offending them, the advice is, you don't have to hate them back or do evil to them. Pray for them and leave the matter into God's hands. God will deal with them for you. If they are in need and come to you for help, do not hesitate, help them, in doing this, you will heap burning coals on their head. If they genuinely repent forgive them and be reconciled to them (Luke 17:3-4).

There are other times when you will have enemies as a result of something bad you did to them. If you know that you have wronged someone in any way, the best thing to do is to ask the person for forgiveness, and take the necessary steps to restore the trust and the friendship that was lost. Go and ask for forgiveness from the person you have wronged:

> Therefore, if you are offering your gift at the altar and there remember that your brother has something against you; leave your gift there in front of the altar. First go and be reconciled to your brother; then come and offer your gift. Settle matters quickly with your adversary who is taking you to court. Do it while you are still with him on the way, or he may hand you over to the judge, and the judge may hand you over to the officer, and you may be thrown into prison. I tell you the truth, you will not get out until you have paid the last penny (Matthew 5:23-26).

It is highly recommended in spiritual practices not to offend anyone. Many professors of faith think that they can offend someone and still expect God to protect them. I am afraid this is not so! God is a just God. He does not show favouritism; He is not partial (2 Chronicles 19:4-7). All wrong doing is sin, whether sin against God or sin against someone.

The story between David, Bathsheba, Uriah, and the prophet Nathan in 2 Samuel 12 is a classic example showing how God does not condone wrong doing even if the act is committed by someone who has built his life on God's principles like King David. God loved David, in fact he describes David as a man after his own heart (Acts 13:23). But when David, committed adultery with Bathsheba, Uriah's wife, God did not keep silent on the issue. God sent the prophet Nathan to confront David with his heinous sin. When David repented he was forgiven although David had to be disciplined by God later on.

The point I am making is this, when you wrong someone, don't snub it, go to the person and make peace so that you don't become an enemy to the person.

There are bad people around us, and some of them are our close friends and relatives. They eat with us, go on holidays with us, some of them are our colleagues at the work places and in our colleges. How can you know your enemy of progress? Who can know the thought of a person? How can you know what your close friend is thinking of you? It is only God who can know the thought of a person and to thwart their evil schemes. This is another benefit you will receive for believing in God. God will protect you from evil people. He will even show you how to avoid their evil schemes.

The story between David and Ahithophel is a classic example. God saved David from the plot of Ahithophel. When someone told David that his adviser Ahithophel was now backing Absalom to rebel against him, David prayed, "O LORD, let Ahithophel give Absalom foolish advice (2 Samuel 15:31). When Ahithophel saw that his advice had not been followed, he saddled his donkey and set out for his house in his hometown. He put his house in order and then hanged himself. So he died and was buried in his father's tomb (2 Samuel 17:23). May the Lord prevent any Ahithophel in your life from harming you!

For people who are not protected by God, those who are outside God's safe dwelling place: the message from God is to come to 'Him, your helper and protector'. For those of you who have put your trust in God, His message to you is to come and sit at His right hand until He makes 'your enemies your footstool' (Psalm 110:10). God says, 'no weapon formed against you will succeed and that you will refute any mouth that accuses you' (Isaiah 54: 15-17).

8.2 Protection from Satan & his demons

Satan and his demons exist and are inflicting pains on people, breaking marriages, causing sicknesses in people's bodies, leading people into darkness and into immoral lifestyles. Many people want to live a good life, and be freed from their addictions, but Satan and his demons have bound some of these people to such lifestyles. In fact looking at the scale and magnitude of evil in our world, it's not difficult to conclude that Satan is in control of the affairs of our world, a fact scripture also confirms:

> We know that we are children of God, and that the whole world is under the control of the evil one (1 John 5:19).

But the good news is that, one of the reasons Jesus came into this world was to destroy the works of Satan in people's lives:

> He who does what is sinful is of the devil, because the devil has been sinning from the beginning. The reason the Son of God appeared was to destroy the devil's work (1 John 3:8).

The evil one cannot harm those who are born again-those who have built their lives on the principles of God.

> We know that anyone born of God does not continue to sin; the one who was born of God keeps him safe, and the evil one cannot harm him (1 John 5:18).

The term 'born of God' in this text is the same as the theme in John 1:13; 'Children born not of natural descent, nor of human decision or a husband's will, but born of God'. Individuals who profess to be born again often state, they have a personal relationship with Jesus Christ. The evil one cannot harm those born of God, in the sense that Satan cannot destroy their soul, although he can disturb them like what he did to Job. What should people do if they think Satan is disturbing? Such people can ask God in prayer to rebuke Satan on their behalf, like how the angel Michael did in Jude1:9:

> But even the archangel Michael, when he was disputing with the devil about the body of Moses, did not dare to bring a slanderous accusation against him, but said, "The Lord rebuke you!

May the Almighty God rebuke any work of Satan in your life, amen!

8.3 Protection from Witches & nocturnal beings

Many people are afraid of witches and wizards. There are some people too, who do not believe that witches and wizards exist. Some people too, end up spending most of their time praying against the activities of these witches and wizards. What should people do?

Scripture makes it clear that witches, wizards and sorcerers exist, and that their practices are detestable to God.

> When you enter the land the LORD your God is giving you, do not learn to imitate the detestable ways of the nations there. Let no one be found among you who sacrifices his son or daughter in the fire, who practices divination or sorcery, interprets omens, engages in witchcraft, or casts spells, or who is a medium or spiritist or who consults the dead. Anyone who does these things is detestable to the LORD, and because of these detestable practices the LORD your God will drive out those nations before you. You must be blameless before the LORD your God (Deuteronomy 18:9-18).

God hates people who practice these heinous activities. Such people will not go to heaven after death unless they change their ways. God has promised this solution to His people:

I will destroy your witchcraft and you will no longer cast spells (Micah 5:12).

Those who are building their lives on the word of God should not be afraid of the activities of witches and wizard, but should continue to pray to God for protection. Witchcraft is not good. Those who practice witchcraft should stop and receive Jesus into their lives.

God has also given believers authority over demonic and witchcraft activities: 'Jesus called his twelve disciples to him and gave them authority to drive out evil spirits and to heal every disease and sickness' (Matthew 10:1). There is a debate whether all believers in Christ have this authority or this authority is reserved for a few strong believers. My position on this debate is that if you are a believer and you think you are not strong enough to drive out evils spirits in your life or in the life of others then please seek help from your church leaders who will help you either to build a strong faith or help you drive out any evil spirits which are disturbing you. The good news is that no weapon formed against God's children will prosper. May God destroy any witchcraft around you in Jesus name!

In this chapter we have discussed some of the benefits people will enjoy for building their lives on the word of God. We have looked at how through scripture people can be protected from evil, bad people, evil spirits & Satan.

Let us look at how scripture can guide us in our pursuit of material things in the next chapter.

Chapter 9

Scripture guidance on materialism

Many people have material wealth but are not happy in life. Others too have little or nothing and blame their unhappiness for lack of enough material resources. What is the way out? Statistics reveal that substantial numbers of UK population are hungry for meaning to life. In 1999, the Henley Centre published, *The Paradox Prosperity*, a detail research project sponsored by the Salvation Army, which gives an overview of the current scene. The research concluded that:

> There is a growing demand for some sort of **alternative approach to life,** for new answers to old questions. This has led to the emergence of a renewed emphasis on spirituality. There is a recognition that true 'wealth' comes from spiritual as well as material resources, and people are drawing up alternative scale of 'value' that will restore meaning to their lives. 27% of people claim to have successfully changed their spiritual life and a further 20% would like to do so.

Many people are beginning to realised that true wealth does not only come from material sources, but also spiritual. In this chapter, we will look at how scripture provides proper guidance on the subject of materialism which can be defined as the excessive desire to acquire and consume material goods. Materialism can also be defined as a way of thinking that gives too much importance to material possessions rather than to spiritual things. We will also look at how scripture is able to guide rich people in overcoming the problems they have such as corruption, greed and selfishness. These attitudes cause them not to enjoy their labour. We will also look at how scripture can guide the needy or a poor person to make a decent living. Finally we will look at how scripture can guide us to have the proper attitude towards materialism.

Some of the most difficult challenges facing us today is having the right attitude towards money or material possessions and what people can do in order to earn a decent living. Is there any relationship between the rich and the poor, because our society tends to divide the rich and the poor? The two groups seem to have little daily contact; it is sometimes a very hard time communicating a single message to both the very rich and the very poor.

Nevertheless, in this book the author has discussed these groups thoroughly, how each group needs God. In one section, the author addresses the haughty, privileged people of wealth, and in the next section he turns to poor people undergoing severe trials looking up to God for help. The two groups have different problems. The wealthy are sometimes selfish. They show insensitivity and snobbishness to the poor. For their part, the poor sometimes respond with grumbling-they seem to blame God for their poverty. Therefore, the poor need God to help them come out of poverty and acquire decent material wealth. The rich on the other hand need God's guidance on how they can be free from corruption, greed and selfishness.

We live in a materialistic society where many people serve money. They spend all their lives collecting and storing it, only to die and leave it behind. Their desire for money and what it can buy far outweighs their commitment to God and spiritual matters. Whatever you store up, you will spend much of your time and energy thinking about. It is comforting for some of us to hear that many people are becoming more aware that the world we have known and read about in the past centuries is changing and that after dominating the thinking of western people especially, materialism is diminishing and is in the process of being replaced by a more spiritual way of being that would take us through the twenty first century, and beyond. This is what Harvey Cox calls the future of faith, the age of Spirit. Some people are beginning to seek spiritual things more than material things.

Materialism is the opposite of spirituality. It is often bound up with a value system which regards social status as being determined by affluence as well as the perception that happiness can be increased through buying, spending and accumulating material wealth. Positively, materialism if handled properly according to God's principles can help one to build a healthy lifestyle. Negatively, it is considered a crass, if not false, value system induced by the spell of unusual need or desire for material (commodity fetishism) and void of more noble and worthy values.

Materialism without the proper balance can lead to idolatry. In both ancient and contemporary times, an idol is anything that takes the place of God in your life. In times of plenty, we often take credit for our prosperity and become proud that our own hard work and cleverness have made us successful. When this happens, it is easy to get so busy collecting and managing wealth that we sometimes push God right out of our lives, which is another form of idolatry.

But it is God who gives us everything we have, and it is God who asks us to manage it for Him. Psalm 24:1 says 'the earth is the LORD'S and everything in it, the world, and all who live in it'. Because of this Paul could say in Colossians 3:23-24' Whatever you do, work at it with all your heart, as working for the Lord, not for men, since you know that you will receive an inheritance from the Lord as a reward. It is the Lord Christ you are serving.'

If your attitude towards God is right, your life will end well because 'He will give you the strength to make wealth appropriately (Deuteronomy 8:18). But if your attitude towards Him is wrong 'your life may end badly, although you can live on your natural strength and abilities to some extent, in times of crisis whom do you fall on?

The purpose of having money through hard work is to help you afford life's necessities such as food, shelter, clothing, education, health insurance, transportation, making contributions to charity work, giving offerings to God to help build His kingdom etc. God is a God of purpose, the reason He will bless you is so that you can live to honour His name. God doesn't want you to go hungry or to go and steal. This is another reason He gave you the ability to make wealth. But wealth, if not handled properly can rob you of spiritual blessings as the following sections will tell.

9.1 Guidance for Rich people: How the rich desperately need God

Who is a rich[17] person? A rich person is someone who has lots of money and possessions. There are many reasons why people aspire to be rich; some people want to be rich because of selfishness and for pleasure, others with right and genuine motives. This is what one blogger said:

> You see, my goals are to become completely debt-free. I'm getting closer and closer to that goal. Within the last few months, I downsized my house, doubled my income, and was able to pay off all of my debts except for the mortgage. So now all I have left is about $100,000 to pay off before I am completely debt-free.

It is scriptural to work hard for your daily necessities; and to be debt free if you can. Proverbs 10:4-5 says 'Lazy hands make a man poor, but diligent hands bring wealth. He who gathers crops in summer is a wise son, but he who sleeps during harvest is a disgraceful son'. Ephesians 4:28 says 'He who has been stealing must steal no longer,

---

[17] According to Dr. Edwin Louis Cole, Wealth and riches are not synonymous. Wealth will get you riches, but riches will never make you wealthy.

but must work, doing something useful with his own hands, that he may have something to share with those in need.

'He who does not work, neither shall he eat' is a Biblical aphorism derived from 2 Thessalonians 3:10. Paul's first letter to the church in Thessalonica affirms that Jesus Christ could return at any time, unexpectedly to take Christian believers to heaven. Evidently, this anticipation had prompted some to quit their jobs and do nothing but wait for the second coming. (Dozens of times religious sects have followed the same pattern in the United States by heading for remote areas to await Christ's return.) To correct the imbalance, in this second letter Paul stresses that certain events must happen before Christ's return to take believers to heaven. He also strongly warns against idleness.

'I'm on the right track toward getting out of debt and becoming rich. I'm doing all of the right things, says someone. Why do people want lots of money? We know intellectually that money doesn't always bring happiness, yet many people strive for more of it, sometimes even at the expense of their families, spiritual life and their relationship with God. There are too many guys who have built very successful businesses and made large amounts of money and had their family fall apart. As one blogger said 'I used to be envious of them and what they had, but now I just feel sorry for them'. They wanted riches so bad that it consumed them. They have nice houses and brand–new cars, yet are completely alone. Many celebrities find themselves in similar circumstances.

Danger in plenty

To be a rich person comes with its own challenges. A lot of people are not able to cope with life when they become rich. Some even end up living a miserable life, others forget and abandon God because they become too independent and secure in life, they think they don't need God's help anymore let alone a relationship with Him. Moses warned the Israelite this: "When you eat and are satisfied, be careful that you do not forget the Lord" (Deuteronomy 6:11-12). It is often most difficult to follow God when life is easy. We can easily fall prey to temptation and fall away from God in times of material abundance. Here are some notable examples of this truth.

In Genesis 3, the first couple on earth Adam and Eve, lived in a beautiful world and had a perfect relationship with God. Their needs were met; they had everything. But they fell to Satan's deception.

In Genesis 9, Noah and his family had survived the flood, and the whole world was theirs. They were prosperous, and life was easy. Noah shamed himself by becoming drunk and cursed his son Ham.

In Judges 2, God had given the nation Israel the Promised Land. They rested at last with no more wandering in the desert. But as soon as brave and faithful Joshua died, they fell into the idolatrous corruptible practices of the Canaanites.

2 Samuel 11 tells us that David ruled well, and Israel was a dominant nation politically, economically, and militarily. But in the midst of prosperity and success, David committed adultery with Bathsheba and had her husband, Uriah, murdered.

King Solomon truly had it all: power, wealth, fame, and wisdom. But his very abundance was the source of his downfall. He loved his pagan idolatrous wives so much that he allowed himself and Israel to copy their detestable religious rites. 'The LORD became angry with Solomon because his heart had turned away from the LORD, the God of Israel, who had appeared to him twice. Although he had forbidden Solomon to follow other gods, Solomon did not keep the LORD'S command. So the LORD said to Solomon, "Since this is your attitude and you have not kept my covenant and my decrees, which I commanded you, I will most certainly tear the kingdom away from you and give it to one of your subordinates' (see 1 Kings 11).

Jesus adds his voice to this theme by saying that it can be very very difficult for a rich person to enter heaven:

> Jesus looked at him and said, "How hard it is for the rich to enter the kingdom of God! Indeed, it is easier for a camel to go through the eye of a needle than for a rich man to enter the kingdom of God." Those who heard this asked, "Who then can be saved?" Jesus replied, "What is impossible with men is possible with God (Luke 18:24-27).

What is impossible with men is possible with God. Rich people, like anyone else desperately need God, else they cannot enter heaven.

Some poor people want to be rich, while some rich people want the simple life of the poor. This is what one rich man said:

> I think about all the weight I could lose if I couldn't afford three meals a day. I mean, it's so hard to have the discipline to skip a meal. But if financial circumstances simply make it impossible to eat, it's like having your own personal diet coach! And without having to worry about teleconferences and meetings all day, poor people are free to spend as much time as they want on their yachts, unburdened by the meaningless demands of the rat race. Without obligations to their shareholders and partners, they can just take off spontaneously to Martha's Vineyard or Cannes whenever they want. Poor people always think it's a cakewalk being rich, but the truth is it's absolutely exhausting. So many possessions to manage and worry about so, many business irons in the fire to keep going. My friends and I are always trying to figure out how to *simplify*, you know? The poor are really lucky, if you think about it. I wish I could have the kind of simplicity, the kind of clear priorities that must come with lacking worldly possessions.

I think every rich person will agree to this honest confession. Building their lives on God's word can help them to deal with such problems, because God's word provides guidance on how to live a balanced life. For example 1 Timothy 6:6-9 reminds us that 'godliness with contentment is great gain. We brought nothing into the world, and we can take nothing out of it. But if we have food and clothing, we will be content with that.' People who want to get rich fall into temptation and a trap and into many foolish and harmful desires that plunge men into ruin and destruction.

Let us briefly discuss the subject of stinginess in this paragraph. There are people who have been blessed with so much money and earthly possessions, but unfortunately are very stingy. As Craig Bloomberg rightly makes the point, 'in wealthy nations such as Britain and the USA, individuals accumulate much wealth through various means and yet are daily exposed to the plight of the poor, whether the homeless on their own city streets or starving children on their TV screens'. What actions should they take on behalf of the poor and the needy? Scripture gives the following advice:

> Command those who are rich in this present world not to be arrogant nor to put their hope in wealth, which is so uncertain, but to put their hope in God, who richly provides us with everything for our enjoyment. Command them to do good, to be rich in good deeds, and to be generous and willing to share. In this way they will lay up treasure for themselves as a firm foundation for the coming age, so that they may take hold of the life that is truly life (1 Timothy 6:17-19).

Rich people need someone to command and guide them on how they are to live a balanced life. This is one of the many benefits in addition to eternal life that a rich person will benefit for building his or her life on the principles of God. Let us talk about the emancipation of the poor and the needy in the next paragraph.

9.2 Guidance for Poor people: How the poor desperately need God

The dictionary defines a poor person as someone who lacks sufficient money to live a standard life considered comfortable or normal in a society. Poor people do not have enough food, clothing, education or healthcare; they live in areas that are prone to diseases, crime and natural disasters. Their basic civil and human rights are often nonexistent. Being a poor person can mean being deprived economically, politically, and socially. How do poor people describe poverty themselves? In Ethiopia they say it is "[living from] hour to hour"; in Jamaica "living in bondage, waiting to be free"; in Cambodia "working for more than 18 hours a day, but still not having enough to feed [yourself]"; in the western countries poverty is described as living from "hand to mouth".

Poor people are not just those who do not have enough or those in need. As Sobrino rightly makes the point in his book Spirituality *of liberation*, 'the poor people are trash and offal of humanity, crucified by the structures of this world. If they resist, they are crucified suddenly and violently. If they do not resist, they are crucified gradually and slowly'. If a poor person does not to help himself or herself with the help of God it is possible that they may die in poverty and pass on their misery to their children. On the other hand, if poor people try to escape their plight, our society unnecessarily makes it very difficult for them to make descent living. But how do people become poor? It is true that some people become poor because they are lazy (Proverbs 10:4). Others too inherit poverty from their parents. Sometimes people become poor because, the system and structure of this world do not favour them, so they end up becoming poor. Poor people are always at a disadvantaged, and so what will they benefit by believing in God?

The poor seem to have special favour from God

The God who created the heavens and the earth is the Father of all mankind. But Of the poor of this world, it can be rightly said that they have hope, and that the struggle for their liberation is with the help of God. Poor people seem to have special favour from God as the following scriptures make clear.

> He who oppresses the poor shows contempt for their Maker, but whoever is kind to the needy honors God (Proverbs 14:31).

> He who is kind to the poor lends to the LORD, and He will reward him for what he has done (Proverbs 19:17).

> If a man shuts his ears to the cry of the poor, he too will cry out and not be answered (Proverbs 21:13).

> For God, who was at work in the ministry of Peter as an apostle to the Jews, was also at work in my ministry as an apostle to the Gentiles. James, Peter and John, those reputed to be pillars, gave me and Barnabas the right hand of fellowship when they recognized the grace given to me. They agreed that we should go to the Gentiles, and they to the Jews. **All they asked was that we should continue to remember the poor, the very thing I was eager to do** (Galatians 2:8-10).

There are many scriptures which confirm the fact that the poor and the needy have a special place in the heart of God. Jesus made this point clear in His manifesto, and He lived to fulfill that promise.

> The Spirit of the Lord is on me, because He has anointed me to preach good news to the poor. He has sent me to proclaim freedom for the prisoners and recovery of sight for the blind, to release the oppressed, to proclaim the year of the Lord's favor (Luke 4:18-19).

Many poor people have managed to overcome some of these handicaps through their resilience and resourcefulness, often helped by their spirituality and philanthropy. Until the 18th century, poverty was seen as inevitable. But since the 1880s the reduction in extreme poverty – from three-quarters to one-fifth of the world's population – shows that the number of poor people in the world can be further reduced, if not eliminated.

There are still many people who do not know what to do in order to earn some money for daily living. In my previous book, *How Unity can benefit you, the family, the church, and the nation,* I have discussed some of the things people can do to earn a descent living. Please get a copy of this book from your local bookstore or Amazon if necessary.

As at February 2014, the number of unemployed young people in the UK stood at almost one million and, unlike adult unemployment, this number has hardly fallen since the recession in 2008. For the UK, higher unemployment leads to lost economic productivity and higher welfare costs. And the costs for the individual are even more profound, unemployment can have scarring effects on wages; increase the likelihood of future spells of unemployment; and affect mental and physical wellbeing. Successive governments have tried and failed to tackle this crisis and one of the aims of this book is to help and encourage people to start thinking of other means of employing themselves. Without any source of money, no one can survive in our modern world. This makes money one of the main pillars of life alongside family life and ultimately faith in God, arguably though.

How can we help the poor? Is it enough to give them food, clothing and shelter usually from the surplus of the rich? In this book I would suggest that, we must do more than providing food and clothing for the needy. We should go a step further, to empower them, and provide opportunities for them to acquire descent living for themselves. The banks and the financial institutions should help the poor and the needy with lower interest rates on loans, overdraft, mortgages, and other credit facilities. There should be less vigour on credit checks for the poor and the needy. Most poor people will always have a bad credit score because they do not have the money to make regular payments. Rich people can easily afford to settle their debts compared to the poor. Unfortunately, rich people get the best interest rates, meaning they pay less on what they borrow. The poor has to pay more on what they borrow. The poor person is always at a disadvantage.

I believe the needy and poor people also have their role to play in emancipating themselves. Yes, it is true that sometimes our world system does not favour them, but they should encourage themselves to persevere, work hard and make good use of the little opportunities that will come their way. They must adopt a winning mentality. They must learn not to remain consumers perpetually. They should stop complaining and put up a brave face. They should not expect the rich to pity them, but rather they should work hard and put their hope in God, because God will never leave them nor forsake them.

We all have a personal responsibility towards materialism, because we live in a materialistic world. Let us discuss this further in the next section.

9.3 Guidance for Your Personal responsibility towards materialism

Responsibility is defined as 'something that one should do because it is morally right or legally required to do so'. We have all been placed in a world which is both material and spiritual. Each and every one of us has their own duty towards the material things they acquire; how they can invest them well and how they can avoid materialism dictating life to them. One becomes a slave to whatever is controlling them. Many people are controlled by material things. Some have become slaves of money instead of money serving them. Some people could not invest what they acquired well, and so they end up becoming poor in the end. Some have also been able to manage the little they were entrusted with, and have left a good inheritance for the generations to come.

Putting God first above money is your responsibility; giving to help the poor is your responsibility; giving to help God's kingdom is your responsibility, not oppressing the poor is your responsibility, and investing wisely is your responsibility. Materialism goes with proper responsibility; this is called stewardship in Christianity. A steward is one who manages the possessions of another. We are all stewards of the resources, abilities and opportunities that God has entrusted to our care, and one day each one of us will be called to give an account on how we have managed what the Master has given us.

Dealing with enemies of Materialism

An enemy is someone or something that harms or threatens someone. Many people are working very hard, but immorality is robbing them of the reward of their hard work. This is a secret enemy in people's life, hardly detected. Immoral lifestyles, sometimes appeals to the flesh and so many people indulge in it without taking into account that they are courting or embracing their enemy of progress. In this section we will be looking at some of these enemies of money: the common ones are pleasure, power, and fame.

1. Pleasure – alcohol, drugs, gambling sexual trek

Pleasure can be defined as a state of gratification. Pleasure can be an enemy of materialism in the sense that, one may have to spend a lot of money in order to experience this state of gratification. Proverbs 21:17 says 'He who loves pleasure will become poor; whoever loves wine and oil will never be rich'. Many people spend money which could have been used on something beneficial on cigarettes, drugs, sexual trek, entertainment, alcohol etc.

2. Power

Power can also be an enemy of materialism in the sense that, people who have money tend to crave for power. They sometimes end up spending all their resources in other avenues to become powerful. Abraham Lincoln once said "Nearly all men can stand adversity. But if you want to test a man's character give him power." **Lord Acton**—was an English Catholic historian, politician, and writer. He is famous for his remark, "Power tends to corrupt, and absolute power corrupts absolutely." Most great men are almost always bad men because of power. Please do not use your resources to obtain power over people. Power over people can be an enemy of materialism. You may end up losing everything. But seek power from above, coming from the Father in heaven.

Power based on love is a thousand times more effective and helpful than the one acquired by any other means. Jesus said "you will receive power when the Holy Spirit comes on you; and you will be My witnesses in Jerusalem, and in all Judea and Samaria, and to the ends of the earth" (Acts 1:8). "For God will not give us a spirit of timidity, but a spirit of power, of love and of self-discipline" (2 Timothy 1:7). Seek power from God to serve humanity in rescuing them from the kingdom of darkness to the kingdom of light in Christ Jesus.

3. Fame

Fame is the state of being known by many people. Fame defines you to a certain degree: "it [can] puff you up, or it [can] shrink you down," said one celebrity. Desiring to be famous can be a dangerous drug. The unfortunate truth, however, is that for each and every celebrity, the fame machine can only churn for so long. As a former famous pop star revealed, "I've been addicted to almost every substance known to man at one point or another and the most addicting of them all is fame." As was evidenced in the recent death of 48-year-old Whitney Houston, fame and being a celebrity can closely mirror substance abuse symptomatology — and over time, result in actual substance abuse, isolation, mistrust, dysfunctional adaptation to fame, and then, too often, untimely death. The examples are familiar: from Judy Garland to River Phoenix, and Michael Jackson to Whitney Houston.

Please do not use your resources to obtain stardom. Humble yourself, and learn how to serve people. Fame is a secret enemy and can destroy you. According to scripture "Anyone who chooses to be a friend of the world becomes an enemy of God." Or do you think Scripture says without reason that the spirit He caused to live in us envies intensely? But He gives us more grace. That is why Scripture says: "God opposes the proud but gives grace to the humble" (James 4:4–16).

There are many more enemies of materialism. Only three have been discussed in this section. The lesson here is that as you strive to make ends meet, it is possible that you will become rich. In case you become rich by accident or by purpose, please be mindful of these enemies. Learn how to live responsibly; acquire the grace to invest wisely.

Wise investments

Investment is time, energy, or matter spent in the hope of future benefits actualized within a specified date or time frame. Investments have different meaning in economics, finance, and religion. The term "sowing and reaping" can be what investment means in Christianity. You reap what you sow:

> Do not be deceived: God cannot be mocked. A man reaps what he sows. The one who sows to please his sinful nature, from that nature will reap destruction; the one who sows to please the Spirit, from the Spirit will reap eternal life. Let us not become weary in doing good, for at the proper time we will reap a harvest if we do not give up. Therefore, as we have opportunity, let us do good to all people, especially to those who belong to the family of believers (Galatians 6:7-10).

How can someone make proper use of their resources? Clues to the answer lie in becoming part of something larger than oneself and dedicating all one's drives and ambitions into making a real difference, in a meaningful way, in the world. If you plant to please your desires on pleasure, power and/or fame, it is likely you will reap a crop of sorrow and disappointment. If you plant to please God on helping others, building your family, donating to support the kingdom of God, winning souls, making the worship of God a priority, you will reap joy and everlasting life.

Invest your drive, talent, energy and money into something bigger than yourself. God is building His kingdom, and He is inviting everyone to be part of it. This is one area to invest your resources, which will be used to train more missionaries and to send them to other parts of the world to preach the gospel. You can start off by thinking of something you can do, which you will also be able to leave behind as a legacy for the next generation. There are numerous opportunities to invest wisely. If there are poor people in your area, you can help them to come out of poverty.

Heavenly Father, thank you for the riches I have in Christ. Help me use what I have to help other people and to extend your kingdom, amen.

You may not need God in order to make money- but this can be very dangerous

Sometimes life can be a mystery! As the title of this section suggests, people can make money without believing in God or without worshipping God, but this can be very dangerous. Many people do not see the need to believe in God because they are of the opinion that, although they do not believe in God life is okay for them. They seem to have good jobs, stable families, healthy lifestyle, just to name a few of the things they pride themselves in: the following reasons throw more light on this assertion.

Firstly, during creation, God endowed mankind with abilities, talents, authority etc. That is why people seem to be doing well although some may not believe in God nor worship Him. Pagans can do great things in this world, although they do not acknowledge God in their lives. This also explains why some rich people do not go to church, or worship God but seem to prosper. These qualities and abilities God has given mankind, however are limited, they are not enough. Therefore whoever tries to live in this world without the influence of God, can certainly achieve something, but he or she will be in serious need or will be found wanting at some point in life, either on this earth or after death on the judgement day. Even a casual look around us, tells that humanity does not have all the answers to our problems, socially, politically, spiritually and individually. This is because at creation, God did not give man all the abilities he will need to live without His influence. The little abilities, talents and authority people have are meant to fade in quality and potency.

Another reason why people can be rich without the influence of God is that, Satan can also make people rich easily. In fact, many people have been made rich through Satan's influence over their lives, directly or indirectly. But this is very dangerous because Satan and all his followers are going to perish one day (Revelation 18:1-8). Sadly, many people are not aware of the sources of their material blessings. No one needs any introduction to the aim of Satan or what Satan is up to. Satan's main agenda is to steal, kill and destroy (John 10:10). Satan steals people from God through deception, enticement, temptation, oppression. He kills people through sickness, accident, suicide, wars, murdering. He destroys people's souls by leading them to hell fire, because hell fire is his final destination. Satan will take all his followers to be with him in hell fire at the judgement day (Revelation 20:7-19). Followers of Satan seem to be many in this world. Why don't you decide to be a follower of God? Join the people of God today!

The third reason why it can be dangerous to make money or to live without the influence of God is that, God is the owner of this world, and He is the one everybody is accountable to (Psalm 24:1; Romans 2:6-11). Therefore God can decide to discipline and strip bad people of their blessings, being money, talents, power or even their lives. I have seen a lot of people of whom God striped off their material blessings because of arrogance and irresponsible living. The following scripture throws more light on this:

> Then Jesus told them a parable, saying, the land of a rich man was fertile *and* yielded plentifully. And he considered *and* debated within himself, what shall I do? I have no place [in which] to gather together my harvest. And he said I will do this: I will pull down my storehouses and build larger ones, and there I will store all my grain *or produce* and my goods. And I will say to my soul, Soul, you have many good things laid up, [enough] for many years. Take your ease; eat, drink, *and* enjoy yourself merrily. But God said to him, You fool! This very night they [the messengers of God] will demand your soul of you; and

all the things that you have prepared, whose will they be? So it is with the one who continues to lay up *and* hoard possessions for himself and is not rich [in his relation] to God (Luke 12:16-21).

To be rich towards God means you have a good relationship with Him. How rich are you in relation toward God? Do you know that God is watching over you? Although people can be rich or live their lives without God, this can be very dangerous. Please follow the discussion to the end.

The danger in boasting about tomorrow

Material things are fleeting. Even though people desire to live for a long time, none can be certain that they will. No one can assure himself or herself of more than the present time. It is assumed that the time of a person's life will be threescore and ten, yet no one can be sure of living that long. We are not to take for granted that the Lord will give us a tomorrow. We must use today to get prepared for tomorrow. As we prepare for tomorrow, we are to continually depend upon the providence of God. We are not to leave God out of our daily plans.

Now listen, you who say, "Today or tomorrow we will go to this or that city, spend a year there, carry on business and make money". Why, you do not even know what will happen tomorrow. What is your life? You are a mist that appears for a little while and then vanishes (James 4: 13-14).

Some business men and women think the future is under their control. They boast about what they can do yet leave God out of the equation only to be disappointed. We can get so used to the daily routine of living our lives that we forget we have no ultimate control over our lives. We get annoyed when the smooth running of our life is disrupted by a tailback on the motorway, a piece of technology which will not work or a domestic emergency or illness.

A Syrian Bishop put it like this: 'I don't know what the future holds, but I do know who holds the future'. We need to live our lives in the full expectation that God may well break in at some stage and change the plans we have made. He is God, after all. Kings Solomon advises us to 'trust in the LORD with all your heart and lean not on your own understanding; in all your ways acknowledge him, and he will make your paths straight. Do not be wise in your own eyes; fear the LORD and shun evil. This will bring health to your body and nourishment to your bones' (Proverbs 3:5-8). We can say this prayer together: Lord, help us not to be so attached to the plans we have made that we have no time for yours, help us Lord!

So far in this chapter, we have looked at how scripture can guide us when it comes to materialism. We have seen how both the rich and the poor need God in their daily lives. We have also made the point that we all have a responsibility to manage our material resources well.

How do you interpret a given document? How do you interpret the Bible? Let us discuss these issues in the next chapter.

Chapter 10

Proper use of God's word: Guidelines

It is quite common to hear people dismiss an interpretation by saying, 'that is your interpretation' or something like 'you are interpreting the Bible that way to make it fit your opinion'. It is true that Christians sometimes have different interpretations of the same biblical passage; it is also true that some interpretations are better than others. In this section an attempt will be made to discuss how one can use the word of God correctly. Using the word of God correctly boils down to how one interpret a particular text in the Bible correclty. This is important because if you are going to build your life on what God has said, then it is important that you get the message right. This will involve the act of interpreting the Bible and its practical application. This is call hermeneutics and practical theology respectively. Hermeneutics is the science of interpretation, especially of the Scriptures or the branch of theology that deals with the principles of Biblical exegesis[18]. Practical Theology on the other hand, as its name implies, is the study of theology in a way that is intended to make it useful or applicable. Its emphasis is on how all the teaching of Scripture should affect the way we live today.

For many years, the major approach to biblical interpretation was to look at the author, the individual book, and the particular section

---

[18] Exegesis is a critical explanation or interpretation or biblical text

in great depth. In some cases this resulted in lengthy discussions of the way in which the book was composed, and in an extreme instances a search for different original sources. More recently, there has been an emphasis on interpreting scripture as it stands and seeing each passage in the context of other scriptures around it. But I think we need to go further and see each of the particular text we are interested in the overall context of scripture.

Let us in a brief moment look at some of the various approaches to biblical interpretations that are in use. The **Historical–grammatical** principle is based on historical, socio–political, geographical, cultural and linguistic / grammatical context. The **Dispensational model** or The **Chronometrical Principle** holds the view that during different periods of time, God has chosen to deal in a particular way with mankind in respect to sin and mankind's responsibility. The **New–Covenantal** model holds the view that the Old Testament Laws have been fulfilled and abrogated or cancelled with Christ's death, and replaced with the Law of Christ of the New Covenant, although many of the Old Covenant laws are reinstituted under the New Covenant. The **Christo–Centric Principle** holds the view that the mind of deity is eternally centered in Christ. All angelic thought and ministry are centered in Christ. All Satanic hatred and subtlety are centered at Christ. All human hopes are, and human occupations should be, centered in Christ. The whole material universe in creation is centered in Christ. The entire written word is centered in Christ. The **Application Principle** holds the view that an application of truth may be made only after the correct interpretation has been made. The **Context Principle** holds the view that God gives light upon a subject through either near or remote passages bearing upon the same subject. In this book, we will make use of some of these techniques, including some of the methods the Jewish people use to interpret scripture.

The Bible is God's book, written through human authors to convey a true and clear message about God and his world. The task of the Bible reader is to continue to seek that sure meaning and respond in trust and obedient living. The meanings of the majority of passages in the Bible are plain and obvious. Some passages in the Bible can be taken at face value, others cannot. Let us look at this passage:

> He [Jesus] said to them, "Go into all the world and preach the good news to all creation. Whoever believes and is baptized will be saved, but whoever does not believe will be condemned. And these signs will accompany those who believe: In my name they will drive out demons; they will speak in new tongues; they will pick up snakes with their hands; and when they drink deadly poison, it will not hurt them at all; they will place their hands on sick people, and they will get well (Mark 16:15-18).

Look at this text, which aspect do you think can be taken at face value and which cannot be taken at face value? It is clear that one can take all the text at face value perhaps except 'they will pick up snakes with their hands; and when they drink deadly poison, it will not hurt them at all'. Of course if you intentionally pick up poisonous snakes with your hands, you are likely to get bitten by these snakes even if you have believed the good news, repented, been baptized and are filled with the Holy Spirit. Therefore this text we just analyzed cannot be taken at face value.

The apostle Peter advices readers of the Holy Scripture thus:

> Bear in mind that our Lord's patience means salvation, just as our dear brother Paul also wrote you with the wisdom that God gave him. He [Paul] writes the same way in all his letters, speaking in them of these matters. His letters contain some things that are hard to understand, which ignorant and unstable people distort, as they do the other Scriptures, to their own destruction (2 Peter 3:15-16).

The Apostle Paul's letters for example, contain some things that are hard to understand, which ignorant and unstable people distort, as they do the other Scriptures, to their own destruction. What principles can one use to interpret a Biblical passage so that one will not distort the message of God to one's own detriment? There are many principles, we should not forget our need to depend on the Holy Spirit to help us understand the scripture, but this will be looked at in detail in a later section. Let us look at our first guiding principles of scripture interpretation.

1. Understanding God's Purpose for all creation

God is a God of purpose. He has his own reason for doing what he does. This notion must be taken into consideration when you interpret any portion of the Bible for your practical application. In the book of Genesis 12:1-13, God purposes can be summarised as:

> I will bless those who bless you, and whoever curses you I will curse; and all peoples on earth will be blessed through you.

From the text just read and others in both the Old and New Testaments, it is clear that the reason God blesses people with good health, family, good job, salvation, and spiritual gifts is to be a blessing to other people, so that as many people as possible can enter his kingdom. Every scripture should be interpreted in the light of God's purpose. So, as you build your life on the word of God, remember that the benefit you will enjoy should not be private but that through you others should also be blessed.

Understanding God's purpose for all creation can help you avoid applying God's principles selfishly. Selfishness is one of the common reasons why many people do not benefit much from practicing God's principles. Many prayers are not answered because such prayers are too self-centred. For example God's word or instructions on marriage is not meant for the benefit of the couples alone, but also for the benefit of God himself, other people and the society as a whole. Most marriages do not do well because the couples live for themselves alone forgetting that God also has an interest in the marriage and that they are to use their marriage to glorify him, help the church, and help other people.

Every benefit one enjoys from building his or her life on God's principles should be received in the light of God's purpose for giving such blessings. In the writings of the prophet Ezekiel and others in the Old Testament, God's purpose or reason why He will make Israel holy and righteous was not because the nation Israel deserves it. But it was because of God's Holy name which the people had profaned among the nations. This assertion is also confirmed in the New Testament, where Paul says in the book of Ephesians that Christ loved the church and gave himself up for her to make her holy, cleansing her by the washing with water through the word, and to present her to himself as a radiant church, without stain or wrinkle or any other blemish, but holy and blameless (Ephesians 5:25-27).

From this text, the reason why people receive the gift of righteousness is so that they can have fellowship with God. God is holy, so those who want to have fellowship with God must be holy as well (Hebrews 12:14). As you put your faith in Jesus Christ, God will help you to become righteous, but remember to use your new spiritual state to glorify God and to help your friends who do not know Jesus as their Lord and saviour.

The main point in this section is that people should always take into account why God blesses them, when they are enjoying the fruit of their labor or when they are applying the Holy Scriptures to their day to day activities. Let us look at the next guidelines people should use when interpreting or applying the scriptures to their lives.

2. Scripture can be interpreted literally

This principle is technically known as the historical-grammatical method of interpreting scripture. This method takes the natural, straightforward sense of a text or passage as fundamental. A 'literal' approach requires that we interpret Scripture:

1. According to the original meaning. God's Word is almost always immediately relevant to the situation to which it was addressed; we need, therefore to uncover as fully as possible

the original setting and meaning before attempting to relate it to ourselves.

2. According to literary form. The Bible is made up of all kinds of literature: poetry, prose, parables, allegory (Ezekiel16), apocalyptic (Revelation), fable (Judges.9:8–15), etc. The type of literature must always be taken into account when interpreting scripture. This is not to say that a poetic section, for example, cannot convey factual material, but it means one will not interpret poetic or visionary material in the same way as historical narrative or doctrinal passages. We must also be sensitive to the use of metaphor and other figures of speech.

3. According to context. The setting of a text or a saying in the section and book of the Bible in which it occurs is fundamental to correct interpretation. It should be noted in this connection that the division of the books in the Bible into chapter and verse are not original.

3. The author intensions for writing the book

Sometimes, in reading the Bible, it is important to find out why the writer wrote that particular book in the Bible or that particular section or verse. We then take our interpretation and relate it to the teaching of Scripture as a whole. In this way, our overall understanding develops. Knowing the authors intensions for writing a particular book in the bible also helps us not to worry about some of the issues the writer did not discussed. For example, John's main aim in writing the book of John is stated thus:

> Jesus did many other miraculous signs in the presence of his disciples, which are not recorded in this book. But these are written that you may believe that Jesus is the Christ, the Son of God, and that by believing you may have life in his name (John 20:30-31).

Here you can see that John selected few events of Jesus' life to prove a point. His main argument is that he wants people to believe that Jesus is the Son of God and that by believing in him, they may have eternal life. There could be other issues John could have addressed, but he did not. In this case, anyone who has any problem or question about the book of John, which the author did not address, can embark on his or her own study to find answers. Always find out the author's intention of writing the book or the passage or that particular verse before you do any application. This will help you to know what he is interested in and what he is not. Let us take another example to illustrate this principle:

Stop drinking only water, and use a little wine because of your stomach and your frequent illnesses (1 Timothy 5:23).

From this text, it is clear that the reason why Paul told Timothy to take 'a little wine' was because of his stomach and frequent illness, for medicinal purpose. Some people unfortunately use this verse to justify alcoholism.

4. The background situation

In reading any book in the Bible, it is sometimes helpful to know the culture of the people, the life conditions of the people and sometimes the geo-location of the people to whom the writer wrote the book to. For example, we can only see the distinctive place and true significance of the books of Amos and Hebrews if we know that the books are addressed to different people in different situations. We shall also understand better why Amos spoke as he did if we know something about the social conditions in Israel during the eight century BC. We shall not feel the full force of the warnings in Hebrews until we have begun to comprehend the pressures faced by first-century Jewish Christians.

5. Using other scriptures to interpret a particular scripture

There are at times when a particular text cannot adequately explain itself. If such case arises, it is a good practice for one to look elsewhere in the bible where the same subject is discussed. For example, Paul's statement:

> ... 'the living God who is the saviour of all men... '(1 Timothy 4:10).

This could be taken as an indication that no one will be lost. But a reading of the rest 1 Timothy 4:10 and John 3:16 for example make it clear that this is completely contrary to Paul's purpose of writng that verse. As another example, let us look at Hebrews 6: 4-6:

> It is impossible for those who have once been enlightened, who have tasted the heavenly gift, who have shared in the Holy Spirit, who have tasted the goodness of the word of God and the powers of the coming age, if they fall away, to be brought back to repentance, because to their loss they are crucifying the Son of God all over again and subjecting him to public disgrace.

This passage has caused many interpreters great difficulty. The question people often ask is, can a believe fall away? People who don't believe in "eternal security" think the passage refers to Christians who fall away from the faith. Others, such as John Calvin, insist that the author of Hebrews must be referring to people who never fully became Christians, because other verses seem to teach the eternal security of those in Christ (see John 5:24; 6:37; Romans 8:1; Hebrews 8:12).

Regardless, the author is writing about a hypothetical situation. He is not describing what happened, but only what could happen: if such a 'falling away' ever did occur, it would be impossible to rescue such people again. To help get a proper understanding, we can look at other books in the Bible which talks about the subject of 'falling away'. In the book of Jude, the writer says ' And the angels who did not keep their positions of authority but abandoned their own home—these he has kept in darkness, bound with everlasting chains for judgment on the great Day (Jude 1:6). Here, one can say that if the angels who were in heaven fell away, then Christians can also fall away beyond recovery. In Genesis 3, we know that Adam and Eve disobeyed God and so they were thrown out of the Garden of Eden. Base on what happened to Adam and Eve, one can say that a believer can also disobey God beyond divine forbearance and could miss heaven as a result. Some people however interpret this text differently.

There may be at times when you may even need a bible dictionary in order to understand a particular text or word of scripture. There are many biblical dictionaries in use these days. Consult your pastor or a church leader before deciding which one to use.

6. Application – Putting into practice what God says

Building your life on God's principles involves putting into practice what God has to say. Practising the word of God is synonymous to taken a medicine. Unless the medicine is taken, the patient cannot experience the healing effect of the medicine. Many people only hear God's word without putting them into practice:

> Why do you call me, 'Lord, Lord,' and do not do what I say? I will show you what he is like who comes to me and hears my words and puts them into practice. He is like a man building a house, who dug down deep and laid the foundation on rock. When a flood came, the torrent struck that house but could not shake it, because it was well built. But the one who hears my words and does not put them into practice is like a man who built a house on the ground without a foundation. The moment the torrent struck that house, it collapsed and its destruction was complete (Luke 6:46-49).

In this text, practicing God's word seems to be more important to Jesus than just listening or even calling upon his name. He describes practicing God's word as building a house on a good foundation which is able to resist the pressures of life. And so in order for one to build their lives on God's principles, one has to put into practice what the Bible says. You can believe all the right things, yet still be dead wrong. That is why James also encourages believers this way:

> Do not merely listen to the word, and so deceive yourselves. Do what it says. Anyone who listens to the word but does not do what it says is like a man who looks at his face in a mirror and, after looking at himself, goes away and immediately forgets what he looks like. But the man who looks intently into the perfect law that gives freedom, and continues to do this, not forgetting what he has heard, but doing it—he will be blessed in what he does (James 1:22-25).

God is more interested in the doing aspect than just the accumulation of knowledge. James says, people deceive themselves if they only listen or read the word of God without putting them into practice. I have seen many Christians whose lives are not built on solid foundation because they don't practice what the Bible says, although they claim to be believers. It is the doing that makes the difference, not just the knowing about the Bible or scripture quotations.

In applying God's word to your day to day life, your behaviour patterns and attitude will be challenged. Love for God and neighbour should be the yardstick by which people are to practice the principles of God.

> Teacher, which is the greatest commandment in the Law? Jesus replied: Love the Lord your God with all your heart and with all your soul and with all your mind. This is the first and greatest commandment. And the second is like it: 'Love your neighbor as yourself. All the Law and the Prophets hang on these two commandments (Matthew 22:36-40).

By fulfilling these two commands, a person keeps all the other commandments of God. Jesus says that if we truly love God and our neighbour, we are naturally keep all the commandments. Because if one loves God, he or she will not be selfish with the benefits he or she receives. This is looking at God's law positively. Sometimes, rather than worrying about all we should not do, we should concentrate on all we can do to show our love for God and others. Let us look at two more principles to guide us in interpreting the Bible.

7. Midrash- Jewish interpretation of the Bible

If one looks at the way the New Testament quotes the Old Testament; it is clear that the apostles did not use western protestant methods of exegesis or interpretation[19]. Jesus was considered a Rabbi. Paul was a Rabbi. They interpreted the Bible in the way other Rabbis did. So in this section we will look at an introduction to "Midrash", one of the methods Jewish people interprets the Bible. The Jewish people were the original recipients of the Holy Scriptures although some of the New Testament books were written by non Jews.

The apostle Paul lamented when his own people as a nation failed to receive Christ as their saviour in his days: 'For I could wish that I myself were cursed and cut off from Christ for the sake of my brothers, those of my own race, the people of Israel. Theirs is the adoption as sons; theirs the divine glory, the covenants, the receiving of the law, the temple worship and the promises. Theirs are the patriarchs, and from them is traced the human ancestry of Christ, who is God over all, forever praised! Amen'[20]. The Jews were the chosen recipients of the Holy Scriptures. It is therefore important that readers of the Bible look at how the Jewish people view the Holy Scriptures.

For example, when we come to consider Biblical prophecy, the western mind says that prophecy consist of a prediction and a fulfilment. But to the ancient Jewish mind, prophecy was not

---

[19] According to James Jacob Prasch in *Grain for Famine*, St. Matthew Publishing, Cambridge, 2000
[20] Romans 9: 3-5

a question of something being predicted, then being fulfilled. That is a wrong view of biblical prophecy, according to the Jewish mind. Rather, to the Jewish, **prophecy was a pattern** which is recapitulated; a prophecy having multiple fulfilment. And each cycle teaches something about the ultimate fulfilments. The ultimate fulfil of every prophecy is in Christ Jesus. The Jewish see the word of God (prophecy) as a pattern with multiple fulfilments, the ultimate fulfilment is in Christ. Once a prophecy has been fulfilled in Christ, there is no need for people to look forward to its fulfilment again. Any reference to such prophecy in terms of its future fulfilment can be considered as a faulty scriptural interpretation.

Let us take some examples to illustrate this principle further. Just as Moses led the Israelites out of Egypt through the water (Red sea) into the Promised Land, so Jesus Christ leads believers out of the world through baptism into heaven. To the New Testament believer, heaven is our Promised Land. In Exodus 15:1, we sing the song of Moses after they had crossed the red sea: *the horse and its rider are thrown into the red sea.* We see the same pattern in Revelations 15:3 where we sing the song of Moses– why? Because everything is a pattern, what happened in the past can and will happen in the future, until it find its fulfilment in Christ. That is why the apostle Paul could say to his Roman readers that, 'Christ is the end of the law' [of Moses] (Romans 10:4).

Let us look at another example. Just as Moses made a covenant with blood and sprinkled it on the people (Exodus 24:8) so did Jesus. Jesus has made a covenant with believers and sprinkled us with his blood (1 Peter 1:2). Moses fasted for forty days; Jesus also fasted for forty days (Luke 4). What can you say about Moses and Jesus Christ? Using Midrash to interpret the word of God it is easy to see that Jesus is the prophet God promised the Israelite in Deuteronomy 18:18 who will be like Moses. Let us take another example. In Amos 8:11 -12 that Bible says:

> The days are coming," declares the Sovereign LORD,
> "when I will send a famine through the land—not

a famine of food or a thirst for water, but a famine of
hearing the words of the LORD. Men will stagger from
sea to sea and wander from north to east searching for the
word of the LORD, but they will not find it.

A lack of food is famine. A lack of the word of God is also considered
as famine. During the Inter-Testaments period which lasted for about
420 years, the people had the Maccabaeus, but they had no prophets.
There were no prophets from the time of Malachi to the time of John
the baptism, and so there was no spoken or written word from God
to the people. There was famine of the word of God in those days.
John the Baptist came in the spirit of Elijah and fed God's people by
preaching God's word during a famine (Luke 1:11-17; Matt 17:10-
13). So it will be before Jesus comes the second time. Because of
persecution, God's servants cannot preach the gospel anymore, there
will be famine for hearing the word of God, until mighty angels give
a final witness of the gospel to the people (read Revelation 14:6-7).

What lesson can you learn from all this? If you are privileged to
hear God's word today, do not hardened your heart, but responds to
God's invitation, and accept him to your life. Build your life on his
word for a better future. It is possible that a time is coming when
you may not have the opportunity to hear God's message again. You
may not have anyone to take personal interest in the salvation of your
soul. You may not have anyone to encourage you to seek God or
to tell you to pray or to go church. You may experience famine of
the word of God if you do not receive God's offer of life now. Don't
forget that there is time for everything under the sun. Today may be
the day God is reaching you with his word that is why perhaps you
are reading this book. I tell you, now is the time of God's favor, now
is the day of salvation. Let us continue our discussion on how you
can interpret scripture using Midrash.

The Use of typology and allegory in Midrash: Midrash sometimes
uses typology and allegory (symbols) – in order to illustrate and
illumine the word of God. Typology is the study and interpretation
of types and symbols, originally especially in the Bible. In typology,

things in the New Testament are prefigured or symbolized by things in the Old Testament. Both typology and allegory use symbols. For examples, Jesus is "the Passover lamb" in the New Testament. That is why Paul could say that 'Christ, our Passover lamb has been sacrificed' (1 Corinthians 5:7). The Passover was first celebrated in Egypt. The blood of this sacrifice sprinkled on the door-posts of the Israelites was to be a sign to the angel of God, when passing through the land to slay the first-born of the Egyptians (Exodus 12:1-28). In fact, the bringing of the Passover sacrifice resumed only after the Israelites had taken possession of the land, and then the sacrifice was made annually until during the times when Solomon's Temple and the Second Temple stood and functioned. During this time there was a definite ritual for the offering, in addition to the regulations prescribed by the Law. But as Paul said,'Christ is the end of the law so that there may be righteousness for everyone who believes' (Romans 10:4). Jesus is your Passover lamb. He has already been sacrificed. If you want to escape death, then accept him as your Lord and saviour.

In Biblical typology, some things typify the Holy Spirit in different aspects. New wind is a liquid which represent the Holy Spirit in the aspect of worship. Another liquid is oil, which speaks of the anointing of the Holy Spirit. But the living water in scripture is always the Holy Spirit out poured. Jesus explained it this way:

> Whoever believes in me, as the Scripture has said, streams of living water will flow from within him." By this he meant the Spirit, whom those who believed in him were later to receive. Up to that time the Spirit had not been given, since Jesus had not yet been glorified (John 7:38-39).

Jesus said directly that the living water is the Holy Spirit outpoured. The incident where Jesus thought about the living water took place at Succoth- the Feast of Tabernacles or Booths (John 7:2; 10). One of the regular events of that feast was the taking of water from the Pool of Siloam in a procession, led by the Levites, to the *Gabbtha* where the water would be poured out on the stones. It was against this background that Jesus identified Himself as the one who would give living water to anyone who was thirsty and willing to come to him to drink. What Jesus said in john 7:36-38 was one of the fulfilments of Isaiah 44:3:

> For I will pour water on the thirsty land, and streams on the dry ground; I will pour out my Spirit on your offspring, and my blessing on your descendants.

Using Midrash, it is easy to understand how some of the Old Testament prophecies are fulfilled in the New Testament. God has promised to pour his Spirit onto people who are thirsty. This is one of the many reasons why I wrote in the earlier chapter urging people to build their spirituality on Jesus. What people are seeking is exactly what Jesus is inviting people to come to receive (John 7:37-40). They should turn to Jesus Christ to quench their spiritual thirst,

At this juncture, you can pause reading this book and pray to God, inviting Jesus into your life. He will filled you with the Holy Spirit and pour his blessings on you and your descendants.

Let us look again at another scripture to see if we can understand what is happening in our world today using Midrash, reading from the book of Amos:

> I also withheld rain from you when the harvest was still three months away. I sent rain on one town, but withheld it from another. One field had rain; another had none and dried up. People staggered from town to town for water but did not get enough to drink, yet you have not returned to me," declares the LORD (Amos 4:7-8).

Why is it that someone like Reinard Bonnke has such tremendous success in Africa in terms of soul winning in his worldwide evangelism campaigns, but nothing much happens when he goes to Germany or England or Australia? The reason is that Reinard Bonnke has success in Africa because it is raining in Africa, it is raining Indonesia, it is raining in Brazil; there is drought in Britain and Australia. The rain here typify the pouring of the Holy Spirit.

The bible says that by God's direction, one place will be rained on, but another place will not be rained on and will dry up. We have seen what was said in Amos 4:7-8 happening over and over again in different generations, countries and even churches, thus the prophecy has had multiple fulfilments, and those who want God to pour his Holy Spirit on them should return to him in prayer, repentance and humanity (2 Chronicles 7: 14).

The Holy Spirit must be poured out before souls could be won for Christ (Acts 1:8). And it does not matter how many programs they have and how much money churches spend they are not going to make it rain. God is sovereign. He can be petitioned but not manipulated (Acts 8:9-25). What have you learnt from this? There are places where God's spirit is pouring out in abundance that is why revival is taken place there. We need to ask God to pour his Spirit on us. This patchy outpouring of God's Spirit will continue until the second coming of Jesus (John 14:15-18).

Let us take another example. In Genesis 24, Abraham sent a servant to get a bride for his Son Isaac. He placed gifts of jewellery on a train of camels to be given to his kinsmen, to prove that the servant was sent by Abraham.

This scripture has many fulfilments in the New Testament: First, God sent John the Baptist (servant) to prepare a people (bride) for the first coming of Jesus Christ (Mark 1:1-8).

Second God sent his Spirit to prepare a bride (the church) for Jesus (Acts 1:8; Ephesians 4: 4-16). Whatever happened in the Old Testament has its fulfilment in the New Testament. It is therefore important that you read the Old Testament not as a history book, but that you read it as a message from God which finds its fulfilment in the New Testament.

This means that to understand the New Testament better, we need to look at the Old Testament. For example, there is no way we will understand the subject of atonement without studying what atonement means in the Old Testament. Before we conclude our discussion on Midrash, let us briefly talk about one other principle in Midrash.

The Principle of kalver homer in Midrash: There is a principle in Midrash called **kalver Homer**. It is a principle which the apostle Paul studied in the school of **Hillel**. This principle is translated as "light to heavy". It means that something that is true in a light situation becomes especially true in a heavy situation. For example Hebrews 10:25 urges us *not give up meeting together, as some are in the habit of doing, but let us encourage one another—and all the more as you see the Day approaching.* Meeting together is always important but in the last days, it becomes especially more important. Things that are generally important become more important as we get closer to the return of Jesus.

Lets us take another example to illustrate the principle of **kalver Homer** in Midrash. On warning the early Christians of backsliders and false believers in the church, this is what Jude had to say:

> But, dear friends, remember what the apostles of our Lord Jesus Christ foretold. They said to you, "In the last times there will be scoffers who will follow their own ungodly desires." These are the men who divide you, who follow mere natural instincts and do not have the Spirit (Jude 1:17-19).

These scoffers and false prophets have been around since the early church, but the main focus of Jude's emphasis is that in the last days they will multiply. The point is this, things that are true at any time in history becomes especially true in the last days. Jesus warned that there will be false teachers and false prophets coming among us (Matthew 24: 23-25). There have always been false prophets and false teachers coming to deceive God's people, but in the last days they will multiply.

In Midrash when two events happen at the same location, it means something; there is a lesson to learn or something to look forward to. In the Jewish way of looking at the Bible, when two things happen at the same geographical location, there is usually a theological and spiritual connection between them. For instance, King David was born at Bethlehem (1 Samuel 16:1); Jesus the 'Son of David' was born at Bethlehem (Matthew 2:1). Elijah, Elisha and John the Baptism, all had the same spirit working in them (2 Kings 2:9-15; Luke 1:17). Does this tell you something? Elijah ended his ministry on the plain of Jericho, Elisha began his ministry on the plain of Jericho and the ministry of John the Baptist took place on the plan of Jericho. Midrash asks the question, where has this happen before. How is it fulfilled in Jesus?

So far we have looked at Midrash, one of the Jewish methods of interpreting the scriptures. The reason why we considered this method of looking at the scripture is because of its usefulness in the early church. Secondly, the Jewish people are the original recipients of the scriptures, and so it is important that we look at how they interpret the scriptures. We thank God that we now have many methods or guidelines for interpreting scripture. As I said earlier, there may be at times when one will need a Bible dictionary in order to understand certain words in the Bible. Let us look at one very important way of interpreting the Bible.

8. Scripture can be interpreted by the Holy Spirit

True understanding is not natural to us; it is God's gift (Mathew 11:25; 16:17) through the work of the Holy Spirit (John16:13). This neither absolves us from hard work, nor implies that we can isolate ourselves from other Christians in our understanding of the Bible. The Holy Spirit is a corporate Spirit, dwelling in all God's true people (1Corithians 12:12ff). It is folly to expect God to teach us through his Word if we neglect his ordained means of bringing us his truth, including the gift exercised by his chosen teachers.

This hermeneutical principle carries a profound spiritual challenge. God's Spirit is holy; therefore what we understand of his truth is related less to the capacity of our brains than to the extent of our obedience. How far one can see depends on how high one has climbed in their relationship with God rather than on how elaborately one is equipped. 'Blessed are the pure in heart, for they will see God' (Matthew 5:8).

The habit of approaching Scripture in an attitude of prayer is entirely correct in this connection. 'Open my eyes that I may see wonderful things in your law' (Psalm.119:18) are appropriate words every time we hear or handle the Bible. We are concerned not so much with 'who God is (or was, or will be)', as if he were some third party external to our conversation or searching. Rather, we are concerned with 'who you are, O God'. We are concerned with the God who is now here, before whom we bow in worship, upon whose power and grace we utterly depend in every moment for life and existence. 'Come, Holy Spirit!'

We can summarise the role of the Holy Spirit in interpreting the Bible as follows:

1. The Holy Spirit works through the Bible's authors to give us the text God wants us to have. Mark 12:36 says' David himself, speaking by the Holy Spirit, declared: '"The Lord said to my Lord: "Sit at my right hand until I put your enemies under your feet'. Acts 1:15-16 says 'In those days Peter stood up among the believers (a group numbering about a hundred and twenty) and said, "Brothers, the Scripture had to be fulfilled which the Holy Spirit spoke long ago through the mouth of David concerning Judas, who served as guide for those who arrested Jesus'. All these scriptures show that the Holy Spirit spoke through the authors of the Bible (see 2 Peter 1:20-22 and2 Timothy 3:15-17). Let us look at another role of the Holy Spirit in scripture interpretation.

2. The Holy Spirit speaks through the text of scripture. For example 1 Corinthians 2: 10-16 says:

> ...but God has revealed it to us by his Spirit. The Spirit searches all things, even the deep things of God. For who among men knows the thoughts of a man except

the man's spirit within him? In the same way no one knows the thoughts of God except the Spirit of God. We have not received the spirit of the world but the Spirit who is from God, that we may understand what God has freely given us. This is what we speak, not in words taught us by human wisdom but in words taught by the Spirit, expressing spiritual truths in spiritual words. The man without the Spirit does not accept the things that come from the Spirit of God, for they are foolishness to him, and he cannot understand them, because they are spiritually discerned. The spiritual man makes judgments about all things, but he himself is not subject to any man's judgment: For who has known the mind of the Lord that he may instruct him? But we have the mind of Christ.

The Holy Spirit speaks through the text of scripture to us. And so we have to be mindful of the importance of God's Spirit when reading the Bible. I believe an attitude of prayer, humility, respect, and a desire to understand what is written can be very helpful.

3. Finally, the Holy Spirit works through our study of the Bible to transform our lives by convicting us that it is God's word:

For we know, brothers loved by God, that he has chosen you, because our gospel came to you not simply with words, but also with power, with the Holy Spirit and with deep conviction. You know how we lived among you for your sake. You became imitators of us and of the Lord; in spite of severe suffering, you welcomed the message with the joy given by the Holy Spirit. And so, you became a model to all the believers in Macedonia and Achaia (Thessalonians 1:4-7).

It is my prayer that as you begin to build your life on God's principles, your whole life will be genuinely transformed and that your faith becomes unshakable no matter how strong the storm may be against your life.

In this chapter, our main concern has been how one can make good use of the word of God in their lives. We have looked at how we can interpret scriptures using various guidelines or methods of interpretation. I hope you will find these discussions useful in your desire to build your life on God's word.

Conclusion

This is the end of this book, *Building your life on the principles of God: the solid foundation.* In what some bible commentators refer to as Paul's 'Letter from Death Row'; Paul could confidently say that he has been faithful to his call to the end: 'For I am already being poured out like a drink offering, and the time has come for my departure. I have fought the good fight, I have finished the race, and I have kept the faith. Now there is in store for me the crown of righteousness, which the Lord, the righteous Judge, will award to me on that day—and not only to me, but also to all who have longed for his appearing'.[21] As he neared the end of his life, Paul could confidently say that he had been faithful to his call. Thus he faced death calmly, knowing that he would be rewarded by Christ. This is my prayer for you as you build your life on the principles of God, the solid foundation.

---

[21] 2 Timothy 4:6–8

Other Books by the author

1. *How Unity can benefit you, the family, the church, and the nation.* London: Authorhose (2013).

2. *The final destination of the Human soul.* London: Authorhouse (2014).

Consulting Books

Astin, A. W., Astin, H., & Lindholm, J. (2011). *Cultivating the Spirit: How College can Enhance Student's inner Lives.* San Francisco: Jossey-Bass.

Atwam, A. B. (2013). *How Unity can benefit.* London: Authorhose.

Atwam, A. (2014). *The final destination of the Human soul.* London: Authorhouse.

Bates, L. (2009). *The New Economic Disorder.* Florida: Excel Books.

Berger, P. (1999). *The Desecularization of the Worl: Resurgent Religion and World Politics.* Michigan: Ethics and Public Centre and Wm. B. Eerdmans Publishing Co.

Blomberg, C., & (ed), C. D. (2006). *Neither Poverty nor Riches.* Illinios: Inter Varsity Press.

Bloomer, G. (2008). *Love Dating Marriage: Tough Questions, Honest Answers.* New Kensington : Whitaker House.

Cox, H. (2009). *The Future of Faith.* Nwe York: Harper Collins Publishers.

Drane, J. (1999). *The Bible Phenomenon: Its Significance in the world of Science and New Age Spirituality.* Oxford: Lion Publishingnplc.

Hansson, M. (2013, Febuary 26). *The Guardian home.* Retrieved April 28, 2014, from The Guardian home : http://www.theguardian.com/society/2013/feb/26/mindfulness-meditation-depression-nhs

Hollenweger, W. (1986). In C. Jones, G.Wainwright, & E. Yarnold, *The Study of Spirituality* (pp. 549-554). London: SPCK.

Houston, D. J., & Cartwright, K. E. (2007). Spirituality and Public Service. *Public Administration Review, 67* (1), 88-102.

International Bible Society. (1999). *The Holy Bible: New International Version.* Nashville: Holman Publishers.

Jeffrey, G. R. (2000). *Surveillance Soceity: The rise of Anti Christ.* Colorado Springs: Waterbrook Press.

Lynn, M. L., Naughton, M. J., & VanderVeen:, S. (2009). Faith at Work Scale (FWS): Justification, Development, and Validation of a Measure of Judaeo-Christian Religion in the workplace. *Journal of Business Ethics,* 227-243.

McGrath, A. (2011). *Why God won't go away: Engaging with the New Atheism.* London: SPCK.

McGrath, A., & C, M. J. (2007). *The Dawkins Delusion?: Atheist Fundamentalism and the the denial of the divine.* London: SPCK.

Sheet, D. (2006). *Authority in Prayer: Praying with power and purpose.* Minnesota: Bethany House Publishers.

Sobrino, J. (1998). *Spirituality of Liberation.* Maryknoll, New York: Orbis Books.

Williams, R. (2012). *Faith in the Public Square.* London: Bloomsbury.